Baroque Poetry

Selected and translated
with an introduction by

J. P. HILL

and

E. CARACCIOLO-TREJO

*Department of Literature
University of Essex*

Dent, London
Rowman and Littlefield, Totowa, N.J.

© Selection, translation and introduction, J. M. Dent & Sons Ltd, 1975
All rights reserved
Made in Great Britain
at the
Aldine Press · Letchworth · Herts
for
J. M. DENT & SONS LTD
Aldine House · 26 Albemarle Street · London

First published 1975
First published in the United States 1975
by ROWMAN AND LITTLEFIELD, Totowa, New Jersey

This book if bound as a paperback is subject
to the condition that it may not be issued
on loan or otherwise except in its original
binding

This book is set in 8 on 9 point Times New Roman 327

Dent edition
ISBN (if a hardback): 0 460 10357 1
ISBN (if a paperback): 0 460 11357 7

Rowman and Littlefield edition
Hardback ISBN: 0-87471-574-1

Contents

Contents

Contents

Contents

Introduction

This anthology seeks to illustrate certain tendencies, obsessions, and favourite topics of poets in England, France, Spain, Italy, Germany and Mexico in the sixteenth and seventeenth centuries. We have not tried to offer any certainties—to provide, for example, firstly a definition of *baroque*, and then to follow it by a selection of poems used as 'evidence' to prove the validity of our definition. The attempt to do so might be valuable, but we doubt whether it could ever be more than a valiant failure, for, like *classicism* or *romanticism*, *baroque* is a term which points to a series of complex and often self-contradictory attitudes towards life which no definition can encompass.

Why, therefore, have we chosen *Baroque Poetry* as the title for this book? Firstly we must look at the alternatives. 'Metaphysical Poetry' seems too parochial, too English, and decades of readers and students have sweated under the load of ambiguities that the word contains. 'Seventeenth Century Poetry' is both too broad and too narrow, since styles which become common in the seventeenth century are prefigured in the early sixteenth (for example the contorted syntax of later writers prefigured in the sonnets of Michaelangelo) and the bland chronology of such a title carries no notion of selectivity. 'Mannerist' still seems too much a figure of art-history, despite attempts, notably in France,[1] to give it some literary sinew.

Baroque, however, in the common tongue, carries some notion of period, some notion of the unusual, dramatic, and inspired portrayal of nature and love and religion, some notion of style and, most important of all, a strong overtone of internationalism.[2]

Seeking to illustrate tendencies in the poetry of western Europe which emerge, submerge, and re-emerge in different countries at different times, we felt that a chronological presentation would be both misleading and rather dull. Similarly, a straight division by country, perhaps ending with a little footnote called 'Mexico and North America', would tend to perpetuate national boundaries within an international style, boundaries which it is the aim of this anthology to question. Of course we recognize

[1] See Raymond, Marcel: *Être et Dire*, especially pp. 63–135, Neuchâtel, 1970.

[2] A very useful discussion of the history of the concept of baroque may be found in Wellek, René: *Concepts of Criticism*, pp. 67–127, Yale, 1963.

that there *are* national differences. (Our selection of poems on man's love and fear of God is dominated by poems in English, and Italian is barely represented, for it seems to us that writers like Donne and Herbert had discovered new and fruitful ways of voicing personal religious feeling, whereas the Italians continued to write skilfully about what had been written skilfully about before, presenting rhetorical paraphrases of set theological topics.) But differences between love poetry in England and France, or differences between the Spanish and Italian ways of describing a landscape, can only be seen when theme and language are placed side by side. And likewise in style: the Spanish poets tend more to 'abstraction' than the English, but similar devices of syntax, antithesis, logic (sometimes correct, sometimes deliberately not) and wit are used by both to present their contrasting responses to the world. Furthermore, in a period when contrast and violent juxtaposition are two common literary techniques, we haven't always been afraid of surprising collocations.

The titles of the five sections ('A Vision of Nature,' 'Artifice', 'Love', 'On Life, Time and Death', 'The Love of God') of course cover the themes of all poetry at all times. But in the period represented, and in the styles for which we claim the blanket-title *baroque*, certain aspects of those themes become dominant, even obsessive, and others are scarcely dealt with. For example, our 'Vision of Nature' contains no poems which deal with the beauty of nature in itself, and no poems which simply use natural harmonies and images to illustrate a moral, religious, or amatory theme. The vision of nature offered here is of nature as an artefact with power over man, the artificer being either God or the poet. And this artefact is a confusing one, for the poet-interpreter can never discover where the reality begins and where his own art ends. 'Which is which?' is a question he can hardly ever answer.

The section opens with a contrast between du Bartas' picture of primeval chaos awaiting the ordering hand of God and Tasso's of primeval happiness before the ordering, and hence constricting, hand of honour and law made men unhappy. Then, after Guarini's reply, we move to the selection from *Gerusalemme Liberata*, where Tasso describes the most beautiful landscape of love imaginable, but where he is careful to show that this landscape is a deceitful mirage, created by the arts of a sorceress in order to pervert the honourable nature of a man. This is followed by a long selection from Góngora's *Las Soledades*, in which the poet's art seeks always to transmute the natural world into an invented vision, with conceit built upon conceit in such an extraordinary way that it almost seems as if the writer is desperate to escape from mere things, mere nature, into a world wholly of his own making . Then comes Milton's picture of Eden before the fall, a picture of the perfect art of God about to be ruined by the wicked art of Satan and the imperfect nature of man.

In other poems in the section we see nature as aesthetic experience ('The Garden'), nature as literary convention ('An Invitation to Phillis'), nature as religious teacher ('Lob Gottes im Luftraum'), and nature as a deliciously decadent sensual relaxation ('La Solitude'). In all these poems there is a determined effort to see reality as something other than itself, something which the arts of the poet can *will* into autonomous existence. And it is that effort of will, differently applied according to the temperament of the poet, which unites such variety, and which is one of the characterizing qualities of verse which may be called 'baroque'. To attempt consistency in anthologizing such a quality would be to weaken and limit the quality itself.

From the use of artifice to present a vision of nature, the next step is towards artifice used for its own sake, merely to prove the wit, skill, and sensitivity of the poet himself. In no other verse is delight in the artificial so lovingly, even hypnotically, cherished, and in these seventeenth-century poems[1] the further the poet can remove himself from reality, the more elegant, the more 'poetical' he seems. Here, the whole of the external world becomes a picture in the imagination, sometimes delicious and erotic, sometimes grotesque and absurd, as all rivers become crystals, all tears oceans, all birds feathered lyres, and all things other than what they are. The beloved herself often ceases to be a woman and becomes a picture, as her actions and physical attributes however small (her sewing and freckles) are isolated and transformed (her needle becomes an arrow, her freckles love's hiding-places) into elegant vignette.[2] The lady has become an excuse for artistic imagination rather than a reason for it.

But the poet knows he is showing off, and his delight in his own skill is one of the constituents of the total effect of the poem. His self-awareness is as important to the poem as its stanza-form, and this self-awareness is most often manifested in his choice of deliberately ridiculous subjects, or in his setting out to prove the most illogical propositions. He may wish to prove that when his mistress sings the whole universe is transformed into a song, and in such a case the reader is on familiar literary ground, aware of a whole tradition of hyperbolic love-poetry. But he may set out to prove something which is logically, literarily, and *emotionally* unusual, such as the proposition that it is better to have an ugly faithless mistress than a lovely faithful one.[3] In either case the poet's obvious pleasure in his own extravagance becomes central to the poem, for the pleasure indicates that enjoyment of art itself can override the normal logical and emotional bases of life. By such art both the beautiful and the ugly become subordinate to skill, and hence the real is defeated by the poem. What is 'proved' nearly always becomes incidental to the finally self-centred delight of the man 'proving' it.

In the section 'Love', however, we have selected poems where the poet uses his wit not for its own sake, but in order to reveal some of the unexpected and often profound perceptions that love can give him. Love itself often binds and harmonizes normally conflicting impulses, reconciles apparent irreconcilables, resolves paradoxes. Two may, in love, be one,

---

[1] The few earlier poems included seek only to establish a historical basis.
[2] See pp. 87 and 104.   [3] See p. 108.

and weakness may, in love, be strength. So there is a consistency between the act of loving and the technique of writing. In the best of these poems we see intellect and emotion perpetually reinforcing each other. But by no means all of them are in praise of love. The emotion may be fear as well as joy; the intellect may lead one to reject as well as to accept, and so their love poems are as various as their poems on nature.

Since so much baroque poetry is concerned with the unreal, and the transient unreal at that (his mistress when walking in the snow makes, for a second, a snowflake already melted by the envy of her beauty re-freeze upon the hem of her dress) [1] it is not surprising that in poems on 'Life, Time and Death' the prevailing tone is a pessimistic one. Continual emphasis upon an artificial vision which the poem both describes and symbolizes seems to point to an overwhelming desire to arrest time, and by arresting it, to escape or master it. So, when dealing with time itself, these poets have to deal with a threat not only to their bodies, which all men have to deal with, but to the very fabric and often the cause of their art and visions as well. Art itself, in for example Shakespeare or Horace, has been seen as the defier of time; the art of the baroque poet appears to be rooted not in a defiance but in an escape from the burdens of temporality. What they can do is not defy time, but document its appalling power, and this they do magnificently and dramatically: Quevedo, for example, sees himself merely as 'present successions of death', his life not a process, but, using language itself as an account of terror, 'un fué, y un será, y un es cansado' ('a was, a will-be, and a weary is').[2]

The only way round the fear of time is through a harmonious celebration of, or a deeply personal account of resolved doubts in, God. In England, Crashaw, Herbert, and Milton found original ways of writing about God— Crashaw with the sensuous adoration of which he, and he alone, was fully capable, Herbert with his absolute honesty and marvellous ear, and Milton with his deep emotional awareness of the intellectual and metaphysical propositions of Christianity. Likewise in Mexico Sor Juana's brilliance, and in America Edward Taylor's dogged honesty still delight. But in mainland Europe, after San Juan de la Cruz and apart from some German poems, we have found little verse which offers a satisfactory account of the workings of God and man's attitudes to Him. It is interesting that the haunted fear of time is so well treated in, for example, Quevedo or Sponde, but that they seem unable to elevate themselves to a vision of time confounded by man's acceptance of the love of God. We open the selection with a poem by a French author, La Ceppède,[3] which treats God, the angels, the Holy Ghost, Jesus, the marriage of the Lamb and the Holy Church, the death of one Pope and the enthronement of another, the assumption of the blessed and the victory over death, and subordinates them all to the aesthetic and emblematic notion of whiteness, leaving the reader with a quasi-symbolist vision of whiteness itself, but

[1] See p. 87.   [2] See p. 203.   [3] See p. 225.

giving him no sense of the emotional or theological vitality of any of
those great concepts. Perhaps it would be instructive to compare that
French poem with either Donne's or Herbert's passionate meditations
upon those themes which La Ceppède treats only artificially and
fleetingly.

What characterizes baroque poetry is the repetition of conceit. The
frequency with which this device is used suggests the near impossibility
of seeing the world as stasis, and the apparent inevitability of seeing the
world as a tense, mobile, changing 'discord'. There is little permanency;
if these poets convey a feeling of harmony, it is usually a facetious one,
which the reader perceives and enjoys for its facetiousness, or which he is
momentarily seduced into believing. What we normally think of as 'real'
is quite dissipated in the overwhelming artificiality of the poem's images,
and so the poem itself seems to demonstrate the dissolution of reality,
to exist as proof that reality is but a fickle dream. The concrete and
tangible are more frequently used to portray the destruction of the body
or the loss of emotion than to consider the state of man or the condition
of his moral or amatory feelings;[1] likewise the poets again and again
describe organic things, flesh, trees, flowers, through artificial images of
inorganic ones, jewels, gold, marble, as though they were willing themselves
to see permanence, wealth, and man-made beauty in all impermanent,
deceptive, natural things.[2] The poet writes his poem, the world that he
knows and the world that he wants cease to be distinguishable; and though
the world that he knows may not endure, the yearned-for world of the
poem just might. It is no accident that the subjunctive and the conditional
are common introductory tenses, any more than it is an accident that
having moved from a reality to an image the poet then moves from that
image to another rather than from that image back to a now transmuted
reality. Even blood itself ceases to be the warm substance of physical
life and becomes a mere colour, which it has in common with rubies,[3] and
through such conceits what is grammatically substantive becomes adjec-
tival or decorative, and carefully contrived syntactical ambiguities and
word-arrangements make the location of the adjective or descriptive
phrase itself ambiguous.[4]

But by no means all poems of conceit are short, passionate, and merely
conceited. There is a continuing use of various extended conventions,
such as the pastoral, the topos of the Golden Age, the long invitation to
love. The poet (for example Cotton[5] or Marino[6]) uses one of these
standard subjects to present a lengthy account of a world totally based
upon literature, an account which hovers tantalizingly between re-enact-

[1] See pp. 160, 162, 164 etc.
[2] See pp. 21, 22, 23, 130 etc.
[3] See p. 95.
[4] See pp. 16, 17, 92, 100 etc.
[5] See p. 43.
[6] See p. 75.

ment of an earlier way of writing which is felt to be valuable, and loving parody of it. We do not feel that Cotton is merely persuading to love, or that Marino is just writing about the loss of love; we feel that both of them are nostalgically, and with some self-doubt, paying a sincere compliment to what they feel to have been a golden age of writing set in what they feel to have been a golden age of nature. Here artifice has become more than conceit, more even than a world of dream; it has become the total reason for the poem and its total subject as well. The poem is openly artificial in language and structure and wholly about artifice. Such verse, whether it be pastiche or parody, is full of reminiscences of other verse, and the reminiscences reinforce the purely literary nature of the experience being offered to the reader. Significantly, in two favourite baroque topics, the echo and the mirror, the echo becomes the cause of the voice, the mirror becomes the creator rather than the reflector of the object.[1]

As in the imagery, so in the syntax. Baroque writers delight in manipulating syntax so as to create either ambiguity or drama.[2] Often one finds oneself in difficulty in construing Milton, even more in translating Góngora, because the poet has contrived that certain phrases or clauses, certain blocks of language, appear by positioning or metre to qualify that which either grammatically or syntactically they cannot qualify. Just as in one of Horace's Odes, the delight and import are to be found in the surprising shifts of vision, changes of awareness, that such ambiguities create in reading the poem. Often in this way one adjective can be made to seem to apply to two nouns, hence linking them together, and forming a kind of word play by word-order alone.

Examples of use of conceits and syntax in these ways, combined with prefigurations of themes which later become dominant, appear very early. Therefore we have felt free to include Michaelangelo, du Bellay, Southwell, San Juan de la Cruz, and others who are not normally considered 'baroque'. Obviously they, and even a writer like Tasso, occupy a borderline position, but when they write, as Michaelangelo does, in such an ambiguous syntax about love and appearance, or as du Bellay does, in such an emblematic way about the metamorphoses of a rose, then we have felt that they found the styles later to be developed and should be briefly represented.

One could say that in excess, in exaggeration, lies one of the central elements of baroque creation. Excess indicates the presence of an energy which seems to burst out of pre-established order. The energy of the Renaissance tended to purity of form, was canalized into canons: baroque energy in comparison seems uncontrolled. The shared acceptance of a norm is absent; rather than dialogue we have the poet's interminable ingenious soliloquy as he examines his private dreams, his literary world, his consciousness. This individualism affords him a special autonomy, the

[1] See pp. 45, 75.
[2] See pp. 15 to 33, and 33 to 36.

freedom of the man completely alone. Such freedom, such loneliness, is simultaneously a liberation and a terror, for all he can know is his own self, and one of the things he knows about it is its transient smallness. And in that freedom we find enacted the drama of the modern man or artist, who, like his baroque predecessor, faces a fragmented and puzzling world with no guide-lines save those of his own making.

Select Bibliography

There is a vast and continually growing mass of material dealing with the baroque period in general and with the concept of baroque, and the number of poets who have been called 'baroque' is enormous. In this small bibliography we list a few of the texts which attempt to characterize baroque in general and European terms. We have omitted works which deal exclusively with individual authors and subsidiary themes, as otherwise the bibliography would be a book in itself.

ALONSO, DÁMASO. *Estudios y ensayos góngorinos*, Madrid 1965

COHEN, J. M. *The Baroque Lyric*, London 1963

CROCE, B. *Storia dell'età barocca in Italia*, Bari 1929

HATZFELD, H. *Estudios sobre el Barroco*, Madrid 1964

LUNDING, E. 'German Baroque Literature', a synthetic view, in *German Life and Letters* 3, 1949/50

DE MORGUES, O. *Metaphysical, Baroque and Précieux Poetry*, Oxford 1953

RAYMOND, MARCEL. *Baroque et Renaissance Poétique*, Paris 1955
Être et Dire, Neuchâtel 1970

ROUSSET, J. *La Littérature de L'Âge Baroque en France*, Paris 1953

SYPHER, W. *Four Stages of Renaissance Style*, New York 1955

TAPIÉ, V. *Le Baroque*, Paris 1961

WARNKE, FRANK J. *Versions of Baroque*, Newhaven 1972

WELLEK, RENÉ. *Concepts of Criticism*, Yale 1963

WÖLFFLIN, HEINRICH. *Renaissance and Baroque*, London 1964

Note on the Texts

Dealing with editions of poems from so many languages we have found that there is a good deal of inconsistency in the amount of modernization of spelling. In these cases, rather than pretend to editorial authority extending over five languages and many authors, we have allowed inconsistencies to stand.

In rare cases where we have been able to find only one text, we have printed it, and in two cases (pp. 159 and 162) where the texts were printed with no punctuation, we have reproduced them, rather than attempted to resolve problems for which we have no manuscript, or any other, evidence.

Note on the Translations

The translations in this book are simply literal versions of the foreign texts, and we do not claim that they have any literary merit. In many of the texts there are ambiguities and puns which cannot be conveyed in English; in such cases we have preferred what seems to us the stronger burden of the ambiguity.

In our versions of poems whose own syntax is often deliberately mannered and contorted we have not always been able to provide simple English; in many instances we hope that the reader will refer to the syntax of the original and see that clumsiness or contortion is not exclusively our own.

Acknowledgements

We owe our thanks to Susanne Flatauer, who helped us with the selection and translation of the German texts, and to Professor Arthur Terry, who most kindly read the typescript and made very useful suggestions. We are also grateful to members of the School of Comparative Studies of the University of Essex, who assisted us in various ways during the preparation of this book.

The poems on pp. 155 and 158 by Henry King are printed by permission of the Clarendon Press, Oxford, from *The Poems of Henry King* edited by Margaret Crum. © 1965 Oxford University Press.

The poems on pp. 97 and 100 by John Cleveland are printed also by permission of the Clarendon Press, Oxford, from *The Poems of John Cleveland*, edited by Brian Morris and Eleanor Withington. © 1967 Oxford University Press.

A Vision of Nature

In their treatments of nature the baroque poets, like their Renaissance predecessors, turned to the concerns of man. One topic, natural beauty, is used in longer poems to point some moral, and in the selections from five long poems which open this section the moral is that nature is an unreliable and dangerous thing. Du Bartas' vision of chaos is a vision of terrifying energy intent on self-destruction, only ordered and held in check by the *mastic* of divine virtue. Matter, he asserts, is basically mutinous, seditious, a killer—only God can control it:

> Tout estoit en brouillis, et ce tas mutiné
> Se fust, seditieux, soy mesme ruiné
> Tout soudain qu'il nasquit, si la vertu divine,
> Esparse dans le corps de toute la machine,
> N'eust servy de mastic, pour ensemble coler
> Le vagueux ocean, le ciel, la terre, et l'air,
> Qui ça et là choquant l'un l'autre, à l'adventure,
> Taschoient faire mourir la naissante nature.[1]

The divine *mastic* which du Bartas claimed to have glued together the chunks of the universe is, in Tasso's chorus from *Aminta*,[2] no more to be found. From a present unhappiness he looks back to a golden age when Love was free, Winter uninvented, and Deceit unknown. However, despite the yearning beauty of his descriptions, the content of the poem is, finally, pessimistic. 'Amiam,' he ends, 'let us love.' The reasons why we should make love are many, but not one of them contains any hint of present happiness: that the world is no longer young; that 'honour' should only concern the mighty, and we are unimportant; that we wish to be left alone (implying that we have no freedoms save anonymity and love-making); that death comes quickly; and, finally, that death is only an eternal night of sleep. In a fallen world, Tasso can offer nostalgia and hopeful hedonism, a hedonism which has as one of its sweetnesses the enjoyment of sadness itself. Guarini, in his *tour de force* of a reply [3] (he repeats every one of Tasso's rhymes in order to arrive at an exactly opposite conclusion), says that all pleasures of the senses are deceits, and the Nature we see here is a

[1] See p. 6.   [2] See p. 6.   [3] See p. 9.

1

snare. We should therefore trust in the only things which are not transient and historical, the laws of God and the gift of Eternity.

Tasso returns to the portrayal of an earthly paradise in his description of the garden of Armida in *Gerusalemme Liberata*.[1] The garden is seen through the eyes of two knights, who recognize it as a temptation which, however seductive, they must resist, and to which one of their company has already succumbed. This paradise is a work of deceiving art, a phantasm created by an enchantress, containing many of the aspects of a hoped-for world of true freedom, such as sexual liberty and eternal fecundity. The calls of its love are almost irresistible, but those calls themselves are memorials of decay and invitations to enjoy now lest tomorrow the mirage be gone:

> Così trapassa al trapassar d'un giorno
> de la vita mortale il fiore e 'l verde;
> né, perché faccia indietro april ritorno,
> si rinfiora ella mai, né si rinverde.
> Cogliam la rosa in su 'l mattino adorno
> di questo dí, che tosto il seren perde;
> cogliam d'amor la rosa: amiamo or quando
> esser si puote rïamato amando.

For Tasso, Armida's garden was a delusion; for Milton pre-lapsarian Eden was a reality catastrophically thrown away. In the passage we have chosen from *Paradise Lost* [2] Satan sits and wonders at the beauty of a world he has come to wreck. It is one of Milton's superlative structural devices to present the great vision of Eden through the eyes of its destroyer (the 'he' of the opening line of this passage is Satan) and then, immediately before the entrance of mankind, to mention Satan again, so casting a dark shadow over Eden, Adam and Eve alike:

> A whole days journey high, but wide remote
> From this *Assyrian* Garden, where the Fiend
> Saw undelighted all delight, all kind
> Of living Creatures new to sight and strange:
> Two of far nobler shape erect and tall,
> Godlike erect, with native Honour clad
> In naked Majestie seemd Lords of all.

Tasso's garden is a dangerous dream, Milton's a pristine reality of which dreams alone remain; between the two we have placed selections from Góngora's *Soledades*. In them we see the most extreme and dominating example of nature transformed into an art-world willed into existence by the poet. The artificial landscape he creates is not sentimental, nor nostalgic, nor even moral; it is an awe-inspiring vision of the complex mag-

[1] See p. 13.　　　　　[2] See p. 35.

2

nificence things might achieve if they were not things, but words. All times, causes, shapes and identities could be that much richer if his syntax and images were the artificers of the world rather than dull truth. But as a dream is more precise than wakefulness, a fairy-tale clearer than a novel, so Góngora, within his imaginative complexities, achieves more precise and tougher visual effects than any other poet in this section. In the light of a lamp the oak-tree seems like a butterfly falling into cinders,[1] the waves of the tide are a centaur of foam,[2] and even the oyster is given a harness of bone rather than a mere shell.[3] Góngora's art has made his vision of nature a super-nature, just as it is the super-natural realism of Salvador Dalí at his best which turns his pictures from documentaries or analyses of life into worlds existing in a timeless imaginative play.

The other poems in the section are less serious, recognizing as they do that Nature may be a relaxation, a fund of images for literary work, or an inspiration to poetry. Marvell finds happiness, amusement, and a possible, but only half-serious, analogue of paradise in the greenery of Appleton House,[4] Saint-Amant derives a deliciously 'romantick' thrill from waterfalls and precipices,[5] and other poets play their variations upon the same tunes. However great their range of seriousness, from Milton at one extreme to de Viau at the other, the poets all seem to agree with Greville that true beauty existed somewhere else at some other time, and only glimpses of it may now be had, if, indeed, it may be glimpsed at all: 'The Golden Age was when the world was young.'[6]

---

[1] See p. 18.   [2] See p. 20.   [3] See p. 23.
[4] See p. 37.   [5] See p. 54.   [6] See p. 64.

Du Bartas

From PREMIERE SEMAINE

. . . .

Ce premier monde estoit une forme sans forme,
Une pile confuse, un meslange difforme,
D'abismes un abisme, un corps mal compassé,
Un chaos de chaos, un tas mal entassé
Où tous les elemens se logeoient pesle-mesle,
Où le liquide avoit avec le sec querelle,
Le rond avec l'aigu, le froid avec le chaut,
Le dur avec le mol, le bas avec le haut,
L'amer avec le doux; brief, durant ceste guerre
La terre estoit au ciel, et le ciel en la terre.
La terre, l'air, le feu se tenoient dans la mer;
La mer, le feu, la terre estoient logez dans l'air;
L'air, la mer, et le feu dans la terre; et la terre
Chez l'air, le feu, la mer. Car l'Archer du tonnerre,
Grand Mareschal de camp, n'avoit encor donné
Quartier à chacun d'eux. Le ciel n'estoit orné
De grand's touffes de feu; les plaines esmaillees
N'espandoient leurs odeurs; les bandes escaillees
N'entrefendoient les flots; des oyseaux les souspirs
N'estoient encor portez sur l'aile des zephyrs.
Tout estoit sans beauté, sans reglement, sans flame;
Tout estoit sans façon, sans mouvement, sans ame.
Le feu n'estoit point feu, la mer n'estoit point mer,
La terre n'estoit terre, el l'air n'estoit point air.
Ou, si jà se pouvoit trouver en un tel monde
Le corps de l'air, du feu, de la terre, et de l'onde,

This first world was a formless form, a confused heap, an unformed mixture, an abyss of abysses, an incoherent body, a chaos of chaos, an unheaped heap where all the elements were jumbled together, where liquid battled with dry, round with sharp, cold with hot, hard with soft, low with high, bitter with sweet; briefly, during this war the earth was in the sky, the sky in the earth. Sea, fire and earth were in the sea; sea, fire, earth, in the air; air, sea, fire in the earth; and the earth in air, fire, and sea. For the Archer of thunder, Field-Marshal of the camp, had not yet given quarter to any of them. The sky was not yet adorned with great clusters of fire; the enamelled plains did not breathe out odours; the scaly herds did not swim the deeps; the sighs of the birds were not yet carried on the zephyr's wings. All was without beauty, without rule, with the flame of life; all was formless, motionless, soulless. Fire was not fire, sea not sea, earth not earth, air not air. Or, if ever in such a world there was to be found the form of air, earth, fire, or water, the air was not clear, the fire not hot, the earth

L'air estoit sans clarté, la flamme sans ardeur,
Sans fermeté la terre, et l'onde sans froideur.
Bref, forge en ton esprit une terre, qui, vaine,
Soit sans herbe, sans bois, sans mont, sans val, sans plaine,
Un ciel non azuré, non clair, non transparant,
Non marqueté de feu, non vousté, non errant,
Et lors tu concevras quelle estoit ceste terre,
Et quel ce ciel encor, où regnoit tant de guerre.
Terre, et ciel, que je puis chanter d'un stile bas,
Non point tels qu'ils estoyent, mais tels qu'ils n'estoient pas.
Ce n'estoit donc le monde, ains l'unique matiere
Dont il devoit sortir, la riche pepiniere
Des beautez de ce Tout, l'embryon qui devoit
Se former en six jours en l'estat qu'on le void.
Et de vray ce monceau confusement enorme
Estoit tel que la chair qui s'engendre, difforme,
Au ventre maternel, et par temps toutesfois
Se change en front, en yeux, en nez, en bouche, en doigts,
Prend icy forme longue, icy large, icy ronde,
Et de soy peu à peu fait naistre un petit monde.
Mais cestuy par le cours de nature se fait
De laid beau, de mort vif, et parfait d' imparfait;
Et le monde jamais n'eust changé de visage,
Si du grand Dieu sans pair le tout-puissant langage
N'eust comme syringué dedans ses membres morts
Je ne sçay quel esprit qui meut tout ce grand corps.
La palpable noirceur des ombres memphitiques,
L'air tristement espais des brouillars cimmeriques,

not firm, and the water not cold. In short, imagine an earth which, useless, is without grass, tree, mountain, valley, plain, an unazure, unclear, untransparent air, not studded with fire, not vaulted, not moving, and then you will conceive what this earth and this sky were like when war reigned supreme, this earth and sky which I can sing in my lowly style not indeed (of items) as they were, but as they were not. It was not then this world, as much as the unique matter from which it had to come, the rich seedbed of the beauties of this All, the embryo which was to form in six days the shape which you can see. And truly, this confusedly enormous stack was of such power that the flesh could engender itself, misshapen, in the maternal womb, and in time always turn itself into forehead, eyes, nose, mouth, fingers, take here a long shape, there a broad one, there a round one, and out of itself make bit by bit a little world. But this in the course of nature made beauty from ugliness, life from death, perfect from imperfect; and the world would never have changed its face if the omnipotent language of the great god without equal had not as it were injected into the dead members I know not what spirit to move the great body. The palpable blackness of these mephitic shades, the air sadly thick with Cimmerian mists, the cloudy smoke

5

La grossière vapeur de l'infernal manoir,
(Et si rien s'imagine au monde de plus noir,)
De ce profond abisme emmanteloit la face.
Le desordre regnoit haut et bas dans la masse,
Tout estoit en brouillis, et ce tas mutiné
Se fust, seditieux, soy mesme ruiné
Tout soudain qu'il nasquit, si la vertu divine,
Esparse dans le corps de toute la machine,
N'eust servy de mastic, pour ensemble coler
Le vagueux ocean, le ciel, la terre, et l'air,
Qui ça et là choquant l'un l'autre, à l'adventure,
Taschoient faire mourir la naissante nature.

. . . .

Tasso

CHORUS *from Aminta*

O Bella età de l'oro,
non già perchè di latte
se'n corse il fiume e stillò mèle il bosco;
non perchè i frutti loro
dièr da l'aratro intatte
le terre, e gli angui errâr senz'ira o tosco;
non perchè nuvol fosco
non spiegò allor suo velo,
ma in primavera eterna
ch'ora s'accende e verna,
rise di luce e di sereno il cielo;
nè portò peregrino
o merce o guerra a gli altrui lidi il pino.

of the infernal dwelling (and nothing blacker can be imagined in this world)
darkened and shrouded the face of this profound abyss. Disorder reigned from
top to bottom of the mass, all was in chaos, and this mutinous pile would have
seditiously ruined itself as soon as it was born, if divine virtue, sown throughout
the body of the whole machine [entity], had not acted as gum, to stick together
the waving ocean, the sky, the earth, the air, which, hither and thither by chance
bouncing off each other struggled to kill nature as it was being born.

O lovely age of Gold, not only because the river flowed with milk and the wood
dripped honey; not because the lands, untouched by the plough, yielded their
fruits, and the snakes wandered by without wrath or poison: nor because dark
cloud did not spread its veil, but in eternal spring, which now either burns or
freezes, the sky laughed with light and brightness; nor did the pine [ship] carry
the wanderer or trade or war to foreign shores.

Mal sol perchè quel vano
nome senza soggetto,
quell'idolo d'errori, idol d'inganno,
quel che da'l volgo insano
onor poscia fu detto,
che di nostra natura il feo tiranno,
non mischiava il suo affanno
fra le liete dolcezze
de l'amoroso gregge:
nè fu sua dura legge
nota a quell'alme in libertate avvezze;
ma legge aurea e felice
che Natura scolpì: S'ei piace, ei lice.

Allor tra fiori e linfe
traen dolci carole
gli Amoretti senz'archi e senza faci:
sedean pastori e ninfe,
meschiando a le parole
vezzi e susurri, e a i susurri i baci
strettamente tenaci;
la verginella ignude
scopria le fresche rose,
ch'or tien ne'l velo ascose,
e le poma de'l seno acerbe e crude;
e spesso in fiume o in lago
scherzar si vide con l'amata il vago.

But only because that empty weightless name, that idol of errors, idol of deceit, which the mad mob thereafter called honour and made a tyrant over our [human] nature, did not adulterate the joyful sweetness of the amorous flocks with its cares nor was its harsh law known to those spirits who delighted in freedom; but only the golden, happy law which Nature wrought: 'If it pleases, it's lawful.'

Then, the cupids danced their sweet carols through the flowers and streams without either bows or torches: the shepherds and nymphs sat, mingling with their words caresses and murmurs, and with their murmurs, kisses tightly clinging; the naked maiden uncovers the fresh roses which now she hides behind her dress, and the bitter, unripened apples of her breast; and often the lover is seen to play with his beloved by the river or lake.

A Vision of Nature

Tu prima, Onor, velasti
la fonte de i diletti,
negando l'onde a l'amorosa sete:
tu a' begli occhi insegnasti
di starne in sè ristretti,
e tener lor bellezze altrui secrete:
tu raccogliesti in rete
le chiome a l'aura sparte:
tu i dolci atti lascivi
festi ritrosi e schivi,
a i detti il fren ponesti, a i passi l'arte:
opra è tua sola, o Onore,
che furto sia quel che fu don d'Amore.

E son tuoi fatti egregi
le pene e i pianti nostri.
Ma tu, d'Amore e di Natura donno,
tu domator de'regi,
che fai tra questi choistri
che la grandezza tua capir non ponno?
Vattene, e turba il sonno
a gl'illustri e potenti:
noi qui negletta e bassa
turba, senza te lassa
viver ne l'uso de l'antiche genti.
Amiam, chè non ha tregua
con gli anni umana vita, e si dilegua.

Amiam: chè'l Sol si muore e poi rinasce:
a noi sua breve luce
s'asconde, e'l sonno eterna notte adduce.

You first, Honour, veiled the fountain of pleasures, denying [its] water to amorous thirst: you taught beautiful eyes to stay downcast, and keep their beauties hidden from the world: the hair which before flowed free in the wind you gather in nets: you turned sweet lascivious acts into shameful and embarrassed ones; you put both a rein on speech, and craft on spontaneity: this is your work alone, o Honour, that what was the gift of Love is now theft.

And your noble deeds are our sorrows and tears. But you, lord of Love and Nature, you conqueror of kings, what are you doing in these cloisters which are not big enough to hold your greatness? Go then, and disturb the sleep of the illustrious and the mighty: leave us here, a forgotten and lowly crowd, leave us to live without you, as the ancients did. Let us love, for human life can make no deal with the [passage of the] years, and ebbs away.

Let us love: for the sun dies and is born again; from us he hides his brief light, and eternal night brings sleep.

Guarini

CHORUS *from Il Pastor Fido*

O bella età d'oro,
  Quand' era cibo il latte
  Del pargoletto mondo, e culla il bosco;
  E i cari parti loro
  Godean le gregge intatte,
  Nè temea il mondo ancor ferro nè tosco!
  Pensier torbido e fosco
  Allor non facea velo
  Al sol di luce eterna:
  Or la ragion, che verna
  Tra le nubi del senso, ha chiuso il cielo;
  Ond' è che pellegrino
  Va l'altrui terra, e'l mar turbando il pino.

Quel suon fastoso e vano,
  Quell' inutil soggetto
  Di lusinghe, di titoli e d'inganno,
  Ch' Onor dal volgo insano
  Indegnamente è detto,
  Non era ancor degli animi tiranno,
  Ma sostener affanno
  Per le vere dolcezze;
  Tra i boschi e tra la gregge
  La fede aver per legge
  Fu di quell' alme, al ben oprar avezze,
  Cura d'onor felice,
  Cui dettava Onestà: 'Piaccia, se lice.'

O lovely age of gold, when milk was the food of the infant world, and the wood its cradle; and the untouched flocks rejoiced in their sweet fields, and the world then still feared neither sword nor poison! No grim and dark thought then veiled the sun of eternal light; now reason, which winters among the clouds of sensuality, has closed the sky [from us]; whence it is that the pine [ship] wanders to other lands, disturbing the sea as it goes.

That pompous empty sound, that useless object of flattery, titles, and deceit, which is unworthily called Honour by the mindless mob, was not yet the tyrant over [our] minds, but they could endure hardship through [their] true sweetness: amongst the groves and flocks to have faith in the laws was the care of those souls, accustomed to doing good, the care of happy honour which Honesty dictated: 'Let it please, if it is lawful.'

9

A Vision of Nature

Allor tra prati e linfe
  Gli scherzi e le carole
  Di legittimo amor furon le faci;
Avean pastori e ninfe
  Il cor nelle parole;
Dava lor Imeneo le gioie e i baci
Più dolci e più tenaci:
Un sol godeva ignude
D'amor le vive rose:
Furtivo amante ascose
Le trovò sempre, ad aspre voglie e crude
O in antro, o in selva, o in lago;
Ed era un nome sol marito e vago.

Secol rio, che velasti
  Co' tuoi sozzi diletti
  Il bel dell' alma, ed a nudrir la sete
Dei desiri insegnasti
  Co' sembianti ristretti,
Sfrenando poi l' impurità segrete!
Così, qual tesa rete
Tra fiori e fronde sparte,
Celi pensier lascivi
Con atti santi e schivi:
Bontà stimi il parer, la vita un' arte,
Nè curi (e párti onore)
Che furto sia, purchè s' asconda, amore.

Ma tu, deh! spiriti egregi
  Forma ne' petti nostri,
  Verace Onor, delle grand' alme donno!

Then, through meadows and streams the sports and carols of legitimate love were the torches; shepherds and nymphs had their hearts in their words: their Hymen gave them sweeter and longer lasting joys and kisses; one alone enjoyed the living, naked roses of love: the furtive lover found them always hidden from his rough, crude, desires, whether in cave, wood, or lake, and husband and lover were the same single name.

Evil age, who have veiled with your base delights the beauty of the soul, have taught [men] to nurse the thirst of desires, and to give free rein to the secret impurities beneath virtuous appearances. Thus, as a net stretches between flowers and scattering leaves, you conceal lascivious thoughts beneath holy and shy acts: you think goodness is an appearance, life an art, you don't care (and it even seems a virtue to you) that love is theft, so long as it remains concealed.

But, Oh, Thou formest noble souls in our breasts, true Honour, Lord of great

10

O regnator de' Regi,
Deh torna in questi chiostri
Che senza te beati esser non ponno.
Déstin dal mortal sonno
Tuoi stimoli potenti
Chi per indegna e bassa
Voglia seguir te lassa,
E lassa il pregio dell' antiche genti.
Speriam, chè 'l mal fa tregua
Talor, se speme in noi non si dilegua:

Speriam, chè il sol cadente anco rinasce;
   E 'l Ciel, quando men luce,
   L'aspettato seren spesso n' adduce.

Tasso

From CANTO XVI *Gerusalemme Liberata* (stanzas 9–18)

. . . .

Poi che lasciâr gli avviluppati calli,
   in lieto aspetto il bel giardin s'aperse;
   acque stagnanti, mobili cristalli,
   fior vari e varie piante, erbe diverse,
   apriche collinette, ombrose valli,
   selve e spelonche in una vista offerse;
   e quel che 'l bello e 'l caro accresce all' opre,
   l'arte che tutto fa, nulla si scopre.

spirits. O King of kings, come, return to these cloisters which cannot be happy without you. Let your powerful goads awake from mortal sleep the man who forsakes you because of unworthy and base desire, and forsakes the glory of the ancients. Let us hope, for evil has to make a truce, as long as our hope does not ebb away:

Let us hope, for the setting sun is born again, and Heaven, even though it shines little, still often brings to us the hoped for peace.

When they have left the entangled paths the lovely garden appears as a joyous vision to their sight; still waters, moving crystals, various flowers, various plants, different herbs, sunny hills, shady valleys, woods and caves offer themselves in a vista; and what increases the beauty and worth of the work is the art which makes it all, and is nowhere to be seen.

11

A Vision of Nature

Stimi (sí misto il culto è co 'l negletto)
  sol naturali e gli ornamenti e i siti.
Di natura arte par, che per diletto
  l' imitatrice sua scherzando imiti.
L' aura, non ch' altro, è de la maga effetto,
  l'aura che rende gli alberghi fioriti:
co' fiori eterni eterno il frutto dura,
e mentre spunta l'un, l'altro matura.

Nel tronco istesso e tra l' istessa foglia
  sovra il nascente fico invecchia il fico:
pendono a un ramo, un con dorata spoglia,
  l'altro con verde, il novo e 'l pomo antico:
lussureggiante serpe alto e germoglia
  la tòrta vite ov' è piú l' orto aprico:
qui l' uva ha in fiori acerba, e qui l'or l' have
e di piropo, e già di néttar grave.

Vezzosi augelli infra le verdi fronde
  temprano a prova lascivette note.
Mormora l' aura, e fa le foglie e l'onde
  garrir, che variamente ella percote.
Quando taccion gli augelli alto risponde;
  quando cantan gli augei piú lieve scote;
sia caso od arte, ora accompagña, ed ora
alterna i versi lor la musica ôra.

You would think (so mixed were wilderness and cultivation) that both the embellishments and the lovely places were the work of nature alone. Art seems like nature, a nature who in delight and in play, imitates her imitator. The air is the creation of the enchantress and of nothing else, the air which makes the bowers bloom; the eternal fruit lasts with the eternal flowers, and while one buds, the other ripens.

On the same trunk and under the same leaf, the fig grows old above a fig just being born; the old and young apple hang on one bough, one with golden flesh, the other with green; luxuriant the twisting vine winds high and buds wherever the garden is sunniest; here it has a bitter grape amongst its flowers, and here a golden grape, a purple grape, already heavy with nectar.

Joyful birds among the green fronds, bring to perfection their little love-songs. The breeze murmurs, and makes the leaves and waters sing wherever it touches them; when the birds are silent, it loudly responds and when the birds sing, it hushes its voice; whether by chance or art now it accompanies, and now it alternates its [own] musical prayer with their songs.

12

Vola, fra gli altri, un che le piume ha sparte
  di colori vari, ed ha purpureo il rostro;
e lingua snoda in guisa larga, e pârte
  la voce sí, ch' assembra il sermon nostro.
Questi ivi allor continovò con arte
  tanta il parlar, che fu mirabil mostro.
Tacquero, gli altri ad ascoltarlo intenti;
e fermaro i susurri in aria i venti.

'Deh mira,' egli cantò, 'spuntar la rosa
  dal verdo suo modesta e verginella,
che mezzo aperta ancóra, e mezzo ascosa,
  quanto si mostra men, tanto è piú bella.
Ecco poi nudo il sen già baldanzosa
  dispiega: ecco poi langue, e non par quella,
quella non par, che desïata avanti
fu da mille donzelle e mille amanti.'

'Cosí trapassa al trapassar d' un giorno
  de la vita mortale il fiore e 'l verde;
né, perché faccia indietro april ritorno,
  si rinfiora ella mai, né si rinverde.
Cogliam la rosa in su 'l mattino adorno
  di questo dí, che tosto il seren perde;
cogliam d' amor la rosa: amiamo or quando
esser si puote rïamato amando.'

A bird with many coloured feathers and a purple beak flies among the others; and opens her throat in broad song, with a voice sounding as if it resembled human speech. And she continued her speech there with such art that it was wonderful to hear. The other birds fell silent, intent on listening, and the winds ceased their sighing in the air.

'Behold', she sang, 'the rose budding from her green [leaves], modest and virginal, still only half-open and half hidden, when the less she is seen, the more beautiful she is. Then see, she boldly displays her naked bosom: and then she languishes, and seems not the same, not the same as she was before, when she was desired by a thousand maidens and a thousand lovers.

'Thus, in the passing of a day, passes the flower and green of mortal life; nor does it ever flower or grow green again to bring back April. Let us gather the rose in the beautiful morning of today, which soon loses its brightness: let us gather the rose of love: let us love now when in loving we can be beloved.'

Tacque; e concorde de gli augelli il coro,
  quasi approvando, il canto indi ripiglia.
  Raddoppian le colombe i baci loro;
  ogni animal d' amar si riconsiglia:
  par che la dura quercia, e'l casto alloro,
  e tutta la frondosa ampia famiglia,
  par che la terra e l'acqua e formi e spiri
  dolcissimi d' amor sensi e sospiri.

Fra melodia sí tenera, e fra tante
  vaghezze allettatrici e lusinghiere,
  va quella coppia; e rigida e costante
  se stessa indura ai vezzi del piacere.
  Ecco tra fronde e fronde il guardo inante
  penetra, e vede, o pargli di vedere;
  vede pur certo il vago e la diletta
  ch'egli è in grembo a la donna, essa a l'erbetta.

Ella dinnanzi al petto ha il vel diviso
  e'l crin sparge incomposto al vento estivo:
  langue per vezzo, e'l suo infiammato viso
  fan biancheggiando i bei sudor piú vivo:
  qual raggio in onda, le scintilla un riso
  ne gli umidi occhi tremulo e lascivo.
  Sovra lui pende: ed ei nel grembo molle
  le posa il capo, e'l vólto al vólto attolle;
  . . . .

She ceased; and the chorus of birds, as if approving, sing in tune [with her] when they take up their song again. The doves redouble their kisses; every living thing is reconciled to love: it seems that the hard oak and the chaste laurel, and all the great leafy family [of trees], it seems that earth and water all create and breathe the sweetest senses and sighs of love.

Through this sweet melody, and through all these alluring and flattering enticements go the two [knights]; and, firm and constant, they harden their hearts against the blandishments of pleasure. See, ahead, their glances peer from grove to grove, and see, or seem to see; then they see clearly on the grass the wandering [knight] and the lovely lady, his head on her lap.

She had undone the veil which covered her breasts and her unbound hair spread in the summer breeze: she was weary from loving, and the beautiful drops of sweat, in their whiteness, refresh her flushed face; like a ray [of sunshine] in water, a tremulous and loving smile sparkles in her moist eyes. She hangs over him: and he rests his head on her soft lap and lifts his face to hers.

Góngora

From SOLEDAD PRIMERA

Era del año la estación florida
en que el mentido robador de Europa
—media luna las armas de su frente,
y el Sol todos los rayos de su pelo—
   luciente honor del cielo,
en campos de zafiro pace estrellas;
cuando el que ministrar podía la copa
a Júpiter mejor que el garzón de Ida,
—náufrago y desdeñado, sobre ausente—
agrimosas de amor dulces querellas
   da al mar; que condolido,
   fué a las ondas, fué al viento
   el mísero gemido,
segundo de Arión dulce instrumento.

Del siempre en la montaña opuesto pino
   al enemigo Noto,
   piadoso miembro roto
—breve tabla—delfín no fué pequeño
al inconsiderado peregrino
que a una Libia de ondas su camino
   fió, y su vida a un leño.

THE FIRST SOLITUDE

It was the flowering season of the year, in which the disguised [lying] robber of Europa—armed on his forehead with a half-moon, the Sun as all the rays of his hide—, the shining honour of heaven, grazes on stars in fields of sapphire, when a youth who could better administer the cup of Jove than the boy of Ida, ship-wrecked, repulsed, separated, gave tearful sweet complaints of love to the sea, so that, [when the sea] had taken pity, the sad groan was to the waves and wind like a second sweet instrument of Arion.

A pitying limb torn from the mountain-pine eternally opposed to the North Wind—a little plank—was no little dolphin to the thoughtless traveller who trusted his way to a Libya of waves, his life to a board.

15

Del Océano pues antes sorbido,
   y luego vomitado
no lejos de un escollo coronado
de secos juncos, de calientes plumas,
   —alga todo y espumas—
halló hospitalidad donde halló nido
   de Júpiter el ave.

Besa la arena, y de la rota nave
   aquella parte poca
que le expuso en la playa dió a la roca:
   que aun se dejan las peñas
isonjear de agradecidas señas.

Desnudo el joven, cuanto ya el vestido
   Océano ha bebido,
restituir le hace a las arenas;
   y al sol lo extiende luego,
   que, lamiéndolo apenas
su dulce lengua de templado fuego,
lento lo embiste, y con süave estilo
la menor onda chupa al menor hilo.

No bien pues de su luz los horizontes
—que hacían desigual, confusamente
montes de agua y piélagos de montes—
   desdorados los siente,

First swallowed by the Ocean, and then vomited up not far from a rock crowned with dry reeds and warm feathers, all seaweed and spume, he found hospitality where the bird of Jupiter had found its nest.

He kisses the sand, and gives to the rock that little part of the shattered ship which had displayed him on the beach; for even cliffs permit themselves to be flattered by signs of gratitude.

The naked youth made his clothing restore as much of the ocean as it had drunk to the sands, [i.e. wrung out his clothes on the beach] and extended it to the sun, which, scarcely licking with his sweet tongue of gentle fire, slowly assails it, and gently sucks the smallest wave from the smallest thread.

No sooner had he seen the horizons lose their gold and light—the horizons which make confusedly unequal mountains into water, and oceans into

cuando—entregado el mísero extranjero
en lo que ya del mar redimió fiero—
entre espinas crepúsculos pisando,
riscos que aun igualara mal, volando,
    veloz, intrépida ala,
—menos cansado que confuso—escala.

    Vencida al fin la cumbre
    —del mar siempre sonante,
de la muda campaña
árbitro igual e inexpugnable muro—,
    con pie ya más seguro
    declina al vacilante
breve esplendor de mal distinta lumbre:
    farol de una cabaña
que sobre el ferro está, en aquel incierto
golfo de sombras anunciando el puerto.

'Rayos—les dice—ya que no de Leda
trémulos hijos, sed de mi fortuna
término luminoso.' Y—recelando
de invidïosa bárbara arboleda
    interposición, cuando
de vientos no conjuración alguna—
    cual, haciendo el villano
la fragosa montaña fácil llano,
    atento sigue aquella
—aun a pesar de las tinieblas bella,
aun a pesar de las estrellas clara—
    piedra, indigna tiara

mountains—when, a miserable exile dressed in what he had rescued from the savage sea, treading upon the twilight amongst thorns, he, less weary than bewildered, scaled rocks that a swift intrepid wing in flight would hardly have reached.

At last, having conquered the summit, the just arbiter and unconquerable wall between the ever sounding sea and the silent plain, he now descended with surer steps towards the flickering brief splendour of a scarcely distinguishable light; [it was] the lantern of a cottage which rode at anchor there, announcing the harbour in that uncertain gulf of shadows.

'Rays', he said to them, 'if you are not the tremulous sons of Leda, be the luminous end of my unhappy fortune.' And, fearing the intervening, invidious, and barbarous trees, or perhaps some conspiracy of the winds, just as the countryman makes the rugged mountain into an easy plain, he intently follows the stone, beautiful despite the darkness, clear despite the stars, which, if

17

—si tradición apócrifa no miente—
de animal tenebroso, cuya frente
carro es brillante de nocturno día:
    tal, diligente, el paso
    el joven apresura,
    midiendo la espesura
    con igual pie que el raso,
fijo—a despecho de la niebla fría—
en el carbunclo, norte de su aguja,
o el Austro brame o la arboleda cruja.

    El can ya, vigilante,
convoca, despidiendo al caminante;
    y la que desviada
luz poca pareció, tanta es vecina,
que yace en ella la robusta encina,
mariposa en cenizas desatada.

Llegó pues el mancebo, y saludado,
sin ambición, sin pompa de palabras,
de los conducidores fué de cabras,
que a Vulcano tenían coronado.

    ¡Oh bienaventurado
    albergue a cualquier hora,
templo de Pales, alquería de Flora!
    No moderno artificio
borró designios, bosquejó modelos,
al cóncavo ajustando de los cielos
    el sublime edificio;

apocryphal tradition doesn't lie, is the unworthy tiara of the animal of night, whose brow is the brilliant chariot of nocturnal day; so, diligently the youth hastened his steps, crossing woods and fields at the same speed, fixed, despite the cold mist, on the carbuncle, the north of his needle, though Auster raged, and the trees cracked.

The vigilant dog called him on, rebuffing the wanderer [i.e. the dog's barking enabled him to fix the position of the shelter, though its intention was to scare him off]; and what from afar had seemed a small light, seemed from near by so large that the tough oak lay within it, [like] a butterfly falling into cinders.

The youth drew near and was greeted, without ambition, or pomp of words, by the goat-herds, who held Vulcan crowned. [i.e. they sat in a circle round the fire (forge of Vulcan) and the glitter of light on the circle of their faces became like a crown on the fire]

O welcome resting-place at any hour, temple of Pales, granary of Flora. No modern architect sketched plans, built models, adjusting the sublime edifice to

retamas sobre robre
tu fábrica son pobre,
do guarda, en vez de acero,
la inocencia al cabrero
más que el silbo al ganado.
¡Oh bienaventurado
albergue a cualquier hora!

No en ti la ambición mora
hidrópica de viento,
ni la que su alimento
el áspid es gitano;
no la que, en vulto comenzando humano,
acaba en mortal fiera,
esfinge bachillera,
que hace hoy a Narciso
ecos solicitar, desdeñar fuentes;
ni la que en salvas gasta impertinentes
la pólvora del tiempo más preciso:
ceremonia profana
que la sinceridad burla villana
sobre el corvo cayado.
¡Oh bienaventurado
albergue a cualquier hora!

the concavity of the skies; rushes over oak are your poor fabric, and innocence instead of steel guards the shepherd, [innocence] better guards the flock than his pipe. O welcome resting-place at any hour.

Ambition, swollen with wind, does not dwell in you, nor she whose food is the Egyptian asp [i.e. Envy], nor she who, beginning in a human face, ends in a savage body, and, a plausible sphinx, tempts today's Narcissus to disdain the streams and pursue echoes; nor she who wastes in impertinent salvoes the powder of a stricter time [i.e. squanders gunpowder in salutes and fireworks]; profane ceremony, at which rustic sincerity leans on its bent crook and laughs. O welcome resting-place at any hour.

19

Tus umbrales ignora
la adulación, sirena
de reales palacios, cuya arena
besó ya tanto leño:
trofeos dulces de un canoro sueño.
No a la soberbia está aquí la mentira
dorándole los pies, en cuanto gira
la esfera de sus plumas,
ni de los rayos baja a las espumas
favor de cera alado.
¡Oh bienaventurado
albergue a cualquier hora!
. . . .

From SOLEDAD SEGUNDA

Éntrase el mar por un arroyo breve
que a recibillo con sediento paso
de su roca natal se precipita,
y mucha sal no sólo en poco vaso,
mas su rüina bebe,
y su fin, cristalina mariposa
—no alada, sino undosa—,
en el farol de Tetis solicita.

Muros desmantelando, pues, de arena,
centauro ya espumoso el Ocëano
—medio mar, medio ría—
dos veces huella la campaña al día,

Your portals know nothing of Adulation, the siren of royal palaces, whose sand is kissed by so much wood, [i.e. have so many ships in their ports], the sweet trophies of a tuneful dream. Nor do flattering lies gild the feet of pride, while she turns in the sphere of her plumes, nor does wax-winged favour fall to the foams from the sunbeams. O welcome resting-place at any hour.

THE SECOND SOLITUDE

The sea comes in through a little stream, which, in order to receive it, hurls itself from its natal rock in a thirsty stride, and drinks not only much salt in its little cup, but also its ruin, and, a crystal butterfly not with wings but waves, begs for its end in the lantern of Tethys.

Then, dismantling the walls of sand, the Ocean, spumy centaur, half sea, half estuary, treads twice a day upon the land, pretending in vain to climb the

escalar pretendiendo el monte en vano
   de quien es dulce vena
   el tarde ya torrente
arrepentido, y aun retrocediente.

Eral lozano así novillo tierno,
   de bien nacido cuerno
   mal lunada la frente,
retrógrado cedió en desigual lucha
a duro toro, aun contra el viento armado:
   no pues de otra manera
   a la violencia mucha
del padre de la aguas, coronado
de blancas ovas y de espuma verde,
resiste obedeciendo, y tierra pierde.

   En la incierta ribera
—guarnición desigual a tanto espejo—,
descubrió la alba a nuestro peregrino
con todo el villanaje ultramarino,
que a la fiesta nupcial, de verde tejo
toldado, ya capaz tradujo pino.

Los escollos el sol rayaba, cuando,
   con remos gemidores,
dos pobres se aparecen pescadores,
nudos al mar de cáñamo fiando.
Ruiseñor en los bosques no más blando,
el verde robre que es barquillo ahora,
   saludar vió la Aurora,

mountain, whose sweet voice is the tardy torrent, now repentant, in retreat.

So might a vigorous bullock, its brow hardly yet a crescent moon with horn, give way in unequal combat to the hard bull, armoured even against the wind; in no different way does the stream oppose but obey and lose ground to the great violence of the father of the waves, crowned with white eggs and green foam.

On the uncertain shore, the unequal frame for such a mirror, Dawn found the wanderer with all the villagers from over the sea, whom a capacious pine had brought to the nuptial feast beneath the canopy of green yew.

The sun shone on the cliffs when, with groaning oars, two poor fishermen appeared, entrusting their hempen knots to the sea. Dawn never saw the nightingale in the woods more sweetly salute the green oak that now is a boat

Que al uno en dulces quejas—y no pocas—
ondas endurecer, liquidar rocas.

Señas mudas la dulce voz doliente
   permitió solamente
a la turba, que dar quisiera voces
a la que de un ancón segunda haya
—cristal pisando azul con pies veloces—
salió improvisa, de una y otra playa
vínculo desatado, instable puente.

   La prora diligente
no sólo dirigió a la opuesta orilla,
mas redujo la música barquilla,
que en dos cuernos del mar caló no breves
sus plomos graves y sus corchos leves.

Los senos ocupó del mayor leño
   la marítima tropa,
   usando al entrar todos
cuantos les enseñó corteses modos
en la lengua del agua ruda escuela,
con nuestro forastero, que la popa
del canoro escogió bajel pequeño.

than he who in sweet and many complaints turns the waters to rock, the rocks to water.

The sweet grieving voice allowed only dumb signs to the crowd who sought to give voice to the second bark which suddenly appeared from the bay, treading the crystal azure with swift feet, the untied knot, the unstable bridge between one shore and the other. [i.e. the crowd, not wanting to disturb the song, made signs to the vessel instead of hailing it]

The diligent prow not only hurried to the opposite shore but brought along with it the musical boat which plunged its heavy leads and light corks into two by no means small horns of sea. [the horns of sea are the waves curling from the prow of a vessel moving at speed]

The maritime troops occupied the bosom of the bigger ship, each of them using upon entry all the courteous manners which the rude school in the language of waters had taught them, to our wanderer, who now chose the poop of the little singing boat.

Aquél, las ondas escarchando, vuela;
éste, con perezoso movimiento,
el mar encuentra, cuya espuma cana
   su parda aguda prora
   resplandeciente cuello
hace de augusta Coya peruana,
a quien hilos el Sur tributó ciento
   de perlas cada hora.
Lágrimas no enjugó más de la Aurora
sobre víolas negras la mañana,
que arrolló su espolón con pompa vana
caduco aljófar, pero aljófar bello.

Dando el huésped licencia para ello,
recurren no a las redes que, mayores,
mucho Océano y pocas aguas prenden,
sino a las que ambiciosas menos penden,
laberinto nudoso de marino
Dédalo, si de leño no, de lino,
fábrica escrupulosa, y aunque incierta,
siempre murada, pero siempre abierta.

Liberalmente de los pescadores
al deseo el estero corresponde,
sin valelle al lascivo ostión el justo
   arnés de hueso, donde
   lisonja breve al gusto
   —mas incentiva—esconde:

The bigger ship, frosting the waters, flies off; the lesser, with a leisurely motion, encounters the sea, [and its] sharp dark prow was made by the grey-headed foam into the splendid throat of the Peruvian queen to whom the South paid as tribute every hour a hundred strings of pearls. Morning did not dry more tears over the black violets of Aurora, than did its bow, with vain pomp, bowl over lovely vanishing pearls. [i.e. the dark prow, as it appeared through the trails of spray, resembled the throat of the queen encircled by pearls, and these pearls, appearing and immediately disappearing were as many as the drops of dew appearing on the black violets of dawn, immediately to vanish in the growing sunshine of morning]

The guest permitting it, they do not resort to the great nets which hold a good deal of ocean but little water, but to the [smaller] ones which hang with less ambition, a knotty labyrinth of marine Daedalus, not of wood but thread, a precise but uncertain [flimsy] fabric, always walled, but always open. [i.e. they use nets of fine mesh for inshore-fishing rather than trawls]

The shallows freely responded to the desires of the fishermen, the closely fitting harness of bone being of no use to the lascivious oyster, where he hides his small but yet incentive flattery from the appetite; perhaps the original

23

contagio original quizá de aquella
  que, siempre hija bella
  de los cristales, una
  venera fué su cuna.

Mallas visten de cáñamo al lenguado,
mientras, en su piel lúbrica fiado,
el congrio, que viscosamente liso,
  las telas burlar quiso,
tejido en ellas se quedó burlado.

Las redes califica menos gruesas,
  sin romper hilo alguno,
pompa el salmón de las reales mesas,
cuando no de los campos de Neptuno,
  y el travieso robalo,
guloso de los Cónsules regalo.

Estos y muchos más, unos desnudos,
otros de escamas fáciles armados,
  dió la ría pescados,
que, nadando en un piélago de nudos,
no agravan poco el negligente robre,
espacïosamente dirigido
al bienaventurado albergue pobre,
que, de carrizos frágiles tejido,
si fabricado no de gruesas cañas,
bóvedas lo coronan de espadañas.

contagion sprang from her, the ever-beautiful daughter of the crystals, whose cradle was a scallop shell.

The hempen meshes clothe the sole, while, trusting to his oily skin the viscously smooth conger sought to trick the nets, but found himself tricked and netted.

The salmon endows the finer nets with its own quality, [the salmon], the pomp of royal tables if not of the fields of Neptune, and the playful robalo, a greedy pleasure for Consuls.

The estuary gave these fish and many more, some naked, others armed with easy scales, which swimming in a sea of knots upset the uncaring oak not a little, as it was spaciously steered to the poor but fortunate resting-place which, woven in fragile rushes, if not of wattles made, is crowned by arches of reed-mace. [i.e. as the nets and catch were dropped on the deck the trim of the boat was upset, but it was still steered spaciously, that is, with plenty of sea-room]

El peregrino, pues, haciendo en tanto
instrumento el bajel, cuerdas los remos,
al céfiro encomienda los extremos
    deste métrico llanto:

    'Si de aire articulado
no son dolientes lágrimas süaves
    estas mis quejas graves,
voces de sangre, y sangre son del alma.
    Fíelas de tu calma,
¡oh mar!, quien otra vez las ha fiado
de tu fortuna aún más que de su hado.

    ¡Oh mar, oh tú, supremo
moderador piadoso de mis daños!:
    tuyos serán mis años,
en tabla redimidos poco fuerte,
    de la bebida muerto,
que ser quiso, en aquel peligro extremo,
ella el forzado y su guadaña el remo.

    Regiones pise ajenas,
o clima propio, planta mía perdida,
    tuya será mi vida,

The wanderer meanwhile, turning the vessel into an instrument, the oars to strings, confided to the zephyr the full gamut of his metrical complaint:
    'If these my grave laments are not sweet grieving tears of articulate air, they are voices of blood, and blood of the soul. I trust them to your calm, O sea, to whose fortune I once trusted them more before than to their fate. [i.e. he once before trusted his complaints to the sea in a storm more than he trusted them to the apparently adverse fate of the wrecking ship, that is to say jumped overboard, so he may now well trust them to the sea when it is calm]
    O sea, thou supreme merciful moderator of my grief, my years shall be yours, redeemed [as they were] on a fragile plank from the brink of death, death herself who wanted to be, in that extreme danger, a galley-slave with a scythe for an oar. [i.e. death wanted to row him away with a scythe; but, though death, unlike the sea, was thirsty, the sea provided a plank for him to float to shore on]
    Whether my lost footsteps be on foreign shores or native land, my life will be

25

si vida me ha dejado que sea tuya
    quien me fuerza a que huya
de su prisión, dejando mis cadenas
rastro en tus ondas más que en tus arenas.

    Audaz mi pensamiento
el cenit escaló, plumas vestido,
    cuyo vuelo atrevido
—si no ha dado su nombre a tus espumas—
    de sus vestidas plumas
conservarán el desvanecimiento
los anales diáfanos del viento.

    Esta, pues, culpa mía
el timón alternar menos seguro
    y el báculo más duro
un lustro ha hecho a mi dudosa mano,
    solicitando en vano
las alas sepultar de mi osadía
donde el sol nace o donde muere el día.

    Muera, enemiga amada,
muera mi culpa, y tu desdén le guarde,
    arrepentido tarde,
suspiro que mi muerte haga leda,
    cuando no le suceda,
o por breve o por tibia o por cansada,
lágrima antes enjuta que llorada.

    Naufragio ya segundo,
o filos pongan de homicida hierro
    fin duro a mi destierro;

thine, if any life, which may be thine, is left me by her who forces me to flee her prison, leaving the mark of my chains more on your waves than on your sands.

My audacious thought scaled the zenith clad in feathers, and its intrepid flight—even if it hasn't given its name to your foams—in plumage dressed will be preserved in the diaphanous annals of the wind.

For a lustrum [five years] this fault of mine has made my doubting hand alternate between the less sure helm and the harder staff, in vain begging to bury the wings of my temerity where the sun is born, or where the day dies.

Sweet enemy, let my guilt die, die, and may your disdain, too late repentant, watch over it with a sigh which would make my death joyful, even if it couldn't be followed by a tear, [a tear] even if it were dried before it were shed by either brevity, indifference, or weariness. [If not a tear, even dried before shed, can be given by her, then just a sigh would make his death joyful.]

Whether a second shipwreck or edges of homicidal iron put a hard end to my

tan generosa fe, no fácil onda,
    no poca tierra esconda:
urna suya el Océano profundo,
y obeliscos los montes sean del mundo.

    Túmulo tanto debe
agradecido Amor a mi pie errante;
    líquido, pues, diamante
calle mis huesos, y elevada cima
    selle sí, mas no oprima,
esta que le fiaré ceniza breve,
si hay ondas mudas y si hay tierra leve.'

No es sordo el mar: la erudición engaña.
    Bien que tal vez sañudo
no oya al piloto, o le responda fiero,
sereno disimula más orejas
    que sembró dulces quejas
—canoro labrador—el forastero
    en su undosa campaña.

Espongïoso, pues, se bebió y mudo
el lagrimoso reconocimiento,
de cuyos dulces números no poca
    concentuosa suma
en los dos giros de invisible pluma
que fingen sus dos alas, hurtó el viento;
Eco—vestida una cavada roca—
solicitó curiosa y guardó avara
la más dulce—si no la menos clara—
    sílaba, siendo en tanto
la vista de las chozas fin del canto.

exile, such generous faith no easy wave, no little earth, shall conceal. Its urn will be the deep ocean, the mountains of the world its obelisks.

Grateful Love owes such a tomb to my errant feet; so let liquid diamond still my bones, and the high-raised mountain-top seal but not oppress these little ashes I entrust to them, if there be a silence in the waves, a lightness in the earth.'

The ocean is not deaf; knowledge deceives. Although sometimes stern it heeds not the pilot, or replies in anger, now, serene, it pretends more ears than there were sweet laments which the traveller, tuneful labourer, cast over its wavy plains.

Spongy and dumb it drank the tearful confession, and a tuneful sum of not a few of its sweet numbers was stolen by the wind in the two gyres of invisible plumage which its two wings pretend. Echo clad in a hollow rock, curiously sought and avariciously kept the sweetest, if not the least clear, syllable, the sight of the huts being finally the end of the song.

Yace en el mar, si no continuada,
ísla mal de la tierra dividida,
cuya forma tortuga es perezosa:
díganlo cuantos siglos ha que nada
sin besar de la playa espacïosa
la arena, de las ondas repetida.

A pesar, pues, del agua que la oculta,
concha, si mucha no, capaz ostenta
de albergues, donde la humildad contenta
mora, y Pomona se venera culta.

Dos son las chozas, pobre su artificio
más aún que caduca su materia:
de los mancebos dos, la mayor, cuna;
de las redes la otra y su ejercicio,
     competente oficina.
Lo que agradable más se determina
del breve islote, ocupa su fortuna,
los extremos de fausto y de miseria
moderando.

                En la plancha los recibe
el padre de los dos, émulo cano
del sagrado Nereo, no ya tanto
porque a la par de los escollos vive,
porque en el mar preside comarcano
al ejercicio piscatorio, cuanto
por seis hijas, por seis deidades bellas,
del cielo espumas y del mar estrellas.

There is an island in the sea, if not a continuation of the land then scarcely
divided from it, shaped like the lazy tortoise; and let as many centuries as there
are tell that it swims without kissing the sand of the broad beach, always sought
by the waves.

Despite the waters hiding it, [the island] showed its shell [like a tortoise], if not
large, at least big enough for dwelling places, where humility dwells content,
and Pomona is worshipped.

The huts are two, crudely built of cruder materials, the larger the cradle of the
youths, the other the adequate storehouse for their nets and trade. Their
fortune occupied the most pleasant part of the island, falling between the two
extremes of wealth and poverty.

The father of the two received them on the shore, grey-haired replica of
sacred Neptune, not so much in that he lived by the rocks, and presided over the
piscatorial trade in the neighbouring seas, but in his six daughters, his lovely
goddesses, the foams of heaven, the stars of the sea.

Acogió al huésped con urbano estilo,
y á su voz, que los juncos obedecen,
tres hijas suyas cándidas le ofrecen,
que engaños construyendo están de hilo.
El huerto le da esotras, a quien debe
sí púrpura la rosa, el lilio nieve.
. . . .

    Aura en esto marina
el discurso, y el día juntamente,
trémula, si veloz, les arrebata,
alas batiendo líquidas, y en ellas
    dulcísimas querellas
de pescadores dos, de dos amantes
en redes ambos y en edad iguales.
    Dividiendo cristales,
en la mitad de un óvalo de plata,
venía a tiempo el nieto de la espuma
que los mancebos daban alternantes
al viento quejas. Órganos de pluma
—aves digo de Leda—
tales no oyó el Caístro en su arboleda,
tales no vió el Meandro en su corriente.
Inficionando pues süavemente
las ondas el Amor, sus flechas remos,
hasta donde se besan los extremos
de la isla y del agua no los deja.
. . . .

He welcomed the youth in a civil manner, and by his voice, which even reeds obey, offered him three of his snow-white daughters, who were weaving deceits from thread [i.e. making nets]; the garden offered him the others, to whom the rose owed its purple, the lily its snow.

Then a sea-breeze, wavering but swift, snatches away the discourse along with the day, beating liquid wings, and in them the sweetest complaints of two fishermen, of two lovers, both in the nets [of love], and both of the same age.
    Dividing the crystals, in the midst of an oval of silver came the grandson of the foam [Cupid] while the youths gave alternating laments to the winds. Such organs of feathers—I mean the birds of Leda [swans]—Caistro did not hear in its glade, nor Meander see in its current. Sweetly poisoning the waves, Love, his arrows oars, leaves them not till the extremes of land and water kiss.

29

Lícidas, gloria en tanto
de la playa, Micón de sus arenas
    —invidia de sirenas,
convocación su canto
de músicos delfines, aunque mudos—
    en números no rudos
    el primero se queja
    de la culta Leucipe,
décimo esplendor bello de Aganipe;
    de Cloris el segundo,
escollo de cristal, meta del mundo.

LÍCIDAS
    ¿A qué piensas, barquilla,
pobre ya cuna de mi edad primera,
que cisne te conduzgo a esta ribera?
A cantar dulce, y a morirme luego.
    Si te perdona el fuego
que mis huesos vinculan, en su orilla,
tumba te bese el mar, vuelta la quilla.

MICÓN
    Cansado leño mío,
hijo del bosque y padre de mi vida
    —de tus remos ahora conducida
a desatarse en lágrimas cantando—,
    el doliente, si blando,
curso del llanto métrico te fío,
nadante urna de canoro río.

Meanwhile Licidas, glory of the shore, Micon of its sands, the siren's envy, his song the convocation of dolphins, musical though dumb; in no rude numbers' the first complained of the sweetly elegant Leucippe, the tenth lovely splendour of Aganippe [i.e. a tenth Muse]; the second of Cloris, the crystal rock, the goal of the world.

Licidas Why do you think, little boat, poor cradle of my youth, that like a swan I steer you to this shore to sweetly sing and die? If the fire which my bones chain forgives you, the sea by its shore will kiss you, you the tomb with the overturned keel. [i.e. if the fire of my love doesn't consume you as well as me, you will remain as a memorial on the beach]

Micon My weary wood, son of the forest and father of my life,—now brought by your oars to break into singing tears—I entrust to you the grieving if sweet course of metrical complaint, to you the swimming urn of the tuneful river.

LÍCIDAS
   Las rugosas veneras
—fecundas no de aljófar blanco el seno,
ni del que enciende el mar tirio veneno—
entre crespos buscaba caracoles,
   cuando de tus dos soles
fulminado, ya señas no ligeras
de mis cenizas dieron tus riberas.

MICÓN
   Distinguir sabía apenas
el menor leño de la mayor urca
que velera un Neptuno y otro surca,
y tus prisiones ya arrastraba graves;
   si dudas lo que sabes,
lee cuanto han impreso en tus arenas,
a pesar de los vientos, mis cadenas.

LÍCIDAS
   Las que el cielo mercedes
hizo a mi forma, ¡oh dulce mi enemiga!,
lisonja no, serenidad lo diga
de limpia consultada ya laguna,
   y los de mi fortuna
privilegios, el mar a quien di redes,
más que a la selva lazos Ganimedes.

MICÓN
   No ondas, no luciente
cristal—agua al fin dulcemente dura—:

Licidas I was seeking, among the curling snails, wrinkled shells, not fertile in
   white-breasted pearl, nor in the poison which inflames the purple sea, when,
   brought to blaze by your two suns, I left the heavy signs of my ashes on your
   shores.
Micon I could scarcely distinguish the smallest bark of the greatest whale
   which, like a sailing ship ploughs one Neptune and the other [i.e. sails on
   both oceans], and I was already dragging your heavy fetters behind me; if
   you doubt what you know, read what my chains have written on your sands
   in spite of the winds.
Licidas May the serenity of a limpid lake, as I consult it, tell of these mercies
   which the heavens endowed upon my form, O my sweet enemy, and let the
   sea tell of the blessings of my fortune [the sea] to which I vowed more of my
   nets than Ganymede vowed snares to the forest.
Micon Let not waves, not lucent crystal—that hard watery sweetness—but

31

invidia califique mi figura
de musculosos jóvenes desnudos.
   Menos dió al bosque nudos
que yo al mar, el que a un dios hizo valiente
mentir cerdas, celoso espumar diente.

LÍCIDAS

   Cuantos pedernal duro
bruñe nácares boto, agudo raya
en la oficina undosa desta playa,
tantos Palemo a su Licore bella
   suspende, y tantos ella
al flaco da, que me construyen muro,
junco frágil, carrizo mal seguro.

MICÓN

   Las siempre desiguales
blancas primero ramas, después rojas,
de árbol que, nadante, ignoró hojas,
trompa Tritón del agua, a la alta gruta
   de Nísida tributa,
ninfa por quien lucientes son corales
los rudos troncos hoy de mis umbrales.

LÍCIDAS

   Esta, en plantas no escrita,
en piedras sí, firmeza honre Himeneo,
calzándole talares mi deseo:

---

let the envious lust of hard muscular youths be the proof of my [beautiful] form. He who made the valiant God cheat the swine gave fewer knots to the wood than I gave, foaming, sharp-toothed, to the sea. [He is lovelier than Adonis. The 'foaming, sharp-toothed' applies equally in Spanish to the boar and the fish hooks, but it is difficult to convey in English. The knots are foaming because they are hauled from the breaking wave.]

Licidas As many mothers-of-pearl as the blunt stones polish and the sharp stones carve in the wavy workshop of the shore, so many does Palaemon give to his fair Lycoris, and the same number she gives to the weak walls which fragile reeds and insecure rushes built for me.

Micon The ever unequal branches, first white and then red, of the swimming tree which knows not leaves [i.e. coral] Triton the trumpeter of the water gave in tribute to the high cavern of Nisida, the nymph through whom the rude trunks of my threshold are now gleaming corals.

Licidas Let Hymen honour this constancy, engraved not on wood but stone, and my desire is to shoe him with the winged sandals [of Mercury]; for time

que el tiempo vuela. Goza, pues, ahora
  los lilios de tu aurora,
que al tramontar del sol mal solicita
abeja, aun negligente, flor marchita.

       MICÓN
  Si fe tanta no en vano
desafía las rocas donde, impresa,
con labio alterno mucho mar la besa,
nupcial la califique tea luciente.
  Mira que la edad miente,
mira que del almendro más lozano
Parca es interïor breve gusano.

. . . .

Milton

From PARADISE LOST (Book IV. 205–324)

. . . .

Beneath him with new wonder now he views
To all delight of human sense expos'd
In narrow room Natures whole wealth, yea more,
A Heav'n on Earth: for blissful Paradise
Of God the Garden was, by him in th' East
Of *Eden* planted; *Eden* stretchd her Line
From *Auran* Eastward to the Royal Towrs
Of Great *Seleucia*, built by *Grecian* Kings,
Or where the Sons of *Eden* long before
Dwelt in *Telassar*: in this pleasant soile
His farr more pleasant Garden God ordaind;
Out of the fertil ground he caus'd to grow
All Trees of noblest kind for sight, smell, taste;

  is flying. Now today enjoy the lilies of your dawn, for at the setting of the sun, the bee, already negligent, unwillingly woos the withered flower.
Micon   If so much faith does not in vain defy the rocks, where carved, the sea strongly kisses it with alternate lips, let the shining nuptial torch be its witness. See, how old age lies, see in the most luscious of almond-trees fate is the tiny interior worm.

And all amid them stood the Tree of Life,
High eminent, blooming Ambrosial Fruit
Of vegetable Gold; and next to Life
Our Death the Tree of Knowledge grew fast by,
Knowledge of Good bought dear by knowing ill.
Southward through *Eden* went a River large,
Nor chang'd his course, but through the shaggie hill
Passd underneath ingulft, for God had thrown
That Mountain as his Garden mould high rais'd
Upon the rapid current, which through veins
Of porous Earth with kindly thirst up drawn,
Rose a fresh Fountain, and with many a rill
Waterd the Garden; thence united fell
Down the steep glade, and met the nether Flood,
Which from his darksom passage now appears,
And now divided into four main Streams
Runs diverse, wandring many a famous Realm
And Country whereof here needs no account,
But rather to tell how, if Art could tell,
How from that Saphire Fount the crisped Brooks,
Rouling on Orient Pearl and sands of Gold,
With mazie error under pendant shades
Ran Nectar, visiting each plant, and fed
Flowrs worthy of Paradise which not nice Art
In Beds and curious Knots, but Nature boon
Pourd forth profuse on Hill and Dale and Plain,
Both where the morning Sun first warmly smote
The open field, and where the unpierc't shade
Imbrownd the noontide Bowrs: Thus was this place,
A happy rural seat of various view;
Groves whose rich Trees wept odorous Gumms and Baum,
Others whose fruit burnisht with Golden Rinde
Hung amiable, *Hesperian* Fables true,
If true, here only, and of delicious taste:
Betwixt them Lawns or level Downs, and Flocks
Grazing the tender herb, were interpos'd,
Or palmie hillock, or the flowrie lap
Of som irriguous Valley spred her store,
Flowrs of all hue, and without Thorn the Rose:
Another side, umbrageous Grots and Caves
Of cool recess, ore which the mantling Vine
Lays forth her purple Grape, and gently creeps
Luxuriant; mean while murmuring waters fall
Down the slope hills, disperst or in a Lake,
That to the fringed Bank with Myrtle crownd
Her crystal mirror holds, unite thir streams.
The Birds thir quire apply; airs, vernal airs,

Breathing the smell of field and grove, attune
The trembling leaves, while Universal *Pan*
Knit with the *Graces* and the *Hours* in dance
Led on th' Eternal Spring. Not that fair field
Of *Enna*, where *Proserpin* gathring flowrs
Her self a fairer Flowre by gloomie *Dis*
Was gatherd, which cost *Ceres* all that pain
To seek her through the world; nor that sweet Grove
Of *Daphne* by *Orontes*, and th' inspir'd
Castalian Spring, might with this Paradise
Of *Eden* strive; nor that *Nyseian* Ile
Girt with the River *Triton*, where old *Cham*,
Whom Gentiles *Ammon* call and *Libyan Jove*,
His *Amalthea* and her Florid Son
Young *Bacchus* from his Stepdame *Rhea*'s eye;
Nor where *Abassin* Kings thir issue Guard,
Mount *Amara*, though this by some suppos'd
True Paradise under the *Ethiop* Line
By *Nilus* head, enclos'd with shining Rock,
A whole days journey high, but wide remote
From this *Assyrian* Garden, where the Fiend
Saw undelighted all delight, all kind
Of living Creatures new to sight and strange:
Two of far nobler shape erect and tall,
Godlike erect, with native Honour clad
In naked Majestie seemd Lords of all,
And worthie seemd, for in thir looks Divine
The image of thir glorious Maker shon,
Truth, Wisdom, Sanctitude severe and pure,
Severe, but in true filial freedom plac't;
Whence true autoritie in men; though both
Not equal, as thir sex not equal seemd;
For contemplation hee and valour formd,
For softness shee and sweet attractive Grace,
Hee for God only, shee for God in him:
His fair large Front and Eye sublime declar'd
Absolute rule; and Hyacinthin Locks
Round from his parted forelock manly hung
Clustring, but not beneath his shoulders broad:
Shee as a veil down to the slender waist
Her unadorned golden tresses wore
Dissheveld, but in wanton ringlets wav'd
As the Vine curls her tendrils, which impli'd
Subjection, but requir'd with gentle sway,
And by her yielded, by him best receiv'd,
Yielded with coy submission, modest pride,
And sweet reluctant amorous delay.

Nor those mysterious parts were then conceal'd,
Then was not guiltie shame, dishonest shame
Of Natures works: honor dishonorable,
Sin-bred, how have ye troubl'd all mankind
With shews instead, mere shews of seeming pure,
And banisht from mans life his happiest life,
Simplicitie and spotless innocence.
So passd they naked on, nor shunnd the sight
Of God or Angel, for they thought no ill:
So hand in hand they passd, the lovliest pair
That ever since in loves imbraces met,
Adam the goodliest man of men since born
His Sons, the fairest of her Daughters *Eve*.

. . . .

Marvell

From APPLETON HOUSE (stanzas 37–43 and 63–77)

. . . .

XXXVII

When in the *East* the Morning Ray
Hangs out the Colours of the Day,
The Bee through these known Allies hums,
Beating the *Dian* with its *Drumms*.
Then Flow'rs their drowsie Eylids raise,
Their Silken Ensigns each displays,
And dries its Pan yet dank with Dew,
And fills its Flask with Odours new.

XXXVIII

These, as their *Governour* goes by,
In fragrant Vollyes they let fly;
And to salute their *Governess*
Again as great a charge they press:
None for the *Virgin Nymph*; for She
Seems with the Flow'rs a Flow'r to be.
And think so still! though not compare
With Breath so sweet, or Cheek so faire.

XXXIX

Well shot ye Firemen! Oh how sweet,
And round your equal Fires do meet;

36

Whose shrill report no Ear can tell,
But Ecchoes to the Eye and smell.
See how the Flow'rs, as at *Parade*,
Under their *Colours* stand displaid:
Each *Regiment* in order grows,
That of the Tulip Pinke and Rose.

XL

But when the vigilant *Patroul*
Of Stars walks round about the *Pole*,
Their Leaves, that to the stalks are curl'd,
Seem to their Staves the *Ensigns* furl'd.
Then in some Flow'rs beloved Hut
Each Bee as Sentinel is shut;
And sleeps so too: but, if once stir'd,
She runs you through, or askes *the Word*.

XLI

Oh Thou, that dear and happy Isle
The Garden of the World ere while,
Thou *Paradise* of four Seas,
Which *Heaven* planted us to please,
But, to exclude the World, did guard
With watry if not flaming Sword;
What luckless Apple did we tast,
To make us Mortal, and The Wast?

XLII

Unhappy! shall we never more
That sweet *Militia* restore,
When Gardens only had their Towrs,
And all the Garrisons were Flowrs,
When Roses only Arms might bear,
And Men did rosie Garlands wear?
Tulips, in several Colours barr'd,
Were then the *Switzers* of our *Guard*.

XLIII

The *Gardiner* had the *Souldiers* place,
And his more gentle Forts did trace.
The Nursery of all things green
Was then the only *Magazeen*.
The *Winter Quarters* were the Stoves,
Where he the tender Plants removes.
But War all this doth overgrow:
We Ord'nance Plant and Powder sow.

. . . .

LXIII

When first the Eye this Forrest sees
It seems indeed as *Wood* not *Trees*:
As if their Neighbourhood so old
To one great Trunk them all did mold.
There the huge Bulk takes place, as ment
To thrust up a *Fifth Element*;
And stretches still so closely wedg'd
As if the Night within were hedg'd.

LXIV

Dark all without it knits; within
It opens passable and thin;
And in as loose an order grows,
As the *Corinthean Porticoes*.
The arching Boughs unite between
The Columnes of the Temple green;
And underneath the winged Quires
Echo about their tuned Fires.

LXV

The *Nightingale* does here make choice
To sing the Tryals of her Voice.
Low Shrubs she sits in, and adorns
With Musick high the squatted Thorns.
But highest Oakes stoop down to hear,
And listning Elders prick the Ear.
The Thorn, lest it should hurt her, draws
Within the Skin its shrunken claws.

LXVI

But I have for my Musick found
A Sadder, yet more pleasing Sound:
The *Stock-doves*, whose fair necks are grac'd
With Nuptial Rings their Ensigns chast;
Yet always, for some Cause unknown,
Sad pair unto the Elms they moan.
O why should such a Couple mourn,
That in so equal Flames do burn!

LXVII

Then as I carless on the Bed
Of gelid *Straw-berryes* do tread,
And through the Hazles thick espy
The hatching *Thrastles* shining Eye,

The *Heron* from the Ashes top,
The eldest of its young lets drop,
As if it Stork-like did pretend
That *Tribute* to *its Lord* to send.

LXVIII

But most the *Hewel*'s wonders are,
Who here has the *Holt-felsters* care.
He walks still upright from the Root,
Meas'ring the Timber with his Foot;
And all the way, to keep it clean,
Doth from the Bark the Wood-moths glean.
He, with his Beak, examines well
Which fit to stand and which to fell.

LXIX

The good he numbers up, and hacks;
As if he mark'd them with the Ax.
But where he, tinkling with his Beak,
Does find the hollow Oak to speak,
That for his building he designs,
And through the tainted Side he mines.
Who could have thought the *tallest Oak*
Should fall by such a *feeble Strok*'!

LXX

Nor would it, had the Tree not fed
A *Traitor-worm*, within it bred.
(As first our *Flesh* corrupt within
Tempts impotent and bashful *Sin*.)
And yet that *Worm* triumphs not long,
But serves to feed the *Hewels young*.
While the Oake seems to fall content,
Viewing the Treason's Punishment.

LXXI

Thus I, *easie Philosopher*,
Among the *Birds* and *Trees* confer:
And little now to make me, wants
Or of the *Fowles*, or of the *Plants*.
Give me but Wings as they, and I
Streight floting on the Air shall fly:
Or turn me but, and you shall see
I was but an inverted Tree.

LXXII

Already I begin to call
In their most learned Original:
And where I Language want, my Signs
The Bird upon the Bough divines;
And more attentive there doth sit
Then if She were with Lime-twigs knit.
No Leaf does tremble in the Wind
Which I returning cannot find.

LXXIII

Out of these scatter'd *Sibyls* Leaves
Strange *Prophecies* my Phancy weaves:
And in one History consumes,
Like *Mexique Paintings*, all the *Plumes*.
What *Rome, Greece, Palestine*, ere said
I in this light *Mosaick* read.
Thrice happy he who, not mistook,
Hath read in *Natures mystick Book*.

LXXIV

And see how Chance's better Wit
Could with a Mask my studies hit!
The Oak-Leaves me embroyder all,
Between which Caterpillars crawl:
And Ivy, with familiar trails,
Me licks, and clasps, and curles, and hales.
Under this *antick Cope* I move
Like some great *Prelate of the Grove*,

LXXV

Then, languishing with ease, I toss
On Pallets swoln of Velvet Moss;
While the Wind, cooling through the Boughs,
Flatters with Air my panting Brows.
Thanks for my Rest ye *Mossy Banks*,
And unto you *cool Zephyr's* Thanks,
Who, as my Hair, my Thoughts too shed,
And winnow from the Chaff my Head.

LXXVI

How safe, methinks, and strong, behind
These Trees have I incamp'd my Mind;
Where Beauty, aiming at the Heart,
Bends in some Tree its useless Dart;

And where the World no certain Shot
Can make, or me it toucheth not.
But I on it securely play,
And gaul its Horsemen all the Day.

LXXVII

Bind me ye *Woodbines* in your 'twines,
Curle me about ye gadding *Vines*,
And Oh so close your Circles lace,
That I may never leave this Place:
But, lest your Fetters prove too weak,
Ere I your Silken Bondage break,
Do you, *O Brambles*, chain me too,
And courteous *Briars* nail me through.

. . . .

Roberthin

FRUEHLINGSLIED

Es kömmt in seiner Herrlichkeit
Der holde Lenz hernieder
Und schenket seine Wonnezeit
Dem Erdenkreise wieder;

Er malt die Wolken mit Azur,
Mit Gold der Wolken Rände,
Mit Regenbogen Tal und Flur,
Mit Schmelz die Gartenwände;

Er kleidet den entblösten Baum,
Deckt ihn mit einer Krone,
Dass unter seinem Schattenraum
Das Volk der Vögel wohne.

SPRING SONG

In his splendour fair spring descends and once again gives his time of delight to the world.

He paints the clouds with azure and their edges with gold, he paints valley and meadow with rainbows, with enamel the garden walls;

he clothes the naked tree, covers it with a crown, so that in its shady bower the birds may dwell.

41

A Vision of Nature

Wie preiset ihrer Lieder Schall
Die Wunder seiner Rechten,
Die Lerch am Tage, Nachtigall
In schauervollen Nächten.

Die Fische scherzen in der Flut,
Die Herden auf der Weide,
Es schwärmt der Bienen junge Brut
Auf der beblümten Heide.

Der Mensch allein, der Schöpfung Haupt,
Vergräbet sich in Sorgen,
Ist immer seiner selbst beraubt,
Lebt immer nur für morgen;

Ihn weckt Auroras güldner Strahl,
Ihm lacht die Flur vergebens,
Er wird, nach selbstgemachter Qual,
Der Henker seines Lebens,

Das ohnehin wie ein Gesicht
Des Morgentraums entfliehet,
Und vor ein schreckliches Gericht
Ihn, den Verbrecher, ziehet.

How the sound of their songs praises the miracle of his right [hand], the lark's in the daytime, the nightingale's in chill nights.

The fish disport themselves in the water, the cattle in the pasture; young bees swarm on the flowering heathland.

Only man, the crown of creation, is buried in cares, bereft of himself he forever lives only for tomorrow.

In vain does Aurora's golden ray wake him, [in vain] do the meadows smile at him, through self-torture he is the executioner of his own life,

which in any case is fleeting like the vision of a morning dream, dragging him, the criminal, before a terrible tribunal.

Cotton

AN INVITATION TO PHILLIS

Come live with mee and be my Love
And thou shalt all the pleasures proove
The mountaines' towring tops can show,
Inhabiting the vales below.
From a brave height my starre shall shine
T'illuminate the desart Clime.
Thy Summer's Bower shall overlooke,
The subtill windings of the Brooke
For thy delight which onely springs,
And cutts her way with Turtle's Wings.
The Pavement of thy Roomes shall shine,
With the Druis'd treasures of the Mine,
And not a Tale of Love, but shall
In Mineture adorne thy wall.
Thy Closett shall Queenes Casketts mock
With rustick jewell of the Rock,
And thyne own light shall make a Gemme,
As bright of these, as Queenes of them.
From this thy Spheare, thou shalt behould
Thy Snowy Ewes troope or'e the mold,
Who yearely pay my Love a peece
Of Tender Lamb, and Silver Fleece.
And when Sols Rayes shall all combine
Thyne to out burne, though not out shine,
Then at the foote of som Greene Hill,
Where Crystall Dove runns murmuring still,
Weele Angle for the bright eyd Fish,
To make my Love a dainty Dish;
Or, in a Cave, by Nature made,
Fly to the Covert of the Shade,
Where all the Pleasures wee will Proove,
Taught by the little God of Love.

And when bright Phebus scorching beames,
Shall cease to Guild the Silver Streames,
Then in the could Armes of the Flood
Wee'le bathing coole the factious blood,
Thy beautious Limbs the Brooke shall grace,
Like the reflex of Cynthia's face,
Whilst all the wondring fry do Greete
The welcom Light, adore thy feet,

A Vision of Nature

Supposeing Venus to be come
To send a kisse to Thetis home.
And following night shall trifled bee,
Sweete; as thou know'st, I promis'd thee;
Thus shall the Summers dayes, and Nights,
Be dedicated to thy delights.
Then live with mee, and be my Love
And all these Pleasures shalt thou proove.

    But when the sapless Season brings
Cold Winter on her shivering wings,
Freezing the Rivers Liquid Face,
Into a Crystall Lookeing-Glass,
And that the Trees theire Naked bones
Together knock, like Skeletons,
Then with softest, whitest Locks,
Spun with the tribute of thy flocks,
We will orecast thy whiter Skin,
Winter without, a Springe within.
Att the first peepe of day Ile rise,
To make the sullen Hare thy prise
And thou with open Armes shalt com
To bidd thy Hunter welcom home.
The Partridge, Plover, and the Poote
Ile with the subtle Mallard shoote;
The Fellfare, and the greedy Thrush
Shall drop from every Hawthorne Bush,
And the slow Heron downe shall fall,
To feede my Fayrest Fayre withall,
The Fether'd People of the Ayre,
Shall fall to be my Phyllis' Fare,
Noe storme shall touch thee, Tempest move;
Then live with mee, and be my Love.

    But from her cloister when I bring,
My Phyllis to restore the Springe,
The Ruffling Boreas shall withdraw,
The Snow shall melt, the Ice shall thaw;
The Ague-ish Plants Fresh Leaves shall shew,
The Earth put on her verdant hue,
And Thou (Fair Phillis) shalt be seene
Mine, and the Summers beautious Queene.
    These, and more Pleasures shalt thou proove;
    Then Live with mee, and be my Love.

Harsdörffer

DER REGEN

Scheint das Himmelwasser teuer,
Ist der Erden Haar geröst:
Ist der Sonnen Strahlenfeuer
Ueber diesen Flur erböst—
Schauet, dort ist unterwegen
Ein so lang erseufzter Regen!
Was verbrennt und ausgerost,
Blumen, Korn, Frucht und Most,
Fühlet nährlich feuchten Trost.

Schauet doch die Himmelstränen,
Die der Frommen Zährenflut
Machet von der Höhe frenen
Auf der heissen Erden Glut.
Schauet Iris' Bogen malen
Die Rubinen und Opalen!
Der vor armen Quellen Saft
Strudelt mit erneuter Kraft
Und den Winzern Freud verschafft.

Nun die trübe Wolke bürstet,
Sind die Felder Jauchzens voll:
Auen, die so lang gedürstet,
Schlürfen sich nun satt und doll.
Wein her! Lasst die Gläser blinken!

THE RAIN

When water from heaven is scarce, the earth's hair is scorched: the sun's fiery rays are angry with this land—look, there comes that long sighed-for rain! All that was burned and scorched, flowers, corn, fruit and the new wine, now feels the nourishing and moist balm.

Look at those tears from heaven which the tears of the faithful have drawn from on high to fall on the hot glowing earth. Look how Iris' arch is painting rubies and opals! The spring which earlier had been dried up now gushes forth with renewed vigour, delighting the wine growers.

Now the dark cloud has burst, the fields are full of joy: meadows which had been thirsty for so long, now drink their fill. Bring wine! Let the glasses gleam!

45

A *Vision of Nature*

Warum sollten wir nicht trinken,
Zecht doch unser Vaterland,
Welches sitzt auf trocknem Land.
Trinken ist der Freundschaft Band.

Höret wie der Regen platschert
Und sich mit den Blättern schlägt,
Lispelt, wüspelt, rauschet, klatschert
Und den Ohren Lust erregt.
Ach dass ein so holdes Flüssen
Möchte mein Gespräch versüssen!
Trinket, aber nicht zu viel,
Saufen ist der Reue Ziel,
Schwätzen ist ein Freudenspiel.

De Viau

LE MATIN

L'Aurore sur le front du jour
Seme l'azur, l'or et l'yvoire,
Et le Soleil, lassé de boire,
Commence son oblique tour.

Ses chevaux, au sortir de l'onde,
De flamme et de clarté couverts,
La bouche et les naseaux ouverts,
Ronflent la lumière du monde.

Why should we not drink, when our country, sitting on dry land, is drinking too. Drinking seals the bond of friendship.

Listen to the rain splashing and hitting the leaves, [hear it] lisping, whispering, rushing, pattering and delighting the ear. Ah, would that my speech could be sweetened by just such a sweet flow! Drink, but not too much, or you will rue it, whereas talking is a delightful pastime.

THE MORNING
Aurora strews azure, gold, and ivory upon the brow of day, and the Sun, weary of drinking, begins his oblique circuit.

His horses, coming from the wave, covered with flame and clarity, mouth and nostrils open, snort the light of the world.

Ardans ils vont à nos ruisseaux
Et dessous le sel et l'escume
Boivent l'humidité qui fume
Si tost qu'ils ont quitté les eaux.

La Lune fuit devant nos yeux;
La nuict a retiré ses voiles;
Peu à peu le front des estoilles
S'unit à la couleur des Cieux.

Les ombres tombent des montagnes,
Elles croissent à veüe d'œil,
Et d'un long vestement de deuil
Couvrent la face des campagnes.

Le Soleil change de sejour
Il pénètre le sein de l'onde,
Et par l'autre moitié du monde
Pousse le chariot du jour.

Desjà la diligente avette
Boit la marjolaine et le thyn,
Et revient riche du butin
Qu'elle a prins sur le mont Hymette.

Je voy le genereux lion
Qui sort de sa demeure creuse
Herissant sa perruque affreuse,
Qui faict fuir Endimion.

Burning they come to our streams and beneath the salt and the spray drink the humidity which smokes as soon as they have left the waters.

The moon flees before our eyes; night has drawn back her veils; little by little the face of the stars is united with the colour of the skies.

Shadows fall from the mountains, they grow before our eyes and cover the face of the land with a long robe of mourning.

The Sun changes his resting-place, he penetrates the bosom of the wave, and drives the chariot of day through the other half of the world.

Already the diligent bee drinks the marjoram and thyme, and returns, rich with the plunder she has captured on Mount Hymettus.

I see the noble lion, who comes from his hollow den, bristling his fearful wig which puts Endymion to flight.

47

A Vision of Nature

Sa dame, entrant dans les boccages,
Compte les sangliers qu'elle a pris,
Ou devale chez les esprits
Errant aux sombres marescages.

Je voy les agneaux bondissans
Sur les bleds qui ne font que naistre;
Cloris, chantant, les meine paistre
Parmy ces costaux verdissans.

Les oyseaux, d'un joyeux ramage,
En chantant semblent adorer
La lumière qui vient dorer
Leur cabinet et leur plumage.

Le pré paroist en ses couleurs,
La bergère aux champs revenue
Mouillant sa jambe toute nue
Foule les herbes et les fleurs.

La charrue escorche la plaine;
Le bouvier, qui suit les seillons,
Presse de voix et d'aiguillons
Le couple de bœufs qui l'entraine.

Alix appreste son fuseau;
Sa mère, qui luy faict la tasche,
Presse le chanvre qu'elle attache
A sa quenouille de roseau.

His lady, going into the groves, counts the wild boar she has captured, or goes down among the spirits wandering in dismal swamps.

I see lambs leaping over the newly-born grass; Cloris, singing, leads them to pasture among these green hillsides.

The birds, in joyous carolling, seem, as they sing, to worship the light which comes to turn their plumage and their bedrooms to gold.

The fields reappear in their colours, the shepherdess, returned to the meadows, drenching her naked leg, treads on herbs and flowers.

The plough cuts through the plain; and the herdsman, following the furrows, urged with his voice and with goads the pair of oxen which pull it.

Alix gets her spindle; her mother, who set her the task, presses the hemp which she fits to her reed distaff.

Une confuse violence
Trouble le calme de la nuict,
Et la lumière, avec le bruit,
Dissipent l'ombre et le silence.

Alidor cherche à son resveil
L'ombre d'Iris qu'il a baisee,
Et pleure en son ame abusee
La fuitte d'un si doux sommeil.

Les bestes sont dans leur tanière,
Qui tremblent de voir le Soleil.
L'homme, remis par le sommeil,
Reprend son œuvre coustumière.

Le forgeron est au fourneau;
Oy comme le charbon s'allume!
Le fer rouge, dessus l'enclume,
Estincelle sous le marteau.

Ceste chandelle semble morte,
Le jour la faict esvanouyr;
Le Soleil vient nous esblouyr:
Voy qu'il passe au travers la porte!

Il est jour: levons nous, Philis;
Allons à nostre jardinage,
Voir s'il est, comme ton visage,
Semé de roses et de lys.

A confused violence troubles the calm of the night; and light and noise dispel shadows and silence.

At his awakening Alidor seeks the shadow of Iris which he kissed, and weeps in his deceived soul for the flight of such a sweet sleep.

The beasts which tremble at the sight of the sun are in their lairs. Man, refreshed by sleep, takes up his daily work.

The blacksmith is in the smithy; listen to the coal catch fire! The red iron on the anvil sparkles under the hammer.

This candle seems dead; day makes it disappear; the Sun comes to dazzle us; watch him pass through the door!

It is day; let us rise, Phyllis, and go to our garden, to see if it, like your face, is strewn with roses and lilies.

49

Von Zesen

DER MORGEN
(The first sixteen lines of an occasional poem on the birthday of a lady)

Der Nächte fahles Häupt, besprüht mit Perlentaue,
Verliert sich allgemach; die junge Rittersfraue
Zieht vor der Himmelsbraut und Sternenkönigin
In Gold aus Ophir her, der Sonnen Marschallin;
Das süsse liebe Bild, das mit so manchen Liedern
Der Lüfte Volk begrüsst, hat selbst den nassen Brüdern
Und Schwestern auf der See ihr schilfischs Häupt vergüldt,
So, dass aus ihrem Krug auch güldnes Wasser quillt.
Der Sterne Herzog selbst, im silberblanken Rocke,
Weicht seiner Königin, die nun als eine Tocke,
Ja Braut aus ihrer Burg ins grossen Königs Saal
Soll werden aufgeführt. Sie schaue doch einmal,
O Schöne, welch ein Glanz und welch ein Blitz sich zeiget
Dort gegen Morgen hin; der Wind wird still und schweiget,
Die Wolken werden klar wie schimmernder Krystall,
Mit Jaspen und Saphir vermischet überall
. . . .

Marvell

THE GARDEN

I

How vainly men themselves amaze
To win the Palm, the Oke, or Bayes;
And their uncessant Labours see
Crown'd from some single Herb or Tree.

THE MORNING
Gradually the pale head of Night is disappearing, sprinkled with pearls of dew; the young noblewoman [i.e. the morning] walks before the celestial bride and the starry queen, [dressed] in gold from Ophir, marshalling in the sun. This delightful picture, greeted with many songs by the folk that live in the air, has spread a golden hue even over the reedy heads of their watery brothers and sisters of the sea, so that golden water pours from their jug too. The duke of stars himself, in his shiny silver coat [the moon] makes way for his queen who is about to be led forth from her castle as a girl, nay, as a bride, into the hall of the great king. Behold, O fair one, the splendour and flashing light there towards the morning; the wind is stilled and silent, the clouds grow limpid like shimmering crystal, suffused with jasper and sapphire throughout . . .

Whose short and narrow verged Shade
Does prudently their Toyles upbraid;
While all Flow'rs and all Trees do close
To weave the Garlands of repose.

II

Fair quiet, have I found thee here,
And Innocence thy Sister dear!
Mistaken long, I sought you then
In busie Companies of Men.
Your sacred Plants, if here below,
Only among the Plants will grow.
Society is all but rude,
To this delicious Solitude.

III

No white nor red was ever seen
So am'rous as this lovely green.
Fond Lovers, cruel as their Flame,
Cut in these Trees their Mistress name.
Little, Alas, they know, or heed,
How far these Beauties Hers exceed!
Fair Trees! where s'eer your barkes I wound,
No Name shall but your own be found.

IV

When we have run our Passions heat,
Love hither makes his best retreat.
The *Gods*, that mortal Beauty chase,
Still in a Tree did end their race.
Apollo hunted *Daphne* so,
Only that She might Laurel grow.
And *Pan* did after *Syrinx* speed,
Not as a Nymph, but for a Reed.

V

What wound'rous Life in this I lead!
Ripe Apples drop about my head;
The Luscious Clusters of the Vine
Upon my Mouth do crush their Wine;
The Nectaren, and curious Peach,
Into my hands themselves do reach;
Stumbling on Melons, as I pass,
Insnar'd with Flow'rs, I fall on Grass.

VI

Mean while the Mind, from pleasure less,
Withdraws into its happiness:
The Mind, that Ocean where each kind
Does streight its own resemblance find;
Yet it creates, transcending these,
Far other Worlds, and other Seas;
Annihilating all that's made
To a green Thought in a green Shade.

VII

Here at the Fountains sliding foot,
Or at some Fruit-trees mossy root,
Casting the Bodies Vest aside,
My Soul into the boughs does glide:
There like a Bird it sits, and sings,
Then whets, and combs its silver Wings;
And, till prepar'd for longer flight,
Waves in its Plumes the various Light.

VIII

Such was that happy Garden-state,
While Man there walk'd without a Mate:
After a Place so pure, and sweet,
What other Help could yet be meet!
But 'twas beyond a Mortal's share
To wander solitary there:
Two Paradises 'twere in one
To live in Paradise alone.

IX

How well the skilful Gardner drew
Of flow'rs and herbes this Dial new;
Where from above the milder Sun
Does through a fragrant Zodiack run;
And, as it works, th' industrious Bee
Computes its time as well as we.
How could such sweet and wholsome Hours
Be reckon'd but with herbs and flow'rs!

Saint-Amant

LA SOLITUDE

A Alcidon

O que j'ayme la solitude!
Que ces lieux sacrez à la nuit,
Esloignez du monde et du bruit,
Plaisent à mon inquietude!
Mon Dieu! que mes yeux sont contens
De voir ces bois, qui se trouverent
A la nativité du temps,
Et que tous les siècles reverent,
Estre encore aussi beaux et vers,
Qu'aux premiers jours de l'univers!

Un gay zephire les caresse
D'un mouvement doux et flatteur.
Rien que leur extresme hauteur
Ne fait remarquer leur vieillesse.
Jadis Pan et ses demy-dieux
Y vindrent chercher du refuge,
Quand Jupiter ouvrit les cieux
Pour nous envoyer le deluge,
Et, se sauvans sur leurs rameaux,
A peine virent-ils les eaux.

Que sur cette espine fleurie,
Dont le printemps est amoureux,
Philomele, au chant langoureux,
Entretient bien ma resverie!

SOLITUDE

O how I love solitude! How those places sacred to the night, far removed from the world and from noise, please my restlessness. My God, how content are my eyes to see these woods, which were here at the beginning of time, and which all the centuries revere, still as beautiful and green as in the first days of the universe.

A gay zephyr caresses them with a sweet, flattering motion; only their great height indicates their age. Formerly Pan and his demi-gods used to look for refuge here, when Jupiter opened the skies to send the deluge upon us, and, escaping on their branches, they scarcely saw the waters.

How [well], on this flowering thorn, beloved by spring, does Philomel, with langorous song, converse with my reverie. How much pleasure do I take in

53

Que je prens de plaisir à voir
Ces monts pendans en precipices,
Qui, pour les coups du desespoir,
Sont aux malheureux si propices,
Quand la cruauté de leur sort,
Les force à rechercher la mort!

Que je trouve doux le ravage
De ces fiers torrens vagabonds,
Qui se precipitent par bonds
Dans ce vallon vert et sauvage!
Puis, glissant sous les arbrisseaux,
Ainsi que des serpens sur l'herbe,
Se changent en plaisans ruisseaux,
Où quelque Naïade superbe
Regne comme en son lict natal,
Dessus un throsne de christal!

Que j'ayme ce marets paisible!
Il est tout bordé d'aliziers,
D'aulnes, de saules et d'oziers,
A qui le fer n'est point nuisible.
Les nymphes, y cherchans le frais,
S'y viennent fournir de quenouilles,
De pipeaux, de joncs et de glais;
Où l'on voit sauter les grenouilles,
Qui de frayeur s'y vont cacher
Si tost qu'on veut s'en approcher.

seeing these mountains, hanging in precipices, which are so tempting for unhappy men, against the blows of despair, when the cruelty of their fate forces them to look for death.

How sweet do I find the wildness of these proud tumbling waterfalls, which hurl themselves in bounds down this green, savage valley. Then, gliding beneath the glades, like serpents through the grass, they are turned to pleasant streams, where some proud Naiad reigns, as in the bed where she was born, upon a throne of crystal.

How I love this peaceful marsh! It is all bordered with rowans, with alders, willows and osiers, which are never harmed by the iron [axe]. Nymphs, looking for a cool place, come here to find reeds, flags and rushes for their distaffs, and one sees frogs jump away to hide themselves in fear, as soon as one tries to approach them.

Là, cent mille oyseaux aquatiques
Vivent, sans craindre, en leur repos,
Le giboyeur fin et dispos,
Avec ses mortelles pratiques.
L'un, tout joyeux d'un si beau jour,
S'amuse à becqueter sa plume;
L'autre allentit le feu d'amour
Qui dans l'eau mesme se consume,
Et prennent tous innocemment
Leur plaisir en cet élement.

Jamais l'esté ny la froidure
N'ont veu passer dessus cette eau
Nulle charrette ny batteau,
Depuis que l'un et l'autre dure;
Jamais voyageur alteré
N'y fit servir sa main de tasse;
Jamais chevreuil desesperé
N'y finit sa vie à la chasse;
Et jamais le traistre hameçon
N'en fit sortir aucun poisson.

Que j'ayme à voir la décadence
De ces vieux chasteaux ruinez,
Contre qui les ans mutinez
Ont deployé leur insolence!
Les sorciers y font leur sabat;
Les demons follets s'y retirent,
Qui d'un malicieux ébat
Trompent nos sens et nous martirent;
Là se nichent en mille troux
Les couleuvres et les hyboux.

There, a hundred thousand water-birds live without fearing, in their repose, the expert, alert fowler, and his deadly practices. One, joyful in such a lovely day, happily preens his feathers; another quells the fire of love, which even burns in water, and all happily take their pleasure in this element.

Neither summer nor cold, ever since both of them existed, have seen a cart or a boat pass through this water; no thirsty traveller has cupped his hand to drink; no desperate deer has here ended his life at the hunt; and the treacherous hook has never drawn out a fish.

O how I love to see the decline of those old ruined castles, against which the mutinous years have vaunted their insolence! Witches hold their sabbath here; mischievous demons come here to deceive our senses and torment us with malicious games; and here in a thousand holes nest snakes and owls.

L'orfraye, avec ses cris funebres,
Mortels augures des destins,
Fait rire et dancer les lutins
Dans ces lieux remplis de tenebres.
Sous un chevron de bois maudit
Y branle le squelette horrible
D'un pauvre amant qui se pendit
Pour une bergère insensible,
Qui d'un seul regard de pitié
Ne daigna voir son amitié.

Aussi le Ciel, juge équitable,
Qui maintient les loix en vigueur,
Prononça contre sa rigueur
Une sentence epouvantable:
Autour de ces vieux ossemens
Son ombre, aux peines condamnée,
Lamente en longs gemissemens
Sa malheureuse destinée,
Ayant, pour croistre son effroy,
Tousjours son crime devant soy.

Là se trouvent sur quelques marbres
Des devises du temps passé;
Icy l'âge a presque effacé
Des chiffres taillez sur les arbres;
Le plancher du lieu le plus haut
Est tombé jusques dans la cave,
Que la limace et le crapaud
Souillent de venin et de bave;
Le lierre y croist au foyer,
A l'ombrage d'un grand noyer.

The screech-owl with its funeral cries, deadly augurers of destiny, makes the goblins laugh and dance in these places filled with darkness; beneath a beam of cursed wood dances the horrid skeleton of a poor lover who hanged himself for an unfeeling shepherdess who would not deign to look on his love with a single glance of pity.

So Heaven, equitable judge who maintains the laws in all their force, pronounced an appalling sentence for her cruelty; around his old bones her shade, condemned to griefs, laments with long-drawn groans her unhappy destiny, having her crime always in front of her to make her terror grow.

There are found on marble stones devices of times past; there age has almost effaced initials carved on trees; the floor of the highest room has fallen down into the cellar, which the slug and toad soil with venom and slime; there the ivy grows on the hearth under the shade of a great walnut.

Là dessous s'estend une voûte
Si sombre en un certain endroit,
Que, quand Phebus y descendroit,
Je pense qu'il n'y verroit goutte;
Le Sommeil aux pesans sourcis,
Enchanté d'un morne silence,
Y dort, bien loing de tous soucis,
Dans les bras de la Nonchalence,
Laschement couché sur le dos
Dessus des gerbes de pavots.

Au creux de cette grotte fresche,
Où l'Amour se pourroit geler,
Echo ne cesse de brusler
Pour son amant froid et revesche.
Je m'y coule sans faire bruit,
Et par la celeste harmonie
D'un doux lut, aux charmes instruit,
Je flatte sa triste manie,
Faisant, repeter mes accords
A la voix qui luy sert de corps.

Tantost, sortant de ces ruines,
Je monte au haut de ce rocher,
Dont le sommet semble chercher
En quel lieu se font les bruïnes;
Puis je descends tout à loisir,
Sous une falaise escarpée,
D'où je regarde avec plaisir
L'onde qui l'a presque sappée
Jusqu'au siege de Palemon,
Fait d'esponges et de limon.

Down there extends a vault so dark that in one certain place I think that
Phoebus, when he goes down there, would not see a thing; Sleep with heavy
eyelids, entranced by a sad silence, sleeps there, well away from all cares, in the
arms of Nonchalance, relaxed upon his back upon poppy-seeds.

In the hollow of this fresh grotto, where even Love could freeze, Echo never
ceases to burn for her cold, rejecting lover. I slip noiselessly into it, and by the
celestial harmony of a sweet lute, taught by her spells, I flatter her sad madness,
making my chords repeat in tune the voice which serves her for body.

Sometimes, leaving these ruins, I climb to the top of this rock, whose summit
seems to seek the place where mountain-mists are born. Then I descend at my
leisure beneath a rugged cliff from where I behold with pleasure the wave which
has almost undermined it as far as the seat of Palemon, made of sponges and
mud.

Que c'est une chose agreable
D'estre sur le bord de la mer,
Quand elle vient à se calmer
Après quelque orage effroyable!
Et que les chevelus Tritons,
Hauts, sur les vagues secouées,
Frapent les airs d'estranges tons
Avec leurs trompes enrouées,
Dont l'eclat rend respectueux
Les ventes les plus impetueux.

Tantost l'onde, brouillant l'arène,
Murmure et fremit de courroux,
Se roullant dessus les cailloux
Qu'elle apporte et qu'elle r'entraine.
Tantost, elle estale en ses bords,
Que l'ire de Neptune outrage,
Des gens noyez, des monstres morts,
Des vaisseaux brisez du naufrage,
Des diamans, de l'ambre gris,
Et mille autres choses de pris.

Tantost, la plus claire du monde,
Elle semble un miroir flottant,
Et nous represente à l'instant
Encore d'autres cieux sous l'onde.
Le soleil s'y fait si bien voir,
Y contemplant son beau visage,
Qu'on est quelque temps à savoir
Si c'est luy-mesme, ou son image,
Et d'abord il semble à nos yeux
Qu'il s'est laissé tomber des cieux.

How lovely a thing it is to be by the side of the sea, when it has just become calm after some terrible storm! And when the long-haired Tritons, rising high above the shaken waves, strike the air with strange noises from their curling trumpets, whose din makes the most impetuous winds respectful.

Sometimes the wave, pounding the sand, murmurs and trembles with wrath, rolling over the pebbles which it brings up, and then drags back. Sometimes, it throws on to its shores, when the ire of Neptune rages, drowned men, dead monsters, ship-wrecked vessels, diamonds, ambergris, and a thousand other valuable things.

Sometimes, the clearest [thing] in the world, it resembles a floating mirror, and shows us at one time other heavens beneath the wave. The sun appears so clearly as he looks at his lovely face there, that one takes some time to find out if it is he himself or his image, and at first it seems to our eyes that he has fallen from the heavens.

Bernières, pour qui je me vante
De ne rien faire que de beau,
Reçoy ce fantasque tableau
Fait d'une peinture vivante.
Je ne cherche que les deserts,
Où, resvant tout seul, je m'amuse
A des discours assez diserts
De mon genie avec la muse;
Mais mon plus aymable entretien
C'est le ressouvenir du tien.

Tu vois dans cette poesie
Pleine de licence et d'ardeur
Les beaux rayons de la splendeur
Qui m'esclaire la fantaisie:
Tantost chagrin, tantost joyeux,
Selon que la fureur m'enflame,
Et que l'objet s'offre à mes yeux,
Les propos me naissent en l'ame,
Sans contraindre la liberté
Du demon qui m'a transporté

O que j'ayme la solitude!
C'est l'element des bons esprits,
C'est par elle que j'ay compris
L'art d'Apollon sans nulle estude.
Je l'ayme pour l'amour de toy,
Connaissant que ton humeur l'ayme;
Mais quand je pense bien à moy,
Je la hay pour la raison mesme:
Car elle pourroit me ravir
L'heur de te voir et te servir.

Bernières, to whom I boast that I have done nothing which is not beautiful, receive this fantastic picture, made from a living painting. I only seek for the deserts, where, dreaming all alone I divert myself with lively discourses between myself and the muse; but my most delightful conversation is the memory of yours.

You see in this poem, full of extravagance and ardour, the beautiful rays of the splendour which illuminates my fantasy: sometimes grieving, sometimes joyful, as the fury inflames me, and as the object appears before my eyes, the subjects are born in my spirit, without confining the liberty of the demon who transports me.

O how I love solitude! It is the element of good men, it is through her that I have learned Apollo's art without study. I love her through love of you, knowing that your humour loves her; but, when I think only of myself, I hate her for the same reason: for she can deprive me of the opportunity of seeing and serving you.

59

Von Spee

LOB GOTTES IM LUFTRAUM

Ach lobe Gott, du reiner Luft,
Du Web gar zart gesponnen!
Zu Nachts bist nur ein schwarzer Tuft
Bis zu der Morgensonnen:
Da zeigest dich in klarem Schein
Viel weisser als die Schwanen,
Wann schon gleich ausgespannet sein
Ihr breite Federfahnen.

Zu dir viel tausend Vögelein
Mit Freud und Jubel schweben,
Zur Sangschul zu dir kommen ein
Und nach dem Kränzlein streben.
Wer will die Stücklein zählen all,
So die dann figurieren?
Concerten, Fugen, Madrigal
Auf hundertfalt Manieren.

In dir auch fliegen rein und zart
Fast aller Ding Gestalten,
So seind von Farben aller Art
Unmerklich abgespalten:
Auch Atem süss von Blumen all,
All Ruch und Kraft der Erden,
All Sang und Klang, all Ton und Schall
In dir gezielet werden.

IN PRAISE OF GOD IN THE AIR

O praise God, pure air, you delicately spun web! At night you are nothing but a black haze until the morning sun: then you display yourself in [its] clear light, whiter than the swans, even when the wide flags of their feathers are spread out.

Many thousands of little birds fly to you with joy and jubilation, they come to the song school to compete for the winner's garland. Who could count the tunes they perform? Concertos, fugues, madrigals, in a hundred different ways.

In you float, pure and delicate, the shapes of almost all things which have become imperceptibly detached from colour: the sweet breath of flowers, all the mist and strength of the earth, all songs and strains, all sounds and rounds, are aimed at you.

Auch lobet Gott, ihr Luftgewächs,
Ihr Wolken hochgeboren,
Ihr Wind, zween uber fünfmal sechs,
Ihr Hagel rund gefroren,
Ihr fliegend Flammen, Donner, Blitz,
Komet uns nit gewogen,
Schnee, Reif und Regen, Kält und Hitz
Und du, gefärbet Bogen.

Der Schnee da kommt wie sanfte Woll
Von Wolken abgekeimet,
Der Hagel wie die Perlen voll,
Von Kälte stark geleimet.
Dann weil die Tropfen seind im Fall,
Vom Frost ertappet werden,
Der backt und härtets wie Krystall—
Da kuglens ab zur Erden.

Der weisse Tau und Regen klar
Gar lieblich kommt gefliessen,
Der Regenbogen immerdar
Sich spannet ohne Schiessen.
Den klaren Blitz wir fürchten mehr,
Wann gross Gewölk sich weget;
Doch lobe Gott nun eben sehr,
Was nur die Luft sich reget.

Praise God also, you airy growths, you high-born clouds, you winds, two over five times six, you hailstones frozen round, you flying flames, thunder, lightning, and comet, not well-disposed towards us, snow, hoar frost and rain, cold and heat, and you, many-coloured arch [rainbow].

Snow comes like soft wool combed from the clouds, and hail like pearls, stiffened by the cold. For as the drops fall, they are caught by the frost which bakes and hardens them like crystals—then they roll down to earth.

The white dew and the clear rain pour down sweetly, the rainbow is drawn without ever firing [an arrow]. We are more afraid of the flash of lightning when heavy clouds are moving [across the sky]. Yet, praise God, whatever moves in the air.

A Vision of Nature

Er legt den Winden Flügel an,
Er gürtet ihn' die Lenden,
Die Blitz er heisst mit Kräften gahn,
Er schüttlet sie von Händen.
Mit Wetter und Unwetter stark
Sein Allmacht er erzeiget;
Vor ihm erschreckt all Bein und Mark,
Vor ihm sich alles neiget.

Benlowes

From *Theophila's Love-Sacrifice*

. . . .

When callow Nature, pluck'd from out her nest
Of causes, was awak'd from rest,
Her shapeless lump with fledg'd effects He trimly drest.

Then new-born day He gilt with glittering sun
(Contracted light); with changing Moon
He night adorn'd, and hung up lamps, like spangled bullion.

The earth, with water mixed, He separates:
Earth plants brought forth, and beasts all mates;
The waters fowl, and fish to yield man delicates.

Then did of th' elements' dust man's body frame
A perfect microcosm, the same
He quickened with a sparkle of pneumatic flame.

More heav'nly specified by life from th' Word;
That, Nature doth, this, Grace afford;
And Glory from the Spirit design'd, as threefold cord.

Man, ere a child; by infusion wise; though He
Was of, yet not for earth, though free
Chanc'llor install'd of Eden's University.

He gives wings to the winds, he girds their loins. From his hands he releases
flashes of lightning, commanding them to depart with great force. He shows his
omnipotence through good and bad weather; all creatures stand in dread of him,
all bow down before him.

His virgin-sister-wife i' th' grove he woo'd
(Heav'n's nursery); new fruit his food,
Skin was his robe: clouds wash'd, winds swept his floor.

Envy, that God should so love man, first mov'd all good.
Satan, to ruin Heav'n's belov'd:
The serpent devill'd Eve, she's dam to Adam prov'd.

Both taste, by tasting, tasteless both became;
Who all would know, knew nought but shame:
They blush for that which they, when righteous, could not name.

Still in our maw that apple's core doth stick,
Which they did swallow, and the thick
Rind of forbidden fruit has left our nature sick.

Now serves our guiltiness as winding sheet,
To wrap up lepers; cover meet;
While thus stern vengeance does our wormships sadly greet.
. . . .

Klaj

LANDSCHAFT

Hellglänzendes Silber! mit welchem sich gatten
Der astigen Linden weitstreifende Schatten!
Deine sanftkühlend-geruhige Lust
Ist jedem bewusst.

Wie sollten kunstahmende Pinsel bemalen
Die Blätter, die schirmen vor brennenden Strahlen?
Keiner der Stämme, so grünlich beziert,
Die Ordnung verführt.

LANDSCAPE

Brightly-shining silver! with which the far-roaming shadows of the branching linden trees are mating! Everybody is conscious of your gently-cooling, serene delight.

How could the brushes of imitating art paint the leaves which give shelter from the burning rays? None of the trunks so greenly adorned breaks this order.

Es lispeln und wispeln die schlüpfrigen Brunnen,
Von ihnen ist diese Begrünung gerunnen.
Sie schauren, betrauren und fürchten bereit
Die schneiichte Zeit.

Greville

From *Caelica*

The Golden Age was when the world was young,
Nature so rich, as earth did need no sowing,
Malice not known, the serpents had not stung,
Wit was but sweet affection's overflowing.

Desire was free, and beauty's first-begotten;
Beauty then neither net, nor made by art,
Words out of thoughts brought forth, and not forgotten,
The laws were inward that did rule the heart.

The Brazen Age is now when earth is worn,
Beauty grown sick, Nature corrupt and nought,
Pleasure untimely dead as soon as born,
Both words and kindness strangers to our thought:

If now this changing world do change her head,
Caelica, what have her new lords for to boast?
The old lord knows desire is poorly fed,
And sorrows not a wavering province lost,
  Since in the gilt age Saturn rul'd alone,
  And in this painted, planets every one.

The gliding wells lisp and whisper, this green adornment has sprung from
them. Already they shiver and mourn and fear the time for snow.

Artifice

This section is devoted to poems of transformation, metamorphosis, and play. The poet either transforms common logical and aesthetic expectations, and writes about such unexpected subjects as appallingly ugly women,[1] combs which turn into sailing-ships,[2] birds which prefer love of a woman to liberty,[3] or he uses the poem itself as a representation of some metamorphosis which he wishes were true. Ronsard wishes to become a bull, or a shower of gold, in order to possess his mistress;[4] Marino laughingly insists that the thread his mistress uses when she is sewing is the thread of his heart,[5] and several poets play with the conceit of the mirror or echo which repeats exactly and yet is different from the repeated object or sound. Many of the poems use hyperbole which the poet himself recognizes as such, so setting up a humorous distance between the author and the poem—du Bellay sees two suns rise in one morning,[6] Strode makes snowflakes into worshippers,[7] Cleveland's lady's red and white cheeks become York and Lancaster, but a York and Lancaster between whom there is not civil war but harmony.[8]

The poets also play with notions of art itself. There are many attempts to make the poem into a little picture, a self-contained and elegant cameo arising from some trivial perception;[9] and there are even more which deal with the beloved as artist, either in dress or the arts of love,[10] or a singer, dancer, or instrumentalist who combines in herself the arts of enchantress and poet:

> Each step trod out a lover's thought
> And the ambitious hopes he brought,
>   Chain'd to her brave feet with such arts,
> Such sweet command and gentle awe,
> As when she ceas'd we sighing saw
>   The floor lay pav'd with broken hearts.[11]

[1] See p. 108.   [2] See p. 92.   [3] See p. 99.
[4] See p. 101.   [5] See p. 87.   [6] See p. 71.
[7] See p. 87.   [8] See p. 100.   [9] See p. 86.
[10] See pp. 90, 93, 99 etc.   [11] See p. 91.

When she dances thus, the natural laws cease to be valid, and she ceases to be mortal; when she plays the lute, only the grace and harmony of her playing are powerful enough to heal the wounds caused by her lovely eyes; and though the poet's wounds are painful, he is happy in his pain:

> Ma felice languir, poiché non tanto
> ferisce il guardo con pungenti ardori,
> quanto con dolce suon risana il canto.[1]

The baroque poets are not, for the most part, concerned to create new conventions, new poetical topics, but to invert the ones already existing, or to find new stratagems for making verse out of them. This may be seen clearly from poems which derive from the convention of a laudatory description of the mistress, and various superficially novel ways of being original in that convention are here represented. Cleveland exaggerates it until it becomes burlesque,[2] Giovanetti isolates the one possible flaw in his lady, the moles on her face, and proves that even they are eternally beautiful:

> Oh care macchie, avventurose e belle!
> Cosí de' prati e de l'eterea spera
> sono ancor macchie i fior, macchie le stelle.[3]

Auvray startlingly reworks the poetical possibility of the mistress being like a saint—his mistress is like one because she is as thin as holy bones in a shrine:

> Ce seroit violer le droit des Trespassez
> De toucher sacrilège à ses membres ethiques,
> Je les baiserois bien s'ils estoient enchassez,
> Comme au travers d'un verre on baise les reliques.[4]

Such flagrant novelties are easily identified; moments when the old convention is just on the verge of being broken down are less easy to see. The section opens with a poem by du Bellay in which the poet plays with the theme of metamorphosis: the lady is turned into a rose. Du Bellay touches upon many conventions of mediaeval and early Renaissance love-poetry—only the man who has chosen virtue as his guide will be able to pluck the rose (deriving its colour from shame, *pudicité*, and its eternal freshness from *honneur*) which has power over sexual love, and which is also the symbol of sexual fertility. But one does not feel that he is seriously interested in the meaning behind the convention, as even a later poet familiar with his work, Spenser, would have been; one senses rather that he is using the pictorial devices, the superficies, of the convention in order to create an elegant

[1] See p. 92. [2] See p. 100. [3] See p. 104.
[4] See p. 110.

formal picture, that his imagination is working to create an ingenious effect aimed at the eye and ear, not the brain:

> Mes cheveulx sont changez en feuilles qui verdoyent,
> Et ces petis rayons, qui vivement flamboyent
> Au centre de ma rose, imitent de mes yeux
> Les feuz jadis égaulx à deux flammes des cieulx.[1]

The poet's skill in making 'new' this old convention is the *raison d'être* of the poem; he is demonstrating his power over words, and the more well-worn the topic, the more his skill, his artifices, can be admired. Du Bellay's concentration upon visual detail is not so different from the concentration upon minutiae of the poets who follow him. To write of the stamens in the middle of a rose, or of a fly flying into the eye of the mistress, is simultaneously to prove one's versatility by showing the reader something previously unnoticed, and to resolve the problems of coping with the greater emotions and visual experiences by ignoring them. If the little thing is done well or wittily, the great may be temporarily ignored.

These poems offer no meaning beyond the meanings of the moment, look for no patterns in nature other than the patterns which the poet's art can self-consciously create: they are entertainments, things of beauty with no justification save the facts of their existence and vitality. Unlike Silesius's rose, these poems are not oblivious of themselves, but self-conscious; like his rose, they are without *why*:

> Die Ros' ist ohn warum; sie blühet, weil sie blühet,
> Sie acht' nicht ihrer selbst, fragt nicht, ob man sie siehet.[2]

[1] See p. 68.   [2] See p. 114.

Du Bellay

MÉTAMORPHOSE D'UNE ROSE

Comme sur l'arbre sec la veufve tourterelle
Regrette ses amours d'une triste querelle,
Ainsi de mon mary le trespas gémissant,
En pleurs je consumois mon aage languissant:

Quand pour chasser de moy ceste tristesse enclose,
Mon destin consentit que je devinsse Rose,
Qui d'un poignant hallier se hérisse à l'entour,
Pour faire résistance aux assaults de l'Amour.

Je suis, comme j'estois, d'odeur naïve et franche,
Mes bras sont transformez en épineuse branche,
Mes piedz en tige verd, et tout le demeurant
De mon corps est changé en rosier bien fleurant.

Les plis de mon habit sont écailleuses poinctes,
Qui en rondeur égalle autour de moy sont joinctes:
Et ce qui entr'ouvert monstre un peu de rougeur,
Imite de mon ris la première doulceur.

Mes cheveulx sont changez en fueilles qui verdoyent,
Et ces petis rayons, qui vivement flamboyent
Au centre de ma rose, imitent de mes yeux
Les feuz jadis égaulx à deux flammes des cieulx.

METAMORPHOSIS OF A ROSE

As the widowed turtle dove on the dry tree weeps for her love in sad complaint so, bewailing the death of my husband, in tears I consumed my years of grief:
    when, to drive this imprisoned sadness from me, my destiny permitted me to become a Rose, which bristles with thorns all round in a prickly copse to resist the attacks of Love.
    I am, as I was, in perfume fresh and free, my arms are turned into a thorny branch, my feet into a green stem, and all the rest of my body is changed into a flowering rose bush.
    The folds of my dress are become scaly brambles, joined all round me in circles: and that which, half-opened, shows a little red, imitates the first sweetness of my smile.
    My hair is changed to green leaves, and these little rays which vividly flame in the middle of my rose imitate the fires of my eyes which formerly resembled two heavenly flames.

Le beauté de mon teinct à l'Aurore pareille
N'a du sang de Vénus pris sa couleur vermeille,
Mais de ceste rougeur que la pudicité
Imprime sur le front de la virginité.

Les graces, dont le ciel m'avoit favorisée,
Or que rose je suis, me servent de rosée:
Et l'honneur qui en moy a fleury si long temps,
S'y garde encor entier d'un éternel printemps.

La plus longue frescheur des roses est bornée
Par le cours naturel d'une seule journée:
Mais ceste gayeté qu'on voit en moy fleurir,
Par l'injure du temps ne pourra dépérir.

A nul je ne défends ny l'odeur ny la veuë,
Mais si quelque indiscret vouloit à l'impourveuë
S'en approcher trop près, il ne s'en iroit point
Sans esprouver comment ma chaste rigueur poingt.

Que nul n'espère donc de ravir ceste rose,
Puis qu'au jardin d'honneur elle est si bien enclose:
Où plus soingneusement elle est gardée encor
Que du Dragon veillant n'estoient les pommes d'or.

Celuy qui la vertu a choisy pour sa guide,
Ce sera celuy seul qui en sera l'Alcide:
A luy seul j'ouvriray la porte du verger,
Où heureux il pourra me cueillir sans danger.

The beauty of my complexion, like that of Aurora, has not taken its crimson colour from the blood of Venus, but from that red which shame prints on the brow of virginity.

The graces, with which heaven favoured me, now that I am a rose are my dewdrops: and the honour which has flowered in me for so long is there kept intact by an eternal Spring.

The longest freshness of roses is bounded by the natural course of a single day: but that gaiety to be seen blooming in me cannot be destroyed by the ravages of time.

I deny to no-one either the sight of me, or my scent, but if some indiscreet man wishes rashly to come too close, he will not go without having discovered how my chaste strictness can prick.

Let no-one then hope to ravish this rose, since she is so well protected in the garden of honour: where she is even more carefully guarded than the golden apples were by the wakeful Dragon.

He who has chosen virtue for his guide, he alone will be Alcides [i.e. the Hercules who can pick the apples of the Hesperides]: to him alone will I open the door of the orchard where, happy man, he will be able to gather me without danger.

Qu'autrement on n'espère en mon cueur faire brèche:
Car je ne crains Amour, ny son arc, ny sa flèche:
J'esteins, comme il me plaist, son brandon furieux,
Le aeles je luy couppe, et debende les yeux.

SONNET

Vent doulx souflant, vent des vens souverain,
Qui voletant d'aeles bien empanées
Fais respirer de soüeves halenées
Ta doulce Flore au visage serain,

Pren de mes mains ce vase, qui est plein
De mile fleurs avec' l'Aurore nées,
Et mil' encor' à toy seul destinées,
Pour t'en couvrir et le front et le seing.

Encependant, au thesor de ces rives
Je pilleray ces emeraudes vives,
Ces beaux rubiz, ces perles et saphirs,

Pour mettre en l'or des tresses vagabondes,
Qui ça et la folastrent en leurs ondes,
Grosses du vent de tes plus doulx soupirs.

Let none hope otherwise to make a breach in my heart: for I do not fear Love, neither his bow, nor his arrow: I can extinguish, as I please, his furious torch, clip his wings, and take the bandage from his eyes.

Sweet, breathing breeze, sovereign breeze among breezes, who, fluttering on feathery wings, make your sweet lovely-faced Flora breathe with soft pantings,
   take from my hands this vase, which is full of a thousand flowers born with Aurora, and a thousand more destined for you alone to cover your head and bosom.
   Meanwhile, I will loot from the treasure of these shores these bright emeralds, beautiful rubies, pearls and sapphires,
   to set them in the gold of her vagabond tresses which frolic to and fro in their waves, heavy with the wind of your sweetest sighs.

SONNET

Deja la nuit en son parc amassoit
Un grand troupeau d'etoiles vagabondes,
Et pour entrer aux cavernes profondes,
Fuyant le jour, ses noirs chevaulx chassoit.

Deja le ciel aux Indes rougissoit,
Et l'Aulbe encor' de ses tresses tant blondes
Faisant gresler mile perlettes rondes,
De ses thesors les prez enrichissoit:

Quand d'occident, comme une etoile vive,
Je vy sortir desus ta verde rive,
O fleuve mien! une Nymphe en rient.

Alors voyant cette nouvelle Aurore,
Le jour honteux d'un double teint colore
Et l'Angevin et l'Indique orient.

Schein

O FILLI, SCHAEFRIN ZART

O Filli, Schäfrin zart,
Wär ich eins deiner Schäfelein,
Würd ich nach Hirtenart
Dir besser angelegen sein;
Aber so tust du mich allweg meiden,
Das bringt mir unaussprechlich Leiden.

Already night was gathering into her park a great herd of vagabond stars, and, fleeing the day, was driving her black horses to enter her deep caverns.

Already the sky of the Indies was turning red and Dawn, making a thousand little round pearls shower down already for her so blonde tresses, was enriching the meadows with her treasures:

when, from the west, like a living star, I saw emerging on to your green shore, O my river, a laughing nymph.

Then, seeing that new Dawn, the day, ashamed, colours with a double hue both the Angevin and Indian sunrise.

O PHYLLIS, GENTLE SHEPHERDESS

O Phyllis, gentle shepherdess, if I were one of your lambs, then, as is the custom among shepherds, I should be closer to you; but now you avoid me always, and that causes me ineffable sorrow.

Artifice

Ach Filli lobesan,
Wär ich ein grünes Bäumelein,
Würdst du dich zu mir nahn,
Unter meinem Schatten schlafen ein;
Aber so ich schlafen muss alleine,
Deswegen seufze, klag und weine.

Ach Filli hochgeborn,
Wär ich ein klein Waldvögelein,
Würd ich dein leise Ohrn
Bewegen mit meinem Stimmelein;
Aber so mein Seufzen, Klag und Flehen
Tut als in Wind vorübergehen.

Ach Filli, Wälder Zier,
Wär ich ein klares Brünnelein,
So badetst du an mir
Dein nackend zartes Leibelein;
Aber so mir nicht zu gut kann werden,
Dass ich dich bloss anseh auf Erden.

Drum, o Cupido blind,
Verwandel mich der Filli mein
Zum Schäfelein geschwind,
Oder zu einem grünen Bäumelein,
Oder lass mich als ein Vöglein singen,
Oder als ein Brünnlein entspringen.

Ah, noble Phyllis, if I were a green-leaved tree, you would come to me and fall asleep in my shade; but now I must sleep alone, and that is why I sigh, lament, and weep.

Ah, well-born Phyllis, if I were a small woodland bird, I would move your ear with my tender voice; but now my sighs, laments and supplications pass like a breeze.

Ah, Phyllis, ornament of forests, if I were a limpid spring, you would bathe your dainty naked body in me; but as things are, I shall not on this earth enjoy gazing at you naked.

Therefore, O blind Cupid, swiftly change me into a lamb, or a green-leaved tree, or let me sing as a bird, or gush forth as a spring.

72

Lord Herbert of Cherbury

A DESCRIPTION

I sing her worth and praises high,
Of whom a poet cannot lie.
The little world the great shall blaze:
Sea, earth her body; heaven her face;
Her hair sunbeams, whose every part
Lightens, inflames each lover's heart,
That thus you prove the axiom true,
Whilst the sun help'd nature in you.

Her front the white and azure sky,
In light and glory raised high;
Being o'ercast by a cloudy frown,
All hearts and eyes dejecteth down.

Her each brow a celestial bow,
Which through this sky her light doth show,
Which doubled, if it strange appear,
The sun's likewise is doubled there.

Her either cheek a blushing morn,
Which, on the wings of beauty borne,
Doth never set, but only fair
Shineth, exalted in her hair.

Within her mouth, heaven's heav'n, reside
Her words: the soul's there glorifi'd.

Her nose th' equator of this globe,
Where nakedness, beauty's best robe,
Presents a form all hearts to win.

Last Nature made that dainty chin,
Which, that it might in every fashion
Answer the rest, a constellation,
Like to a desk, she there did place
To write the wonders of her face.

In this celestial frontispiece,
Where happiness eternal lies,
First arranged stand three senses,
This heaven's intelligences,
Whose several motions, sweet combin'd,
Come from the first mover, her mind.

The weight of this harmonic sphere
The Atlas of her neck doth bear,
Whose favours day to us imparts,
When frowns make night in lovers' hearts.

Two foaming billows are her breasts,
That carry rais'd upon their crests

73

The Tyrian fish: more white's their foam
Than that whence Venus once did come.
　Here take her by the hand, my Muse,
With that sweet foe to make my truce,
To compact manna best compar'd,
Whose dewy inside's not full hard.
　Her waist's an invers'd pyramis,
Upon whose cone love's trophy is.
　Her belly is that magazine
At whose peep Nature did resign
That precious mould by which alone
There can be framed such a one.
　At th' entrance of which hidden treasure,
Happy making above measure,
Two alabaster pillars stand,
To warn all passage from that land;
At foot whereof engraved is
The sad *Non ultra* of man's bliss.
　The back of this most precious frame
Holds up in majesty the same,
Where, to make music to all hearts,
Love bound the descant of her parts.
　Though all this Beauty's temple be,
There's known within no deity
Save virtues shrin'd within her will.
As I began, so say I still,
I sing her worth and praises high,
Of whom a poet cannot lie.

Fleming

From ECHO

. . . .
Als Echo ward zu einem Schalle,
Zu einer unbeleibten Luft,
Die durch das Tal mit halbem Halle
Die, so sie rufen, wieder ruft,
Da ward der hohle Wald voll Klage,
Das feige Wild stund als betört,
Die Nymphen ruften Nacht und Tage,
Wo bist du, Lust, die man nur hört?
. . . .

When echo turned into a sound, into disembodied air, calling with half-resounding voice in answer to those who call her across the valley, the deep forest began to lament, the shy deer stood as if stunned, and nymphs call night and day, where are you, delight that can only be heard?

Marino

ECO

In un bosco frondoso,
presso un antro solingo,
secretario fedel de' suoi dolori,
tra dolente e pensoso,
l'infelice Siringo,
stanco omai di seguir l'empia Licori,
pose freno agli errori;
e, poi ch'assai si tacque,
a lo speco si volse,
e sì dolce si dolse,
che ne sospirâr l'aure e pianser l'acque.
Le note udì Selvaggio,
e scolpille in un faggio.
    —Ninfa,—dicea—già ninfa,
or voce ignuda e tronca,
pronta seguace degli estremi accenti;
tu, che con questa linfa
da la cupa spelonca
ragioni e con gli augelli e con gli armenti;
tu, che, de' miei lamenti
pietosa e de' martìri,
obliando i tuoi stessi,
sì come pur volessi
porgere aita a' miei stanchi sospiri,
le mie pene accompagni
ed al mio piagner piagni;

In a leafy wood, near a lonely cave, the faithful secretary of his griefs, between thoughtfulness and grieving, unhappy Syringo, still weary with pursuing the pitiless Lycoris, ended his wanderings; and, after he had been silent he turned to the cavern and lamented so sweetly that the winds sighed with his lament, and the waters grieved. Selvaggio heard his notes, and carved them on a beech-tree.
    —Nymph—he said—once a nymph, now a naked, broken voice, the ready follower of accents [of] extreme [grief]; you who with this lymph [i.e. sacred water, elixir] from the hollow cave speak to both the birds and the beasts; you who, merciful to my laments and sufferings, forgetting your own, quite as if you wished to tender aid to my weary sighs, are companion to my pains, and grieve for my griefs;

Artifice

   oracolo de' boschi,
anima de le selve,
cittadina de l'ombre, ombra sonante;
tu, che per entro i foschi
alberghi de le belve
segui il fugace tuo, querula amante,
lieve spirito errante,
stridul' aura infelice,
de l'altrui parlar vago
invisibile imago,
degli inospiti orrori abitatrice;
se del mio duol ti dole,
odi le mie parole.
   Le mie parole ascolta
da quest'ombrosa grotta;
ma non ridire altrui ciò ch'io ragiono.
Tu, da le membra sciolta,
voce flebile e rotta,
accogli pur de le mie voci il suono;
ma, se care ti sono,
teco le chiudi e serba,
e questa pietra oscura,
ch'a te fu sepoltura,
e de la pena tua grave ed acerba
ancor freme e rimbomba,
del mio dolor sia tomba.
   Non perché 'l mio cordoglio
resti occulto e secreto,
e l'altrui ferità non si rivele,
misero! ma non voglio,
s'è del mio mal sì lieto,
ferir con suon pietoso il Ciel crudele;

   oracle of the woods, soul of the forests, dweller in the shadows, speaking shadow; you who within the dark dens of the wild beasts pursue your fugitive, [you] complaining lover, light wandering spirit, unhappy, piercing breath of wind, invisible image of the wandering voice of others, inhabitant of the inhospitable horrors, if you care for my cares, hear my words.

   Hear my words from this shady grotto; but do not let others laugh at what I tell you. You, loose-limbed, plaintive, broken-voiced, receive therefore the sound of my songs; but, if they are dear to you, enclose and keep them with you, and let this dark rock, that was your sepulchre, still trembling and resounding from your harsh, bitter pain, be the tomb of my grief.

   Not that my anguished heart should remain hidden and secret, and should not be revealed to the ferocity of others, woe is me, but I do not want to wound cruel Heaven with a piteous sound, if it is so joyful in my sorrow: nor that sad

né che triste querele
vadan tra gente allegra
turbando l'altrui festa
con memoria sì mesta.
Qui dunque, qui, tra l'ombra opaca e negra,
fuor di gioia e di speme
stiamo piangendo insieme.
   Se di chi 'l cor ti strinse
membri l'antiche offese,
sai ben quant'è conforme il nostro stato.
Egual amor n'avinse,
egual beltà n'accese,
egualmente adorammo idolo ingrato.
Tu sei conversa in fiato,
e 'n gemiti ti struggi;
io l'ore e i giorni spendo
sospirando e languendo.
Tu da la gente e da la luce fuggi;
io dal sole e dal mondo
in quest'orror m'ascondo.
   E 'l fanciul parimente,
non meno altier che bello,
quanto la bella mia fiamma pareggia!
Anch'ella assai sovente
nel vicino ruscello
del mio fuoco gentil l'esca vagheggia.
Deh! s'è destin che deggia
in disusata guisa
amar la propria stampa,
perché pur non avampa
di quella che nel cor io porto incisa?
perché non ama almeno
se stessa nel mio seno?

complaints should go amongst happy men, disturbing the gladness of others with so sad a memory. Here, then, here among the thick black shadow, far from joy and hope, let us weep together.

If you remember the old offences of him who gripped your heart, you know well how similar is our condition. An equal love binds us, an equal beauty fires us, equally we adore an ungrateful idol. You are turned to a breath of wind, and consume yourself in groans; I pass the hours and the days sighing and languishing. You flee from men and the light: I in this horror hide myself from the sun and the world.

And equally that boy, no less proud than lovely, how much does he resemble my own flame [his Lycoris]! She also very often in the neighbouring brook gazes at the tinder of my gentle fire. Oh! if it is destiny which allows [her] to love her own image in this unusual way, why then does she not burn for that image I bear carved in my heart? Why at least does she not love herself in my heart?

77

Artifice

Ma, se di doglia umana
qualche pietà ti move,
dal tuo ricetto omai fuggi veloce:
lascia pur questa tana
di fere, e vanne dove
fera stassi più fera e più feroce.
Fiedi con rauca voce
l'inique orecchie, e quivi,
de la tua spoglia scinto,
sospiretto indistinto,
gridando sempre e mormorando vivi;
ché, s'ami i sassi, ahi lasso!
anch'ella è un vivo sasso.
I' so pur che talora,
quando al più lungo giorno
il sol di mezzo il ciel fère la piaggia,
a l'onda, a l'ombra, a l'ôra,
qui sola a far soggiorno
ne suol quella venir, che sì m'oltraggia,
fera bella e selvaggia.
Qui canta e qui favella; e tu cotanto
d'udirla ti compiaci,
che non rispondi, e taci;
o, se rispondi pur, del dolce canto
formi interi i concetti,
non tronchi ed imperfetti.
Or, s'avien che 'l bel piede
per sorte amica e destra
qui soletto il mio sol fermi già mai,
cheggioti per mercede
(se 'n questa rupe alpestra
pur sostenere i raggi suoi potrai):

But, if some pity for human grief moves you, now quickly fly from your refuge: leave this den of beasts, and go where a fiercer and more ferocious wild beast lies. You wound wicked ears with your harsh voice, and then, deprived of your body, an indistinct little sigh, you live forever in cries and murmurs; for, if you love rocks, alas, she whom I love is a living rock.

I know well that sometimes when on the longest day the sun in the midst of the sky strikes the shore, that here, to the waves, to the shades, and to the breeze she regularly comes to rest alone, that lovely, wild heartless one who so hurts me. Here she sings and chatters; and you are so pleased to hear her, that you do not reply, but keep silent; or if you do reply, from the sweet song you form concepts that are harmonious, not broken and imperfect.

Now, if it happens, through a happy and friendly chance, that my sun, alone, should never set her lovely foot here, I implore you, for pity's sake, (if you can only bear her rays in this alpine rock) you, who feel and know it, tell her how

tu, che 'l senti e che 'l sai,
narragli quant'io provo
ne l'alma affanno e foco,
come tu prendi a gioco
gli aspri miei casi e com'ognor ti trovo
di mia lunga fatica
e compagna e nemica.
   Digli sì come spesso
co' miei lamenti i tuoi,
alto chiamando il suo bel nome, accordo;
che s'un giorno da presso
m'udisse, i' so che poi
fôra assai men de la mia morte ingordo.
Digli come t'assordo,
come mi stempro e sfaccio,
come ai miei pianti, ai prieghi
pace or prometti, or nieghi;
come talor, mentr'io non parlo e taccio,
usa ai continui stridi,
tu per te stessa gridi.
   Se ciò farai, prometto
mille ghirlande offrirti
del trasformato tuo vago Narciso,
e 'n quest'ermo boschetto
mille tra lauri e mirti
simulacri piantar del suo bel viso.
E se là sul Cefiso,
mentr'ei visse pastore,
fu già sì crudo teco,
qui presso al fido speco
vo' che tu 'l goda almen rivolto in fiore;
e fien tuo specchio terso
le lagrime ch'io verso.

much hurt and fire I undergo in my soul, how you mock my harsh fortune, and how I always find you both the companion and enemy of my long weariness.

Tell her how often, calling aloud her lovely name, I harmonize your laments with my own; [tell her] that if one day, from nearby, she hears me, I know that then I would be much less eager for my death. Tell her how I deafen you, how I dissolve and undo myself, how you either promise or deny peace to my griefs and prayers; and how, sometimes, when I fall silent, used to continual cries you cry for yourself.

If you do that, I promise to offer you a thousand garlands of your lovely, transformed Narcissus, and in this solitary dell to plant, between the laurels and myrtles, a thousand imitations of his lovely face. And if there, by the river Cefiso, while he lived there as a shepherd, he was so cruel to you, here, by this faithful cavern, I want you at least to enjoy him [now that he has been] transformed into a flower; and let the tears I shed be your shining mirror.

79

Artifice

Così l'umano velo,
placata alfin, Giunone
omai ti renda, e la favella intera!
Così ti renda il cielo
l'amato tuo garzone
ne la leggiadra sua forma primiera;
e l'aria ombrosa e nera
di quest'antro riposto,
ch'oggi risona solo
del tuo profondo duolo,
deggia de' baci suoi risonar tosto,
ed a parlar s'avezze
de le vostre dolcezze!
    Lasso! dove son io?
chi di senno mi priva?
Stolto! a cui parlo? Misero! che tento?
Racconto il dolor mio
a l'insensata riva,
a la mutola selce, al sordo vento.
Oh novo aspro tormento!
Tu, che già mai non manchi,
che 'nfaticabil sei,
gli ultimi accenti miei,
quasi importuni, a replicar ti stanchi.
Ahi, ch'altro non risponde
che il mormorar de l'onde!
    O de le balze alpine
garruletta romita,
ninfa de' verdi e solitari chiostri,
sarà conforme il fine
de l'aspra nostra vita
com'è conforme il suon de' detti nostri?

So Juno, finally placated, will yet restore your body, and full speech! So heaven will restore your beloved boy in his graceful first form; and the shadowy, dark air of this secret cavern, which today resounds only with your profound grief, will then have to resound with his kisses, and accustom itself to speak of your bliss!

Alas! Where am I? Who drives me mad? Fool! to whom do I speak? Wretch! What am I doing? I tell my grief to the unfeeling river bank, to the dumb flint, to the deaf wind. O new and bitter torment! You, who are always present, indefatigable, are weary of answering my last words, as if they were importunate. Alas that nothing replies to me but the murmuring of the waters.

O solitary chatterer from the mountainous cliffs, nymph from the green and lonely cloisters, will the end of our cruel life be as similar as the sound of our

Oimè! perché ti mostri
scarsa a me di favella?
Crudo scherzo, empio scherno!
Dunque al mio strazio eterno
la voce istessa è senza voce? e quella,
ch'ognor geme e languisce,
per me solo ammutisce?
    Vana figlia de l'aere e de la lingua,
teco pur ti trastulla:
ben veggio che sei nulla.

Góngora

Del túmulo que hizo Córdoba en las honras de la señora reina doña Margarita

    Máquina funeral, que desta vida
nos decís la mudanza estando queda,
pira, no de aromática arboleda,
sí a más gloriosa fénix construída;
    bajel en cuya gavia esclarecida
estrellas, hijas de otra mejor Leda,
serenan la Fortuna, de su rueda
la volubilidad reconocida,
    farol luciente sois, que solicita
la razón, entre escollos naufragante
al puerto; y a pesar de lo luciente,
    oscura concha de una Margarita,
que, rubí en caridad, en fe diamante,
renace en nuevo Sol, en nuevo Oriente.

voices? Woe is me! Why do you deny your voice to me? Cruel jest, impious
mockery! Why then is your own voice voiceless to my eternal torment? and that
[voice] which always moans and languishes, only for me is muted?
    Vain daughter of the winds and tongue, you only entertain yourself: I clearly
see that you are nothing.

On the tomb erected by Córdoba in honour of Her Majesty Margarita
Funeral edifice, who, though yourself unmoving, tells us of the mutability of
life; pure, not of aromatic wood, but raised for a more glorious phoenix;
    vessel on whose noble topsail the stars, daughters of another greater Leda,
still the well-known fickleness of Fortune's wheel,
    you are a shining light, which reason seeks when drowning among the reefs at
the mouth of the harbour; and in spite of its light,
    the dark shell of a Margarita [Pearl] who, a ruby in charity, a diamond in
faith, is reborn into a new sun, a new Orient.

81

D'Aubigné

SONNET

Qui void le dieu aux blonds cheveux
En quittant la mer, son hostesse,
Friser en l'air l'or de sa tresse,
Voilé de son chef pretieux,

Qui void l'aether proche des cieux
Ou bien la forme menteresse,
La pluie d'or et la finesse
Du plus adultere des dieux,

Cestuy là verra la peinture
De l'or et de la cheveleure
Qui efface, passe et surmonte

Le soleil, et abbaisse encor,
En mesprisant la pluie d'or,
L'aether qui se cache de honte.

D'Etelan

SONNET DU MIROIR

Miroir, peintre et portrait qui donne et qui reçois,
Et qui porte en tous lieux avec toi mon image,
Qui peux tout exprimer, excepté le langage,
Et pour être animé n'as besoin que de voix;

Whoever sees the golden-haired god, leaving his hostess, the sea, curling the
gold of his tresses in the air which is dimmed by his precious head,
   whoever sees the aether, next to the heavens, or else the deceptive form, the
shower of gold and the trickery of the most adulterous of gods,
   he will have seen [merely] the painting of the gold and of the hair which
effaces, surpasses and outdoes
   the sun, and humbles also, despising the shower of gold, the aether which
hides in shame.

MIRROR SONNET

Mirror, painter and portrait, giving and receiving, and carrying my image
everywhere with you, [mirror] who can express everything but language, and
needs only a voice to be a living thing;

Tu peux seul me montrer quand chez toi je me vois,
Toutes mes passions peintes sur mon visage;
Tu suis d'un pas égal mon humeur et mon âge,
Et dans leurs changemens jamais ne te deçois.

Les mains d'un artisan au labeur obstinées,
D'un penible travail font, en plusieurs années,
Un portrait qui ne peut ressembler qu'un instant.

Mais toi, peintre brillant, d'un art inimitable,
Tu fais sans nul effort un ouvrage inconstant
Qui ressemble toûjours, et n'est jamais semblable.

Marino

SPECCHIO DELL'AMATA

Qualor, chiaro cristallo,
vago pur di mirar quel vivo sole
che 'n te specchiar si sòle,
in te le luci affiso,
ahi, ch'altro non vegg'io che 'l proprio viso!
Specchio fallace, ingrato,
se vagheggiar t'è dato
volto fra gli altri il più ridente e vago,
non dovresti serbar sì trista imago!

you only can show me when I see myself in you, all my passions painted on
my face; you follow in step my humour, my years, and never are deceived in
their changes.

A workman's hands in stubborn labour, after arduous toil make in many
years a portrait which is only accurate for a second.

But you, brilliant painter, with inimitable art, you effortlessly make an
inconstant picture which always resembles, and is never the same.

ON HIS BELOVED'S LOOKING-GLASS

When, clear crystal, I come to gaze on that living sun who often stares at herself
in you, I fix my eyes on you, and, alas, see nothing but my own face! Deceptive,
ungrateful glass, if it is your fate to gaze lovingly at the most laughingly lovely
face of all, you ought not to contain such a sad image.

Habert de Cérisy

From *Métamorphose des Yeux de Philis en astres*

. . . .

Au milieu de ce bois un liquide cristal
En tombant d'un rocher forme un large canal,
Qui comme un beau miroir, dans sa glace inconstante,
Fait de tous ses voisins la peinture mouvante

. . . .

C'est là, par un chaos agreable, et nouveau,
Que la terre et le ciel se rencontrent dans l'eau;
C'est là que l'oeil souffrant de douces impostures,
Confond tous les objects avecque leurs figures,
C'est là que sur un arbre il croit voir les poissons,
Qu'il trouve les oyseaux auprès des ameçons,
Et que le sens charmé d'une trompeuse idole
Doute si l'oyseau nage, ou si le poisson vole.
C'est là qu'une bergère estallant ses attraits,
Fait en se regardant de plus nobles portraits,
Quand, le genou courbé sur les fleurs du rivage,
Elle vient arrouser celles de son visage,
Qui remplissant les eaux de feux et de clartez
Pour un peu d'ornement leur rend mille beautez.
Partout où d'un regard elle échauffe les ondes,
En de noueveaux appas elle les rend fécondes,
Elle n'est plus unique et les flots embelis
Aussi bien que la terre ont une autre Philis.

. . . .

In the midst of this wood a liquid crystal, in falling from a rock, forms a broad canal, which, like a lovely mirror, in its inconstant glass, makes a moving painting of all its surroundings . . . It is there, by a novel, agreeable chaos, that sky and earth meet in the water; it is there that the eye, suffering from sweet impostures, confuses all objects with their reflections, it is there that it thinks it sees fish on a tree, it finds birds next to fish-hooks, and that the sense, charmed by a deceitful idol, is unsure whether the bird swims, or the fish flies. It is there that a shepherdess, displaying her charms, makes, as she looks at herself, the most noble portraits, when, kneeling on the flowers of the riverbank, she comes to water the flowers of her face, which, filling the waters with fires and brilliance, gives them a thousand beauties in exchange for a scrap of ornament. Wherever with a glance she fires the waves she makes them pregnant with new delights; she is no longer one, and the beautified ripples, just like the earth, possess a new Phyllis. . . .

Carew

ON THE SIGHT OF A GENTLEWOMAN'S FACE IN THE WATER

Stand still, you floods! do not deface
    That image which you bear:
So votaries from every place
    To you shall altars rear.

No winds but lovers' sighs blow here,
    To trouble these glad streams,
On which no star from any sphere
    Did ever dart such beams.

To crystal then in haste congeal,
    Lest you should lose your bliss;
And to my cruel fair reveal
    How cold, how hard she is!

But if the envious nymphs shall fear
    Their beauties will be scorn'd,
And hire the ruder winds to tear
    That face which you adorn'd.

Then rage and foam amain, that we
    Their malice may despise;
When from your froth we soon shall see
    A second Venus rise.

Góngora

SONNET

¡Oh claro honor del líquido elemento,
dulce arroyuelo de corriente plata
cuya agua entre la yerba se dilata
con regalado son, con paso lento!

O clear honour of the liquid element, sweet streamlet of running silver, whose
water spreads through the grass with a soft cadence, with a slow step!

85

Pues la por quien helar y arder me siento,
mientras en ti se mira, Amor retrata
de su rostro la nieve y la escarlata
en tu tranquilo y blando movimiento,
    véte como te vas; no dejes floja
la undosa rienda al cristalino freno
con que gobiernas tu veloz corriente;
    que no es bien que confusamente acoja
tanta belleza en su profundo seno
el gran señor del húmido tridente.

Giovanetti

BELLA NINFA SI LAVAVA IN UN LAGO

Allor che l'alba dal mar d'Adria inalza
la face per fugar l'ombra notturna,
a solitario lago, incolta e scalza,
col canestro sen va Fille e co'l'urna.
    Per bagnarsi il bel piè, con mano eburna
i lembi de la veste accoglie ed alza;
e l'onda, ch'era immota e taciturna,
con garrula allegrezza al sen le balza.

Since, while she for whom I feel myself freeze and burn sees herself in you, love paints the snow and scarlet of her face in your tranquil and gentle movement,
    go as you go; do not slacken the undulating reins from the crystal bit with which you guide your swift current,
    for it is not fitting that the great lord with the dripping trident should receive such beauty confusedly in his deep bosom.
[The conceit of the two tercets may be paraphrased: 'continue to move at the same speed, and no faster, for if you accelerate the ripples will confuse the picture of the lady, so spoiling the beauty of the reflection, which will hence become an unfitting gift or tribute to Neptune.']

A BEAUTIFUL NYMPH WASHING HERSELF IN A LAKE

Now, as dawn lifts her torch over the Adriatic to put to flight nocturnal shadow, Phyllis, barefoot and hair in disarray, comes to a solitary lake with her basket and pitcher.
    To wash her lovely foot, she gathers and lifts the skirts of her dress with an ivory hand, and the wave, which before was motionless and silent, leaps with garrulous joy into her bosom.

A l'apparir de lei sopra la sponda,
al discoprir de gli animati avori,
al folgorar de l'aurea chioma bionda,
    alga o scoglio non è, che non s'infiori;
fiore, che non si specchi entro quell'onda;
onda, che non sfavilli a tanti ardori.

Marino

DONNA CHE CUCE

È strale, è stral, non ago
quel ch'opra in suo lavoro,
nova Aracne d'amor, colei ch'adoro;
onde, mentre il bel lino orna e trapunge,
di mille punte il cor mi passa e punge.
Misero! e quel sì vago
sanguigno fil che tira,
tronca, annoda, assottiglia, attorce e gira
la bella man gradita,
è il fil de la mia vita.

Strode

ON A GENTLEWOMAN WALKING IN THE SNOWE

I saw faire Cloris walke alone
Where feather'd raine came softly downe,
And Jove descended from his tower
To court her in a silver shower;
The wanton snowe flewe to her breast
Like little birds into their nest,
And overcome with whiteness there
For greife it thaw'd into a teare,
Thence falling on her garment's hem
For greife it freez'd into a gem.

At her appearance on the shore, at the uncovering of the living ivories, at the glittering of her golden yellow hair,
    there is no weed or wave which does not burst into flower, no flower which is not reflected in that wave, no wave which does not glisten at so many fires.

ON A LADY SEWING

It is an arrow, an arrow, and not a needle which she is using at her work, she whom I adore, the new Arachne of love; with which, while she beautifies and embroiders the beautiful linen, she pierces and runs my heart through in a thousand places. Alas! And that so delicate, bleeding thread which she pulls, cuts, knots, stretches, twists and winds with her beautiful elegant hand, is the thread of my life.

87

D'Aubigné

SONNET

Auprès de ce beau teinct, le lys en noir se change,
Le laict est bazané auprès de ce beau teinct,
Du signe la blancheur auprès de vous s'esteinct
Et celle du papier où est vostre louange.

Le succre est blanc, et lorsqu'en la bouche on le range
Le goust plaist, comme fait le lustre qui le peinct.
Plus blanc est l'arcenic, mais c'est un lustre feinct,
Car c'est mort, c'est poison à celuy qui le mange.

Vostre blanc en plaisir taint ma rouge douleur.
Soyez douce du goust, comme belle en couleur,
Que mon espoir ne soit desmenty par l'espreuve

Vostre blanc ne soit point d'aconite noircy,
Car ce sera ma mort, belle, si je vous treuve
Aussi blanche que neige, et froide tout ainsi.

Randolph

ON THE DEATH OF A NIGHTINGALE

Goe solitary wood, and henceforth be
Acquainted with no other Harmonie,
Then the Pyes chattering, or the shreeking note
Of bodeing Owles, and fatall Ravens throate.

Beside this lovely hue the lily turns black, milk is sunburned beside this lovely hue, the swan's whiteness is extinguished beside you, and the whiteness of the paper where lies your praise.

Sugar is white, and when it melts in our mouths the taste pleases, as does the lustre which paints it. Whiter still is arsenic, but that is a deceitful lustre, for it is death and poison to whoever eats it.

Your whiteness with pleasure dyes my red grief. Be as sweet to taste as you are beautiful in colour, let not my hopes be contradicted by the proof,

let not your white be blackened by aconite, for it will be my death, my lovely, if I find you as white as snow and as cold.

Thy sweetest Chanters dead, that warbled forth
Layes, that might tempests calme, and still the North;
And call downe Angels from their glorious Spheare
To heare her Songs, and learne new Anthems there.
That soule is fled, and to *Elisium* gone;
Thou a poore desert left; goe then and runne,
Begge there to stand a grove, and if shee please
To sing againe beneath thy shadowy Trees;
The soules of happy Lovers crown'd with blisses
Shall flock about thee, and keepe time with kisses.

Marvell

THE FAIR SINGER

I

To make a final conquest of all me,
Love did compose so sweet an Enemy,
In whom both Beauties to my death agree,
Joyning themselves in fatal Harmony;
That while she with her Eyes my Heart does bind,
She with her Voice might captivate my Mind.

II

I could have fled from One but singly fair:
My dis-intangled Soul it self might save,
Breaking the curled trammels of her hair.
But how should I avoid to be her Slave,
Whose subtile Art invisibly can wreath
My Fetters of the very Air I breath?

III

It had been easie fighting in some plain,
Where Victory might hang in equal choice,
But all resistance against her is vain,
Who has th' advantage both of Eyes and Voice,
And all my Forces needs must be undone,
She having gained both the Wind and Sun.

Ronsard

SONNET

Le soir qu'Amour vous fist en la salle descendre
Pour danser d'artifice un beau ballet d'Amour,
Voz yeux, bien qu'il fust nuict, ramenerent le jour,
Tant ils sceurent d'esclairs par la place respandre.

Le ballet fut divin, qui se souloit reprendre,
Se rompre, se refaire, & tour dessus retour
Se mesler, s'escarter, se tourner à l'entour,
Contre-imitant le cours du fleuve de Meandre.

Ores il estoit rond, ores long, or' estroit,
Or' en poincte, en triangle, en la façon qu'on voit
L'escadron de la Gruë evitant la froidure.

Je faux, tu ne dansois, mais ton pied voletoit
Sur le haut de la terre: aussi ton corps s'estoit
Transformé pour ce soir en divine nature.

Lovelace

GRATIANA DANCING AND SINGING

See! with what constant motion,
Even and glorious as the sun,
    Gratiana steers that noble frame,
Soft as her breast, sweet as her voice,
That gave each winding law and poise,
    And swifter than the wings of Fame.

The evening when Love made you descend to the ballroom to dance the artifice of a beautiful ballet of Love, your eyes, although it was night, brought back day, so many lights could they make glitter through the house.

The dance was divine, as it was taken up again, broken, remade, and turn upon turn mixed, diverted, returned to the circle, counterfeiting the course of the river Meander.

Now it is round, now long, now narrow, now pointed, now triangular, resembling sight of a squadron of cranes taking flight from the cold.

I err, you were not dancing, but your foot fluttered above the earth: so your body was transformed by the evening into divine nature.

She beat the happy pavement
By such a star made firmament,
  Which now no more the roof envies,
But swells up high with Atlas ev'n
Bearing the brighter, nobler heav'n,
  And, in her, all the deities.

Each step trod out a lover's thought
And the ambitious hopes he brought,
  Chain'd to her brave feet with such arts,
Such sweet command and gentle awe,
As when she ceas'd, we sighing saw
  The floor lay pav'd with broken hearts.

So did she move; so did she sing
Like the harmonious spheres that bring
  Unto their rounds their music's aid;
Which she performed such a way,
As all th'enamour'd world will say
  The Graces danced, and Apollo play'd.

Marino

BELLA SONATRICE

Duo archi adopra e con duo archi offende
questa ch'arciera e Musa il mondo ammira:
un con la bella man ne move e tira,
un nel ciglio seren ne curva e tende.
  D'ebeno l'un, l'altro d'avorio splende,
Febo l'un, l'altro Amor sostiene e gira;
l'un porge spirto armonico a la lira,
l'altro ai miseri amanti il fura e prende;

A LOVELY PLAYER

She uses two bows, and wounds with two bows, she, archer and Muse whom the
world admires; she moves and draws one with her lovely hand, curves and bends
the other in her serene eyebrow.
  One is a shining ebony, one shining ivory, Phoebus holds and moves one,
Love the other; one endows a spirit of harmony upon the lyre, the other cap-
tures and drives mad the unhappy lovers;

91

diletta l'un con numeri canori,
l'altro con crudi strazi invita al pianto;
l'un saetta le corde e l'altro i cori.

Ma felice languir, poiché non tanto
ferisce il guardo con pungenti ardori,
quanto con dolce suon risana il canto.

Waller

OF A TREE CUT IN PAPER

Fair hand! that can on virgin paper write,
Yet from the stain of ink preserve it white;
Whose travel o'er that silver field does show
Like track of leverets in morning snow.
Love's image thus in purest minds is wrought,
Without a spot or blemish to the thought.
Strange, that your fingers should the pencil foil,
Without the help of colours or of oil!
For though a painter boughs and leaves can make,
'Tis you alone can make them bend and shake;
Whose breath salutes your new-created grove,
Like southern winds, and makes it gently move.
Orpheus could make the forest dance; but you
Can make the motion and the forest too.

Fontanella

PETTINE ROTTO

Candida e delicata navicella,
ch'era di terso avorio opra gioconda,
d'una chioma fendea dorata e bella
l'aurato flutto e la tempesta bionda.

one delights with tuneful numbers, the other beckons to grief with many
torments; one arrows the chords, the other hearts.

But to languish is happy, for her look does not madden with as many burning
ardours, as her song cures with its sweet sound.

THE BROKEN COMB

A little ship, white and delicate, the merry work of soft ivory, parted the gilded
wave and blonde tempest of a golden, lovely, head of hair.

Guidata da una man polita e monda,
prendea de' miei sospir l'aura novella;
ed un cristallo ch'ebano circonda
innanzi avea per tramontana stella.

Vago di gir con peregrino errore,
senza temer di rimanere assorto,
v'ascese incauto il semplicetto core.

Ecco, mentre attendea vicino il porto,
per quello biondo pelago d'amore,
si divise la nave, e restò morto.

Lord Herbert of Cherbury

UPON COMBING HER HAIR

Breaking from under that thy cloudy veil,
  Open and shine yet more, shine out more clear,
  Thou glorious golden-beam-darting hair,
Even till my wonder-strucken sense fail.

Shoot out in light, and shine those rays on far,
  Thou much more fair than is the Queen of Love
  When she doth comb her in her sphere above,
And from a planet turns a blazing star.

Nay, thou art greater too, more destiny
  Depends on thee than on her influence,
  No hair thy fatal hand doth now dispense,
But to someone a thread of life must be.

While, gracious unto me, thou both dost sunder
  Those glories which, if they united were,
  Might have amazed sense, and show'st each hair,
Which if alone had been too great a wonder.

Steered by a white and polished hand, it captured the fresh wind of my sighs;
and a crystal surrounded by ebony led ahead like the pole star.
  Wishing to go wandering to far places, my simple trusting little heart goes
aboard you with no fear of being drowned.
  Behold, while it lies just outside the harbour, the ship is split in two by that
blonde ocean of love, and it lies dead.

And now, spread in their goodly length, sh'appears
  No creature which the earth might call her own,
  But rather one that in her gliding down
Heav'n's beams did crown, to show us she was theirs.

And come from thence, how can they fear Time's rage,
  Which, in his power else on earth most strange,
  Such golden treasure doth to silver change,
By that improper alchemy of age?

But stay, methinks new beauties do arise,
  While she withdraws these glories which were spread
  Wonder of beauties, set thy radiant head,
And strike out day from thy yet fairer eyes.

Carew

CELIA, BLEEDING, TO THE SURGEON

Fond man, that canst believe her blood
  Will from those purple channels flow;
Or that the pure untainted flood
  Can any foul distemper know;
Or that thy weak steel can incise
The crystal case wherein it lies:

Know, her quick blood, proud of his seat,
  Runs dancing through her azure veins;
Whose harmony no cold nor heat
  Disturbs, whose hue no tincture stains:
And the hard rock wherein it dwells
The keenest darts of love repels.

But thou repli'st 'behold, she bleeds!'
  Fool! thou'rt deceiv'd, and dost not know
The mystic knot whence this proceeds,
  How lovers in each other grow:
Thou struck'st her arm, but 'twas my heart
Shed all the blood, felt all the smart.

Quevedo

A Aminta, que teniendo un clavel en la boca, por morderle se mordió los labios, y salió sangre

Bastábale al clavel verse vencido
del labio en que se vio (cuando, esforzado
con su propria vergüenza, lo encarnado
a tu rubí se vio más parecido),

sin que en tu boca hermosa dividido
fuese de blancas perlas granizado,
pues tu enojo, con él equivocado,
el labio por clavel dejó mordido;

si no cuidado de la sangre fuese,
para que, a presumir de tiria grana,
de tu púrpura líquida aprendiese.

Sangre vertió tu boca soberana,
porque, roja victoria, amaneciese
llanto al clavel y risa a la mañana.

Stigliani

APE MORTA

Una pecchia, volata
della mia Lidia al bel labro gentile,
gliel punse e, come è stile,
nel ritrar l'ago vi rimase uccisa.

To Aminta holding a carnation in her mouth, when in biting it she bit her own lips, and shed blood

It was enough for the carnation to see itself defeated by the lip on which it found itself, when its own embarrassment made it blush, and more resemble your ruby [mouth],
without being divided in your lovely mouth and hailed upon by white pearls; for your anger, mistaking it, left the lip bitten instead of the carnation.
If it was not the blood's intention that it should learn from your liquid purple to aspire to the condition of Tyrian crimson.
Your sovereign mouth shed blood, so that a red victory should dawn, as tears on the carnation, laughter on the morning.

ON A DEAD BEE

A honey-bee, having flown on to the lovely, gentle lip of my Lidia, stung her, and, as is their wont, was killed on retracting its sting. O happy, blessed one

95

Oh felice, oh beata
chi ebbe mai tal sorte:
morir dal paradiso infra le porte!

BACI

Se son, come tu dici,
Lidia, le labbra mie siepi spinose,
le tue son molli rose.
Dunque, perché mi vieti
ch'io con soavi baci
queste a quelle congiunga ed avicine?
Stan pur presso alle rose ognor le spine.

Fleming

WIE ER WOLLE GEKUESST SEIN

Nirgends hin alse auf den Mund,
Da sinkt's in des Herzens Grund.
Nicht zu frei, nicht zu gezwungen,
Nicht mit gar zu fauler Zungen.

Nicht zu wenig, nicht zu viel,
Beides wird sonst Kinderspiel.
Nicht zu laut und nicht zu leise,
Bei dem Mass ist rechte Weise.

who could ever have such a fate—to die within the gates of paradise!

KISSES

If my lips are, as you say, Lidia, thorny hedges, then yours are soft roses. Therefore why do you say me nay when I draw near and join mine to yours in sweet kisses? Roses always lie side by side with thorns.

HOW HE WOULD LIKE TO BE KISSED

Nowhere but on the mouth, from where it goes straight to the bottom of your heart. Not too freely, not too forcedly, and not with a lazy tongue either.

Not too little, not too much, else either turns into a children's game. Not too noisily, not too quietly, the golden mean is the right way.

Not too near, not too far apart, the latter causes sorrow, the former suffering; not too drily, not too moistly, [but a kiss] just as Adonis gave to Venus.

Nicht zu nahe, nicht zu weit;
Dies macht kummer, jenes Leid,
Nicht zu trocken, nicht zu feuchte,
Wie Adonis Venus reichte.

Nicht zu harte, nicht zu weich,
Bald zugleich, bald nicht zugleich.
Nicht zu langsam, nicht zu schnelle,
Nicht ohn Unterschied der Stelle.

Halb gebissen, halb gehaucht,
Halb die Lippen eingetaucht.
Nicht ohn Unterschied der Zeiten,
Mehr alleine, denn bei Leuten.

Küsse nun ein jedermann,
Wie er weiss, will, soll und kann.
Ich nur und die Liebste wissen,
Wir wir uns recht sollen küssen.

Cleveland

UPON PHILLIS WALKING IN A MORNING BEFORE SUN-RISING

The sluggish morne, as yet undrest,
My *Phillis* brake from out her East;
As if shee'd made a match to runne
With *Venus* Usher to the sunne.
The trees like yeomen of her guard,
Serving more for pomp then ward,
Rank't on each side with loyall duty,
Weave branches to inclose her beauty.

Not too hard, not too gently, sometimes using both together, at other times not. Not too slowly, not too quickly, not without consideration of place.

Half bite, half breath, half lip in lip. Not without consideration of time, better alone than among people.

Now let everybody kiss any way he knows, wants, must and can. Only I and my mistress know how we two like to kiss.

97

The Plants whose luxurie was lopt,
Or age with crutches underpropt;
Whose wooden carkases were grown
To be but coffins of their owne;
Revive, and at her generall dole
Each receives his antient soule.
The winged Choristers began
To chirp their Matins: and the Fan
Of whistling winds like Organs plai'd,
Untill their Voluntaries made
The wakened earth in Odours rise
To be her morning Sacrifice.
The flowers call'd out of their beds,
Start, and raise up their drowsie heads:
And he that for their colour seekes,
May finde it vaulting in her cheekes,
Where roses mix: no Civill War
Betweeen her *Yorke* and *Lancaster*.
The Mary-gold whose Courtiers face
Eccho's the sunne, and doth unlace
Her at his rise, at his full stop
Packs and shuts up her gaudy shop,
Mistakes her cue, and doth display.
Thus *Phillis* antidates the day.
   These miracles had cramp't the sunne,
Who thinking that his Kingdom's wonne,
Powders with light his frizled locks,
To see what Saint his lustre mocks.
The trembling leaves through which he plai'd,
Dapling the walke with light and shade,
Like Lattice-windowes, give the spye
Room but to peep with halfe an eye;
Least her full Orb his sight should dim,
And bid us all good-night in him,
Till she would spend a gentle ray
To force us a new fashion'd day.
But what religious Paulsie's this
Which makes the boughs divest their bliss?
And that they might her foot-steps strawe,
Drop their leaves with shivering awe.
Phillis perceiv'd, and (least her stay
Should wed October unto May;
And as her beauty caus'd a Spring,
Devotion might an Autumne bring)
With-drew her beames, yet made no night,
But left the Sun her Curate-light.

Marino

NELLA FUGA DI UN UCCELLO

Esca porgea di propria mano un giorno
a vezzoso usignuol Lilla cortese,
quando per l'uscio aperto il volo ei prese,
ed a l'aria natia fece ritorno.
    Con amaro sospir, che l'aure intorno
tutte d'amore e di pietate accese,
tardi e 'ndarno la destra al vento stese,
scolorando le rose al viso adorno.
    —Ove, a rischio di morte, in man nemica
ne vai,—dicea con lagrimose note
— e fuggi chi t'apprezza e ti nutrica?—
    L'augello udilla, e 'n spaziose rote
l'ali rivolse a la prigione antica:
tanto di bella donna il pianto pote.

Giovanetti

BELLA DONNA VESTITA DA TURCA DI CARNEVALE

Ecco la mia bellissima guerriera,
trovando al suo rigor conformi spoglie,
entro fasce barbariche raccoglie
d'attorto e bianco lin la chioma altera;

ON THE FLIGHT OF A BIRD

One day lovely Lilla fed with her own hand her pretty nightingale, when he took flight through the open cage, and returned to his native air.

With a bitter sigh, which burned all the air around with love and tenderness, too late and in vain she stretched her hand to the wind, which blanched the roses of her lovely face.

'Where are you going, at the risk of death, to an enemy hand,' she said in mournful tones 'and why do you run away from her who loves and feeds you?'

The little bird heard her, and beat its wings in wide circles back to its former prison: the grief of a lovely woman can perform so much.

A BEAUTIFUL LADY IN THE CARNIVAL COSTUME OF A TURK

Behold my loveliest warrior, finding a raiment to fit her cruelty, as she wraps her haughty hair in barbarous bands of white and twisted linen [i.e. in a turban]

e con sembianza vaga, ancor che fera,
fra quei lacci d'orrore Amore accoglie;
ché barbara impietà grazia non toglie
a questa sol di cor barbara arciera,

che, contra me cercando arme novella,
or con arco di Tracia arma la mano,
fatta turca d'amore, empia e rubella.

E s'a caso talor l'arco inumano
falla in lanciar le rapide quadrella,
l'arco del ciglio non saetta invano.

Morando

BELLA DONNA VESTITA A DUOLO

S'io miro il manto e il velo
che la fronte serena e il sen v'ingombra,
bella, io vi stimo un cielo
cui fosca notte adombra;
ma se lo sguardo affiso
in sì bel viso e di tai raggi adorno,
voi mi sembrate un sol che porti il giorno.

Cleveland

A FAIRE NIMPH SCORNING A BLACK BOY COURTING HER

Nymph. Stand off, and let me take the aire,
      Why should the smoak pursue the faire?
Boy. My face is smoak, thence may be guest
      What flames within have scorch'd my brest.

and, eager and fierce in appearance, she takes Love in those lassoos of terror; and the barbarous impiety does not take away the grace of the barbarous archeress who shoots at hearts alone,

who anew seeking arms against me, now arms her hand with a Thracian bow, become a Turk of love, impious and bloody.

And if, perchance, such an inhuman bow fails to launch its swift darts, the bow of her eye does not shoot in vain.

ON A BEAUTIFUL WOMAN DRESSED IN MOURNING

If I look at the weeds and veil which shadow your serene forehead and your bosom, lovely one, I see you as a sky darkened by a gloomy night, but if I stare on such a lovely face adorned with such rays, you appear to be a sun bringing the day.

Nymph. The flame of love I cannot view,
      For the dark Lanthorne of thy hue,
Boy. And yet this Lanthorne keeps loves Taper
      Surer then yours, that's of white paper.
      Whatever Midnight hath been here,
      The Moon-shine of your face can cleare.
Nymph. My Moon of an Ecclipse is 'fraid,
      If thou should'st interpose thy shade.
Boy. Yet one thing (sweet-heart) I will ask,
      Take me for a new fashion'd Mask.
Nymph. Done: but my bargaine shall be this,
      I'le throw my Maske off when I kiss.
Boy. Our curl'd embraces shall delight
      To checquer limbs with black and white.
Nymph. Thy inke, my paper, make me guesse,
      Our Nuptiall bed will prove a Presse;
      And in our sports, if any come,
      They'l read a wanton Epigram.
Boy. Why should my Black thy love impaire?
      Let the darke shop commend the ware:
      Or if thy love from black forbeares,
      I'le strive to wash it of with teares.
Nymph. Spare fruitless teares, since thou must needs
      Still weare about thee mourning weeds:
      Teares can no more affection win,
      Then wash thy Æthiopian skin.

Ronsard

SONNET

Je vouldroy bien richement jaunissant
En pluye d'or goute à goute descendre
Dans le beau sein de ma belle Cassandre,
Lors qu'en ses yeulx le somme va glissant.

I would like, richly turning to yellow, to fall drop by drop in a shower of gold,
into the lovely breast of my beautiful Cassandra, when slumber creeps into her
eyes.

Je vouldroy bien en toreau blandissant
Me transformer pour finement la prendre,
Quand elle va par l'herbe la plus tendre
Seule à l'escart mille fleurs ravissant.

Je vouldroy bien afin d'aiser ma peine
Estre un Narcisse, & elle une fontaine
Pour m'y plonger une nuict à sejour:

Et vouldroy bien que ceste nuict encore
Durast tousjours sans que jamais l'Aurore
D'un front nouveau nous r'allumast le jour.

Stolle

DIE VERLIEBTE VERWANDLUNG

Du hast, o Liebe, mich erst in ein Reh verkehrt,
Das seines Jägers Pfeil in zarter Brust getragen;
Hernach in einen Schwan, der sich zu Tode singt;
Und dann in eine Blum', in die die Flamme dringt,
So von der Sonne kommt und allen Saft verzehrt;
Hierauf verlor ich mich in einen Tränenregen,
Und jetzund muss ich, mir zur Pein,
Ein Salamander sein,
Der in der Strahlenglut, so Daphnens Augen hegen,
Verschmachtet, und doch auch sein schmachtend Herze nährt.

I would like to turn myself into a white bull gently to capture her when she goes through the tenderest grass, alone yet ravishing the thousand flowers around her.

I would indeed, to ease my pain, that I were a Narcissus, and she a fountain, where I could plunge myself for one night's stay,

and I truly wish that that night should last forever, without Dawn ever brightening our day with a new face.

THE AMOROUS METAMORPHOSIS

At first, O love, you changed me into a deer, carrying in its tender breast its hunter's arrow; thereafter into a swan, singing unto death; and then into a flower into which penetrates the flame which comes from the sun, absorbing all my sap; thereupon I dissolved into a shower of tears, and now, for my pains, I must be a salamander, languishing in the searing rays of Daphne's eyes, which yet sustain its languishing heart. And yet I should not in the least wish to

Jedennoch wollt ich mich in mindsten nicht beklagen,
Wenn deine Wundermacht,
Die mir bisher nicht Süsses zugedacht,
Mir endlich noch die Gunst gewährte,
Und mich vor meinem Tod in Daphnens Schatz verkehrte.

Carew

A FLY THAT FLEW INTO MY MISTRESS HER EYE

When this fly liv'd, she us'd to play
In the sunshine all the day;
Till, coming near my Celia's sight,
She found a new and unknown light,
So full of glory as it made,
The noonday sun a gloomy shade.
Then this amorous fly became
My rival, and did court my flame;
She did from hand to bosom skip,
And from her breath, her cheek, and lip,
Suck'd all the incense and the spice,
And grew a bird of paradise.
At last into her eye she flew,
There scorch'd in flames and drown'd in dew
Like Phaëton from the sun's sphere,
She fell, and with her dropp'd a tear,
Of which a pearl was straight compos'd,
Wherein her ashes lie enclos'd.
Thus she receiv'd from Celia's eye
Funeral, flame, tomb, obsequy.

UPON A MOLE IN CELIA'S BOSOM

That lovely spot which thou dost see
In Celia's bosom was a bee,
Who built her amorous spicy nest
I' th' Hyblas of her either breast.

complain if your wondrous power which so far has intended no delights for me, would at long last grant me one favour and change me, before I die, into Daphne's lover.

But from close ivory hives she flew
To suck the aromatic dew
Which from the neighbour vale distils,
Which parts those two twin-sister hills.
There feasting on ambrosial meat,
A rolling file of balmy sweat
(As in soft murmurs before death
Swan-like she sung) chok'd up her breath;
So she in water did expire,
More precious than the phoenix' fire.
    Yet still her shadow there remains
Confin'd to those Elysian plains,
With this strict law, that who shall lay
His bold lips on that milky way,
The sweet and smart from thence shall bring
Of the bee's honey and her sting.

Giovanetti

BELLA DONNA CON MACCHIE ROSSE SUL VOLTO

Quegli, Fillide mia, vermigli nèi,
che la natura sì minuti e spessi
ha negli avori del tuo volto impressi,
non macchie, no, ma fregi io li direi.
    Perché con lor vie più leggiadra sei:
giungon grazie al tuo volto i falli stessi,
e sotto insidie ascoso Amore in essi
affina strali più pungenti e rei.
    Oh care macchie, avventurose e belle!
Cosí de' prati e de l'eterea spera
sono ancor macchie i fior, macchie le stelle.

A BEAUTIFUL LADY WITH RED MOLES ON HER FACE

My Phillida, these crimson moles, so tiny, so many, which nature has stamped upon the ivory of your face, I will call not moles, no, but adornments.

    Because you are more attractive through them, the very faults themselves lend graces to your face, and under the snares Love is hidden, and sharpens in them more piercing, more treacherous arrows.

    O sweet moles, seductive, lovely! So are the flowers moles of the meadow, the stars the moles of the ethereal sphere.

E ne le selve ircane ogni aspra fera
lusinga pur con dilettosa pelle,
sparsa di belle macchie, empia pantera.

Donne

THE ANAGRAM

Marry, and love thy *Flavia*, for, shee
Hath all things, whereby others beautious bee,
For, though her eyes be small, her mouth is great,
Though they be Ivory, yet her teeth be jeat,
Though they be dimme, yet she is light enough,
And though her harsh haire fall, her skinne is rough;
What though her cheeks be yellow, her haire's red,
Give her thine, and she hath a maydenhead.
These things are beauties elements, where these
Meet in one, that one must, as perfect, please.
If red and white and each good quality
Be in thy wench, ne'r aske where it doth lye.
In buying things perfum'd, we aske; if there
Be muske and amber in it, but not where.
Though all her parts be not in th'usuall place,
She'hath yet an Anagram of a good face.
If we might put the letters but one way,
In the leane dearth of words, what could wee say?
When by the Gamut some Musitions make
A perfect song, others will undertake,
By the same Gamut chang'd, to equall it.
Things simply good, can never be unfit.
She's faire as any, if all be like her,
And if none bee, then she is singular.
All love is wonder; if wee justly doe
Account her wonderfull, why not lovely too?
Love built on beauty, soone as beauty, dies,
Chuse this face, chang'd by no deformities.
Women are all like Angels; the faire be
Like those which fell to worse; but such as thee,
Like to good Angels, nothing can impaire:
'Tis lesse griefe to be foule, than to'have beene faire.

And in the Hyrcanian woods, every fierce beast is tempted by the wicked
panther with its most delightful skin, speckled with beautiful spots.

105

For one nights revels, silke and gold we chuse,
But, in long journeyes, cloth, and leather use.
Beauty is barren oft; best husbands say,
There is best land, where there is foulest way.
Oh what a soveraigne Plaister will shee bee,
If thy past sinnes have taught thee jealousie!
Here needs no spies, nor eunuches; her commit
Safe to thy foes; yea, to a Marmosit.
When Belgiaes citties, the round countries drowne,
That durty foulenesse guards, and armes the towne:
So doth her face guard her; and so, for thee,
Which, forc'd by businesse, absent oft must bee,
Shee, whose face, like clouds, turnes the day to night,
Who, mightier than the sea, makes Moores seem white,
Who, though seaven yeares, she in the Stews had laid,
A Nunnery durst receive, and thinke a maid,
And though in childbeds labour she did lie,
Midwifes would sweare, 'twere but a tympanie,
Whom, if shee accuse her selfe, I credit lesse
Than witches, which impossibles confesse,
Whom Dildoes, Bedstaves, and her Velvet Glasse
Would be as loath to touch as Joseph was :
One like none, and lik'd of none, fittest were,
For, things in fashion every man will weare.

Morando

BELLA SPOSA DI MARITO DEFORME

Mopso, che brutto il ceffo, il pelo ha folto,
sgangherate le membra, ìmpari il piede,
dàssi a Lidia la bella, in cui si vede
oro il crin, latte il seno e rose il volto.

    Ad un Tersite, ad un Esopo incolto
un'Elena gentil fia giunta in fede;
di lui, che Pane in rustichezza eccede,
fia costei ch'a Siringa il pregio ha tolto.

THE LOVELY WIFE OF A DEFORMED HUSBAND

Mopsus, with his ugly face, his bristling hair, gangling limbs and feet of
different sizes, gave himself to lovely Lidia, with golden hair, milky breasts, and
rosy cheeks.

    A lovely Helen was faithfully joined in matrimony to a Thersites, to a crude
Aesop; she who took the prize of beauty from Syrinx was his, who was more
rough and common than Pan.

Sì dolce miel cibo è d'un orso insano,
sì ricca gemma in fango vil si pone,
sì bella rosa è d'un bifolco in mano.
    Disegual paragon, strana unïone;
ecco congiunta Venere a Vulcano,
maritata Proserpina a Plutone.

Randolph

TO HIS WELL TIMBRED MISTRESSE

Sweet, heard you not fames latest breath rehearse
How I left hewing blocks to hack at verse,
Now growne the master Log, while other be
But shavings, and the chips of Poetry.
And thus I saw Deale-boards of beauty forth,
To make my Love a warehouse of her worth.
Her leggs are heart of Oake, and columnes stand
To beare the amorous bulke; then *Muse* command
That Beech be work'd for thighs unto those leggs,
Turn'd round and carv'd, and joynted fast with peggs.
Contrive her belly round, a dining roome,
When Love and Beauty will a feasting come.
Another story make from wast to chinne,
With breasts like Pots to nest young sparrowes in.
Then place the Garret of her head above,
Thatcht with a yellow haire to keep in Love.
Thus have I finisht beauties master prize
Were but the Glasier here *t*o make her eyes.
Then gentle *Muse* her out-works cease to raise,
To worke within, and wainscot her with praise.

Such sweet honey is the food of a horrible bear, such precious gem is found in such vile dirt, such a lovely rose in the hand of an oaf.
    Unequal paragon, strange union; behold Venus married to Vulcan, Proserpine to Pluto.

Artifice

Suckling

THE DEFORMED MISTRESS

I know there are some fools that care
Not for the body, so the face be fair;
Some others, too, that in a female creature
Respect not beauty, but a comely feature;
And others, too, that for those parts in sight
Care not so much, so that the rest be right.
Each man his humour hath, and, faith, 'tis mine
To love that woman which I now define.
First I would have her wainscot foot and hand
More wrinkled far than any pleated band,
That in those furrows, if I'd take the pains,
I might both sow and reap all sorts of grains:
Her nose I'd have a foot long, not above
With pimples embroider'd, for those I love;
And at the end a comely pearl of snot,
Considering whether it should fall or not:
Provided, next, that half her teeth be out,
Nor do I care much if her pretty snout
Meet with her furrow'd chin, and both together
Hem in her lips, as dry as good whit-leather:
One wall-eye she shall have, for that's a sign
In other beasts the best: why not in mine?
Her neck I'll have to be pure jet at least,
With yellow spots enamell'd; and her breast,
Like a grasshopper's wing, both thin and lean,
Not to be touch'd for dirt, unless swept clean:
As for her belly, 'tis no matter, so
There be a belly, and—
Yet if you will, let it be something high,
And always let there be a tympany.
But soft! where am I now? here I should stride,
Lest I fall in, the place must be so wide,
And pass unto her thighs, which shall be just
Like to an ant's that's scraping in the dust.
Into her legs I'd have love's issues fall,
And all her calf into a gouty small:
Her feet both thick and eagle-like display'd,
The symptoms of a comely, handsome maid.
As for her parts behind, I ask no more:
If they but answer those that are before,
I have my utmost wish; and, having so,
Judge whether I am happy, yea or no.

108

Greflinger

AN EINE JUNGFRAU

Versichert Euch, mein Lieb, ich bin Euch so verpflicht',
So tief, so lang, so breit, Ihr glaubt es selber nicht.
Wie soll ich Euch nicht lieben?
Ihr seid so wunderfein,
Ihr gleichet Euch den Sieben,
Die gross von Löchern sein.

Das Haar ist rabenweiss, die Augen wie Rubin,
Der Mund ist himmelblau, so sticht die Nase hin,
Des Elefanten Schnabel,
Die Zähne sind wie Gold
Und kurz wie eine Gabel—
Ich bin Euch trefflich hold.

Auvray

From CONTRE UNE DAME TROP MAIGRE

Non, je ne l'ayme point ceste carcasse d'os,
Qu'on ne m'en parle plus, quoy qu'il y ait du lucre,
J'ayme autant embrasser l'image d'Atropos
Ou me laisser tomber tout nud dans un sepulcre.

Dés la premiere nuict de nos embrassemens,
J'imaginay sa chambre estre un grand cimetiere,
Son corps maigre sembloit un monceau d'ossemens,
Son linceul un suaire et sa couche une biere.

TO A YOUNG LADY

Rest assured, my love, I am so much obliged to you, so deep, so long, so wide, you would not believe it yourself. How could I not love you? You are so exceedingly fair, you resemble a sieve which is full of holes.

Your hair is ravenwhite, your eyes are like rubies, your mouth is sky-blue, your nose protrudes like an elephant's beak, your teeth are like gold and short like a fork—I am exceedingly fond of you.

AGAINST A WOMAN WHO WAS TOO THIN

No, I do not love this carcass of bones any more; let no-one mention her to me again, although she has plenty of lucre, I would as soon kiss the image of Atropos, or throw myself naked into a sepulchre.

After the first night of our embraces I imagined her chamber was a huge cemetery; her thin body seemed to be a heap of bones, her sheets a shroud and her bed a coffin.

Artifice

Ce seroit violer le droit des Trespassez
De toucher sacrilege à ses membres ethiques,
Je les baiserois bien s'ils estoient enchassez,
Comme au travers d'un verre on baise les reliques.

Belle, dis-je, (tastant la peau de son teton)
Pour ne me point blesser lors que je vous embrasse,
Il faudroit vous garnir les membres de cotton,
Ou que je fusse armé d'un bon corps de cuirasse.

Quand je touche aux rasoirs de vostre hastelet,
Je n'oserois mesler mes os avec les vostres,
Vostre mere vous fit disant son Chapelet
Puis que tout vostre corps n'est que des patinostres.

Au châlit innocent j'eusse dit ces propos:
Pourquoy faut-il jaloux que si haut tu caquettes?
Mais, je cogneus la Dame au cliquetis des os,
Comme on connait un ladre au bruit de ses cliquettes.
. . . .

Ayres

ON A FAIR BEGGAR

Barefoot and ragged, with neglected hair,
She whom the Heavens at once made poor and fair,
   With humble voice and moving words did stay,
   To beg an alms of all who pass'd that way.

It would be to violate the rights of the dead to commit sacrilege on her consumptive [it also means 'ethical': rendering the pun is impossible] limbs; I would kiss them, however, if they were enshrined, as one kisses the relics [of saints] through a glass.

My beauty, I say, fingering the skin of her tit, so as not to hurt me when I embrace you, your limbs will have to be covered with cotton-wool, or I would have to be wearing good armour-plate.

When I feel the razors of your skewers [hips], I wouldn't dare to mix my bones with yours; your mother conceived you while she was telling her rosary, for all your body is made of paternosters.

To the innocent bedstead I would say this: Why do you have to be jealous, and clank so loudly? I recognized the lady from the clicking of her bones, as one recognizes a leper from the noise of his rattle.

110

But thousands viewing her became her prize,
Willingly yielding to her conquering eyes,
　　And caught by her bright hairs, whilst careless she
　　Makes them pay homage to her poverty.

So mean a boon, said I, what can extort
From that fair mouth, where wanton Love to sport
　　Amidst the pearls and rubies we behold?
Nature on thee has all her treasures spread,
Do but incline thy rich and precious head,
　　And those fair locks shall pour down showers of gold.

ON THE PICTURE OF LUCRETIA STABBING HERSELF

Lucrece inflam'd with anger, grief and shame,
Despising life, yet careful of her fame,
Wounds her fair breast, tho' arm'd with Innocence
Could suffer Death, but could not the offence.

Her steel was sharp, her end with glory crown'd,
She sought revenge, and valu'd not the wound;
This so appeas'd her rage, that being dead,
She look'd like one reveng'd, not injurèd.

'Twas Beauty sinn'd, said she, then let it die,
That forc'd me to this last extremity;
Were't not for Beauty I had guiltless been
For it was that made lustful Tarquin sin.

So I to violence a prey was made,
No tears avail'd when virtue was betray'd.
Haughty he was, my Beauty proud as he,
They made me slave, but thus myself I free.

Marino

VIRGINIA

Deh, stringi il ferro, stringi,
fa ciò che fai ardito, o genitore:
meglio è ferir il petto che l'onore.

Now take up the sword, take it up, do what you are bold [enough] to do, O
father: better a wounded breast than a wounded honour. Thus, although my

111

Artifice

Anzi, mentre di sangue il sen mi tingi,
di mille fregi il nome mi dipingi;
e vie più ti devrò, da te svenata,
che da te generata.
Se son tua, puoi ferire,
se son mia, vo'morire.

MEDEA

Fuggite, amanti, Amor. Chi può d'Amore
vincer le forze o contrastar con lui?
Signoreggiar la passïon del core
invan tentai, se ben reina io fui;
né trovar seppi al mio proprio dolore
quel rimedio che spesso io porsi altrui:
ché non valse virtù di pietra o d'erba
la mia piaga a saldar cruda ed acerba.

   Vinsi le stelle con possenti versi,
Amor non vinsi invitto e trionfante;
indietro i fiumi rapidi conversi,
non d'un ingrato le fugaci piante;
i mostri umilïai fieri e perversi,
non un crudele e disleale amante;
fu l'inferno da me frenato e domo,
non fui bastante a soggiogare un uomo.

   Vidi moversi i monti a le mie note,
non disasprirsi un animato sasso;
potei del vago sol fermar le rote,
non arrestar d'un fuggitivo il passo.

bosom is stained with blood my name will be depicted on a thousand friezes:
and I will owe you more lives, when I am killed by you than [I owed you] when
I was begotten by you. If I am yours, then strike, if I am mine, I want to die.

Lovers, fly from love. Who can conquer the force of love or stand against Him?
I tried in vain to lord it over the passion of the heart, although I was a queen;
nor did I know how to find for my own pain that remedy I often gave others:
and the virtù of stones and herbs availed not my cruel and bitter wounds.
   I conquered the stars with powerful verses but I didn't conquer undefeated,
triumphant love; I turned swift rivers back on their courses, but not the fleeting
tears of an ungrateful man; I humbled wild, savage monsters, but not a cruel
and disloyal lover: hell was held and tamed by me: but I wasn't strong enough
to subdue a man.
   I saw mountains move at my [singing] notes but [I didn't see] the softening
of that animate rock: I could stop the wheels of the wandering sun, but not the

112

Desperato disdegno, ahi, che non pote
in cor di donna addolorato e lasso?
Uccisi alfin, da grave duolo oppressa,
padre, sposo, fratel, figli e me stessa.

Saint-Amant

LE PARESSEUX

Accablé de paresse et de melancholie,
Je resve dans un lict où je suis fagote,
Comme un lievre sans os qui dort dans un pasté,
Ou comme un Dom-Quichot en sa morne folie.

Là, sans me soucier des guerres d'Italie,
Du comte Palatin, ny de sa royauté,
Je consacre un bel hymne à cette oisiveté,
Ou mon ame en langeur est comme ensevelie.

Je trouve ce plaisir si doux et si charmant,
Que je croy que les biens me viendront en dormant,
Puis que je voy des-jà s'en enfler ma bedaine,

Et hay tante le travail, que les yeux entr'ouvers,
Une main hors des draps, cher BAUDOIN, à peine
Ay-je pû me resoudre à t'escrire ces vers.

step of a fugitive. Desperate disdain, is there nothing you cannot do in the
grieving and weary heart of a woman? In the end I killed, oppressed with grave
sorrow, my father, husband, brothers, sons, and self.

THE IDLER

Weighed down with laziness and melancholy, I dream in a bed where I am
crumpled up like a boned hare sleeping in a pie, or a Don Quixote in his dismal
madness.

There, not bothering about the Italian wars, the Count Palatine, or his
royalty, I consecrate a lovely hymn to this laziness, in which my soul, languishing, is as if buried.

I find this pleasure so sweet and charming that I think the good things of life
will come to me as I sleep, for I can see already that my belly is swollen with
them,

and I hate work so much, that with half-open eyes, a hand outside the sheets,
dear Baudoin, scarcely have I been able to resolve myself to write you these
verses.

113

Von Logau

DER MAY

Dieser Monat ist ein Kuss, den der Himmel gibt der Erde,
Dass sie jetzo seine Braut, künftig eine Mutter werde.

EIN RÄTSEL UND SEINE LOESUNG

Die Mutter frisst das Kind: Dass dieser Stamm vergeh,
So frisst ihn Erd und Wind.—Es regnet in den Schnee.

Angelus Silesius

OHNE WARUM

(From the collection of Epigrams *The Cherubinical Wanderer*)

Die Ros' ist ohn warum; sie blühet, weil sie blühet,
Sie acht' nicht ihrer selbst, fragt nicht, ob man sie siehet.

MAY

This month is a kiss which heaven gives to earth, to make her now his bride and
later a mother.

RIDDLE AND ANSWER

A mother devours her child: to make this line disappear, earth and wind devour
it.—Rain falling on snow.

WITHOUT 'WHY'

The rose is without 'why'; it blooms because it blooms, it is oblivious of itself,
and does not care whether anyone looks at it.

114

Love

Many poems in the preceding section deal, ostensibly, with love. Many poems in this section display an obvious taste for artifice. The dividing line is thin. However, in this section we offer a sequence of poems where it seems to us that the poets are more concerned with making some statement about the conditions and situations of the lover than with invention, wit, and artifice for their own sake. The statements they make range in tone from the ecstatic and worshipping to the cynical and brutally dismissive; and it is interesting that in many poems one senses that attraction and revulsion intermingle. In the first poem, 'Definiendo El Amor',[1] Quevedo, after a series of Petrarchan oxymorons, turns to the reader and says

> Este es el niño, Amor, este es tu abismo:
> Mirad cual amistad tendrá con nada,
> el que en todo es contrario de sí mismo.

That love itself is a potent nothing, an opposition, a paradox, is not so explicitly or economically stated elsewhere, but one often suspects behind the noble assertions of timeless ecstasy, such as 'Il Riso'[2] by Salomoni, there lies an almost desperate desire to find some coherent meaning, however far-fetched, in an emotion which the poet does not fully trust. And likewise in poems explicitly dismissing the value of love, such as Góngora's exquisite sonnet 'La dulce boca que a gustar convida,'[3] it is noticeable that love's dangerousness is its main attraction. In poems such as these, there seems to be an unresolved and irresoluble subconscious debate taking place; the poet wishes clearly to praise or clearly to condemn, but his gestures of praise or condemnation are checked by an awareness of the other possibilities of love, possibilities which he may not consciously declare, but which he cannot exclude.

Other kinds of debate are simpler, that between 'spiritual' and 'physical' love being the most common. Firstly, there are poems which humorously take the side of the flesh, pretend there is nothing to be debated, and dismiss all aspects of love other than the sexual in a witty, man-of-the-world, way:

> For shame thou everlasting Woer,
> Still saying Grace, and ne're fall to her!
>
> (Cleveland, 'The Antiplatonick')[4]

[1] See p. 119.   [2] See p. 126.   [3] See p. 130.
[4] See p. 143.

115

Having adopted such a simple stance, the poem must stand or fall upon humour and ingenuity of argument, upon the success with which the poet can keep his audience laughing, and hence, by laughter, ingratiate himself and prove that he is a good, down-to-earth chap. And, not surprisingly, few poets succeed; Cleveland with his slangy impertinence and irreverent vocabulary is one who does:

> Give me a Lover bold and free,
> Not Eunuch't with formality;
> Like an Embassador that beds a Queen,
> With the Nice Caution of a sword between.[1]

Scipione Errico with his roué's ingenious pseudo-sophistication is another:

> Non vuol filosofia de l'amar l'arte,
>
> . . . .
>
> perché tocca e non mira il cieco nume.[2]

But more interesting is the poem written jointly by Thomas Carew and John Suckling [3] in which, before the inevitable erotic finale, Carew first presents a lovely version of the pastoral hyperbole that the mistress creates beauty wherever she goes, and then Suckling dismisses it as just the sort of thing a poet would say about that simple object, a woman:

> Tom. Didst thou not find the place inspir'd,
> And flowers, as if they had desir'd
> No other sun, start from their beds,
> And for a sight steal out their heads?
> Heard'st thou not music when she talk'd?
> And didst not find that as she walk'd
> She threw rare perfumes all about,
> Such as bean-blossoms newly out,
> Or chafed spices give?—

> J.S. I must confess those perfumes, Tom,
> I did not smell: nor found that from
> Her passing by aught sprung up new:
> The flowers had all their birth from you.

The need for love, of whatever kind, combines, in the best poems here, with the fear of death. That fear may press the poet to ask for more

---

[1] See p. 144.   [2] See p. 145.   [3] See p. 125.

eroticism, since he believes, or affects to believe, that only the power of love can, temporarily, ward off decay:

> Das Mündlein von Korallen
> Wird ungestalt,
> Die Händ als Schnee verfallen,
> Und du wirst alt.
> Drum lass uns jetzt geniessen
> Der Jugend Frucht,
> Eh dann wir folgen mussen
> Der Jahre Flucht.   (Opitz)[1]

In such poems on the *carpe diem* theme love becomes the opposition of death; the great elegies of the period claim that love may move beyond death, may, by its strength, outlast it and hence render it almost irrelevant.

> Mais en vain les destins mon bel ange ont ravi
> Notre parfaite amour d'une même aile vole
> Et par tout l'Univers l'un de l'autre est suivi
> Sa memoire est mon jour, mon coeur est son mausole
> (Anonymous)[2]

The orthodox Christian viewpoint that physical love may be a cause of spiritual death is the starting point for the great and agonized speculations of Michelangelo and Sor Juana. Both see a conflict between the world of the eternal reason and the world of the senses and limited perception; and both find partial resolution of the dilemma in the very fact of there being a dilemma—if it still remains, it must prove that human reason, although weak and vulnerable, is unconquerable, and cannot be drowned in the attractive but unsatisfactory world of physical love. The pain is the proof, and the greater the pain, the more seductive the temptation, the more noble and eternal is the resistance:

> Cuando fuera, amor, te vía
> no merecí de tí, palma;
> y hoy que estás dentro del alma
> es resistir valentía.
> Córrase, pues, tu porfía
> de los triunfos que te gano,
> pues cuando ocupas, tirano,
> el alma sin resistillo
> tienes vencido el castillo
> e invencible el castellano.

[1] See p. 152.   [2] See p. 160.

Love

> Invicta razón alienta
> armas contra tu vil saña
> y el pecho es corta campaña
> a batalla tan sangrienta.
> Y así, amor, en vano intenta
> tu esfuerzo loco ofenderme,
> pues podré decir, al verme
> espirar sin entregarme,
> que conseguiste matarme
> mas no pudiste vencerme.[1]

The poems of seduction and the meditations of Sor Juana are often based upon the same premises—that the pleasures of the body are overwhelmingly attractive, transient, perhaps even mad. Their deductions are different: the libertines concluding either tacitly or openly that since all things are mad and transient the pleasures should be indulged; Sor Juana that since all things save right reason are transient they should be resisted; but they reach their deductions in the same way, through a tense and vital logic, sometimes funny, sometimes profound, which is rare outside the seventeenth century.

In Davenant's little lyrical debate between a philosopher and a lover the two sides are epigrammatically presented, and the resolution left aptly unsolved:

Lover   Lovers, (Whose Priests all Poets are)
      Think ev'ry Mistress, when she dies,
     Is chang'd at least into a Starr:
      And who dares doubt the Poets wise?

Philosopher But ask not Bodies doom'd to die,
      To what abode they go:
     Since Knowledge is but sorrows Spy,
      It is not safe to know.[2]

---

[1] See p. 137–8.   [2] See p. 173.

Quevedo

DEFINIENDO EL AMOR

Es hielo abrasador, es fuego helado,
es herida, que duele y no se siente,
es un soñado bien, un mal presente,
es un breve descanso muy cansado.

Es un descuido, que nos da cuidado
un cobarde con nombre de valiente,
un andar solitario, entre la gente,
Un amar solamente ser amado.

Es una libertad encarcelada,
que dura hasta el postrero parasismo,
enfermedad, que crece si es curada.

Este es el niño, Amor, este es tu abismo:
mirad cual amistad tendrá con nada,
el que en todo es contrario de sí mismo.

Michelangelo

SONNET

Deh fammiti vedere in ogno loco!
Se da mortal bellezza arder mi sento,
a presso al tuo mi sarà foco ispento,
e io nel tuo sarò, com' ero, in foco.

DEFINING LOVE

It is burning ice, it is freezing fire, it is a wound which hurts and is not felt, it is a dreamed good, a present ill, it is a brief and much wearied rest.

It is a carelessness which brings us care, a coward with the reputation for valour, a solitary walk in a crowd, only a love of being loved.

It is a liberty in prison which lasts until the last paroxysm, a disease which grows if it is cured.

This is the child, Love, this is your abyss: look, what friendship can he have with anything at all, he who in all things is the opposite of himself?

Oh, make me see you wherever I go! If I feel I am burning from a mortal beauty next to yours my fire will be extinguished and I will be burning in your fire, as I was in mine.

Love

Signor mio caro, i' te sol chiamo e 'nvoco
contro l'inutil mio cieco tormento:
tu sol puo' rinnovarmi fuori e dentro
le voglie, e 'l senno, e 'l valor lento e poco.

Tu desti al tempo ancor quest'alma diva,
e 'n questa spoglia ancor fragil' e stanca
l'incarcerasti, e con fiero destino.

Che poss' io altro, che così non viva?
Ogni ben senza te, Signor, mi manca.
Il cangiar sorte è sol poter divino.

SONNET

Non vider gli occhi miei cosa mortale
Allor che ne'bei vostri intera pace
Trovai; ma dentro, ov'ogni mal dispiace,
Chi d'amor l'alma a sè simil m'assale.
E se creata a Dio non fusse eguale,
Altro che'l bel di fuor, ch'agli occhi piace,
Più non vorria; ma perch'è sì fallace,
Trascende nella forma universale.

Dear Lord [refers initially to his beloved, and only by metaphor to God], I only call and invoke you against my useless, blind torment: you alone can remake me inwardly and outwardly: my desires, my wisdom and my scanty, slow courage.

Still, you gave to time this divine soul; in these walls of flesh, feeble and weary, you imprisoned it and also in this harsh destiny.

What else can I do so as not to live like this? Without you, every gift fails me. Only the power of God can alter fate.

My eyes did not see anything mortal when in your beautiful [eyes] I found complete peace; but within, where all evil displeases [they saw] Him who assails my soul with love like Himself.

And if it [the soul] had not been created equal to God, it would not wish for anything more than the beautiful appearance which pleases the eye: but since that [i.e. the appearance] is so deceptive, it [the soul] transcends [reality and goes] into universal form.

Io dico, ch'a chi vive quel che muore
Quetar non può disir; nè par s'aspetti
L'eterno al tempo, ove altri cangia il pelo.
Voglia sfrenata el senso è, non amore,
Che l'alma uccide; e'l nostro fa perfetti
Gli amici qui, ma più per morte in cielo.

SONNET

Ben può talor col casto e buon desio
Di par la speme non esser fallace;
Ch'ogni affetto fra noi s'al ciel dispiace,
A che fin fatto arebbe il mondo Iddio?
S'i' t'amo e reverisco, o signor mio,
Anzi s'i'ardo, è per divina pace
Che ne'begli occhi tuoi s'alberga e giace,
Nimica e schiva d'ogni pensier rio.
Non è amor quel che qui nasce e muore
Con la beltà ch'ogni momento scema,
Ond'è suggetto al cangiar d'un bel viso:
Ma quello è ben, che'n un pudico core
Nè per cangiar di scorza o d'ora estrema
Non manca, e qui caparra il paradiso.

I say that that which dies cannot quench the desire of living man; nor does it seem that the universal is visible in time, where men change their hair [but not their habits].

The [world of] sense is unbridled lust, not love, and it kills the soul; but our [love] makes our friends perfect here, but even more so, through death, in heaven.

Sometimes hope, along with good and chaste desire, may well appear not to be [a] deceitful [thing]; if every one of our affections displeased heaven, to what end should God have made the world?

If I love and revere you, O my lord, and if [I] even burn for you, it is for the divine peace which lodges and lies in your lovely eyes, the enemy and avoider of every evil thought.

That is not love which is born and dies here with the beauty that diminishes at every moment whence it is subjected to the changing of a beautiful face:

but that is really love, which, in a chaste heart, fails neither through a change in outward appearance nor even in the hour of death, and here [below] gives a foretaste of Paradise.

121

Desportes

SONNET

Beaux noeuds crespes et blonds, nonchalamment espars,
Dont le vainqueur des dieux s'emprisonne et se lie;
Front de marbre vivant, table claire et polie,
Où les petits Amours vont aiguisant leurs dars;

Espais monceau de neige, aveuglant les regars,
Pour qui de tout objet mon oeil se desallie;
Et toi, guerriere main, de ma prise embellie,
Qui peux, nue, acquerir la victoire de Mars;

Yeux pleuvans à la fois tant d'aise et de martyre;
Sous-ris, par qui l'Amour entretient son empire;
Voix, dont le son demeure au coeur si longuement;

Esprit, par qui le fer de nostre âge se dore;
Beautés, graces, discours, qui m'allez transformant,
Las! connaissez-vous point comme je vous adore?

Weckherlin

VON IHREN UEBERSCHOENEN AUGEN

Ihr Augen, die ihr mich mit einem Blick und Blitz
Scharpf oder süss nach Lust könnt strafen und belohnen,
O liebliches Gestirn, Stern', deren Licht und Hitz
Kann, züchtigend den Stolz, der Züchtigen verschonen:

Lovely, curling, yellow knots of hair negligently unloosed, where the conqueror of the gods is emprisoned and bound: forehead of living marble, bright polished tablet where the little loves go sharpening their darts;

deep drift of snow, blinding our glances, for which my eye can see nothing else: and thou, warrior hand, enriched by my capture, which, bare, can win the victory over Mars;

eyes raining so much contentment and so much martyrdom together: smiles by which love maintains his empire: voice whose sound remains so long in the heart;

wit, through which the iron of our age is turned to gold: beauties, graces, speech, which transform me, alas, do you know at all how I adore you?

ON HER MORE THAN BEAUTIFUL EYES

O eyes, in whose power it is to punish or reward me with one lightning glance, cruel or tender, just as it pleases you, O lovely constellation, stars whose light and heat, chastising pride, can spare the chaste:

Und ihr, der Lieb Wergzeug, Kundschafter unsrer Witz,
Augbrauen, ja vielmehr Triumphbogen, nein, Kronen,
Darunder Lieb und Zucht in überschönem Sitz,
Mit brauner Klarheit Schmuck erleuchtet, leuchtend wohnen!

Wer recht kann eure Form, Farb, Wesen, Würkung, Kraft,
Der kann der Engeln Stand, Schein, Schönheit, Tun und Gehen,
Der kann der wahren Lieb Gewalt und Eigenschaft,

Der Schönheit Schönheit selbs, der Seelen Freud und Flehen
Und der Glückseligkeit und Tugenden Freundschaft
In euch (der Natur Kunst besehend) wohl verstehen!

Von Zesen

AUF DIE AUGEN SEINER LIEBEN

Ihr Augen voll von Glut! Was Glut? Karfunkelstrahlen:
Auch nicht! Sie sein ein Blitz, der durch die Lüfte sprüht
Und sich aus ihrem Aug bis in die meinen zieht.
Nicht Blitze: Bolzen seins, damit sie pflegt zu prahlen,

Damit sie pflegt den Zoll der Liebe bar zu zahlen.
Nicht Bolzen: Sonnen seins, damit sie sich bemüht
Zu blenden andrer Licht, die keiner ihmals sieht,
Der nicht gestraft muss sein. Nicht Sonnen, Sterne tahlen

and you, love's tools, spies of our wit, eyebrows, no, rather triumphal arches, no, crowns under which dwell, resplendent in their more than beautiful abode, love and modesty, illumined by those jewels of limpid brown!

Whoever can appreciate your form, colour, essence, effect and power, can surely appreciate the angels' state, splendour, beauty and actions,

[and also] the beauty of beauty itself, the joy and longing of the soul, and the friendship of bliss and virtues in you (gazing upon the art of Nature)!

ON THE EYES OF HIS LOVE

You eyes so full of fire! No, not fire: diamonds that glitter: no, not that either! They are lightning, flashing through the air, from her eyes into mine. Not lightning: they are darts with which she is wont to show off,

with which she is wont to pay love's tribute in coin. Not darts: they are suns with which she endeavours to outshine the light of others, and which no one ever beholds but that he must be punished for it. They are not suns or stars that play

Vom Himmel ihrer Stirn: auch nicht: was seh ich schimmern,
Dann Glut ist nicht so feucht, Karfunkel strahlt nicht so,
Der Blitz hat minder Kraft, der Pfeil macht ja nicht froh,
Die Sonn ist nicht so stark, ein Stern kann nicht so glimmern,

Warum dann siehet sie des Volkes Aberwahn
Vor Glut, Karfunkel, Blitz, Pfeil, Sonn und Sternen an?

Stigliani

DONO AVUTO D'UN FIORE

Splendea d'alta finestra il viso adorno,
in cui natura ogni sua grazia pose;
qual, coronata di celesti rose,
appar l'aurora dal balcon del giorno.

   Io, che sempr'erro al car'albergo intorno,
qual fanno intorno ad urna ombre dogliose,
fermo era, quando, avvista, ella s'ascose,
tutta vermiglia d'amoroso scorno.

   E gettommi in ritrarsi un fior dal seno,
in atto che fu studio e parve errore;
di che augurio prend'io felice appieno

   che, forse, appresso al picciolo favore
verrà l'intera grazia un dì, non meno
che venir soglia il frutto appresso al fiore.

from the heaven of her forehead: not that either: as what I can see shimmering, fire is not as intense, diamonds not as glittering, lightning not as powerful, arrows not as joy-bestowing, the sun is not as powerful, a star cannot shine as brightly,

why then, in their delusion, do people regard them as [mere] fire, diamonds, lightning, darts, sun and stars?

HAVING RECEIVED THE GIFT OF A FLOWER

The beautiful face, in which nature places all her grace, shines out of the high window, just as dawn, crowned with celestial roses, appears from the balcony of the day.

I, who always haunt that beloved spot, as grieving shades haunt the funeral urn, had stopped there, when, as she was seen, she vanished, crimson with amorous shame.

As she retired, she threw me a flower from her bosom, with a gesture which was rehearsed, but which appeared to be a mistake; from which I derived the very happy premonition

that, perhaps, the whole blessing would follow on the heels of the little favour, as the fruit usually follows on the heels of the flower.

124

Suckling, Carew

UPON MY LADY CARLISLE'S WALKING IN HAMPTON COURT GARDEN
Dialogue

T(HOMAS) C(AREW)   J(OHN) S(UCKLING)

Tom.   Didst thou not find the place inspir'd,
        And flowers, as if they had desir'd
        No other sun, start from their beds,
        And for a sight steal out their heads?
        Heard'st thou not music when she talk'd?
        And didst not find that as she walk'd
        She threw rare perfumes all about,
        Such as bean-blossoms newly out,
        Or chafed spices give?—

J.S.   I must confess those perfumes, Tom,
        I did not smell; nor found that from
        Her passing by aught sprung up new:
        The flow'rs had all their birth from you;
        For I pass'd o'er the selfsame walk,
        And did not find one single stalk
        Of any thing that was to bring
        This unknown after-after-Spring.

Tom.   Dull and insensible, couldst see
        A thing so near a deity
        Move up and down, and feel no change?

J.S.   None and so great were alike strange.
        I had my thoughts, but not your way;
        All are not born, sir, to the bay;
        Alas! Tom, I am flesh and blood,
        And was consulting how I could
        In spite of masks and hoods descry
        The parts deni'd unto the eye:
        I was undoing all she wore;
        And had she walk'd but one turn more,
        Eve in her first state had not been
        More naked, or more plainly seen.

Tom.   'Twas well for thee she left the place;
        There is great danger in that face;

125

> But hadst thou view'd her leg and thigh,
> And upon that discovery
> Seach'd after parts that are more dear
> (As fancy seldom stops so near),
> No time or age had ever seen
> So lost a thing as thou hadst been.

Salomoni

IL RISO

Qualor da bel desio
tratto gli occhi e la mente,
gli occhi e la mente al mio bel sole affiso,
sì dolce al guardo mio
si scopre e sì lucente,
che da me dolce il cor resta diviso.
D'oro è il crin, d'ostro il viso;
ma più che l'oro e più che l'ostro eletto
il crine arde e fiammeggia,
il viso arde e lampeggia;
d'alabastro è la man, d'avorio il petto,
e nel bel ciglio splende
fiamma d'amor che mille fiamme accende.
    Ma se per mia ventura
riso lucente e chiaro
scopre fra tanti rai sue fiamme accese,
luce mirar più pura,
raggio trovar più caro,
non san le luci a rimirarlo intese.
Riso vago e cortese,
riso figlio del cor, pregio sovrano

THE LAUGH

When, through beautiful desire, I tell of [her] eyes and mind, I fix my eyes and mind upon my beautiful sun, and she appears so sweet and shining to my gaze that my heart is sweetly parted from me. Gold is her hair, scarlet are her cheeks; but more than gold and more than choice scarlet her hair burns and flames, her face burns and flashes lightning; her hand is alabaster, her bosom ivory, and in her lovely eye shines the flame of love which kindles a thousand flames.

But if through my good fortune a clear and shining laugh discloses its kindled flames from so many rays of light, the lights [eyes] made for beholding it do not know how to gaze on a yet purer light, or find a yet dearer ray. Fleeting, courteous laughter, laughter the son of the heart, the sovereign prize

126

di natura e splendore
di bellezza e d'amore,
teco contende, a te s'agguaglia invano
bianco sen, nero ciglio,
bianca man, biondo crin, volto vermiglio.
    Tu, dolcemente uscendo
fuor per gli interni calli,
quasi da fosco ciel chiaro baleno,
e dolce un uscio aprendo
di perle e di coralli,
m'apri soavemente il core e 'l seno.
Quel tuo dolce sereno
sì dolce foco entro il suo lume asconde,
ch'ognor più l'alma mia
accesa esser desia;
sì chiari ognor, sì dolci ognor diffonde
quei raggi ond'io m'accieco,
che tanto veggio sol quanto son cieco.
    Tu l'alma ardente e vaga
feri e pungi a tua voglia,
e sei fulmine al cor, se' lampo a gli occhi;
ma sì dolce è la piaga,
sì soave la doglia,
che d'estremo piacer vien ch'io trabocchi.
Sì dolce il cor mi tocchi,
riso dolce e gentil, sì vago sei,
che spesso in fra i martìri
ridono i miei sospiri,
ridon nel cor ridente i dolor miei,
e dolcemente intanto
ne le luci e nel cor ride il mio pianto.

of nature, and splendour of beauty and love, the white bosom, the black eyebrow, the white hand, golden hair, crimson cheeks, contend with you and match themselves against you in vain.

You, sweetly issuing from the internal pathways of the heart like the clear lightning from a dark sky, and opening a door of pearls and corals, sweetly open my heart and bosom. That serene, sweet, so sweet fire of yours hides in its own light so that my soul desires to be thus kindled evermore; always so clearly, always so sweetly does it diffuse those rays which blind me that I can see so much only when I am blind.

You wound and pierce the loving ardent soul at will, and you are a thunderbolt in the heart, a flash of lightning in the eyes; but so sweet is the wound, so gentle the pain, that it happens I overflow with ecstasy. You touch my heart so gently, sweet and gentle laugh, you are so loving that often my sighs laugh among their torments, my griefs laugh in the laughing heart, and meanwhile my pain laughs sweetly in my eyes and heart.

127

Quanto dal ciel si serra,
quanto è nel cielo accolto
ride e nel riso sol vago si mostra.
Ridente è della terra
il verde grembo e 'l volto,
e di ridenti fior s'orna e s'inostra.
Ne la sua cupa chiostra
con crespo volto il mar ride ed affrena
l'aura che stride e geme,
l'onda che piange e freme.
Ride al riso del mar l'aria serena,
e ne gli aerei campi
ridon le nubi, e son lor riso i lampi.
　　Ride spiegando il velo
e di ridenti orrori
la notte il chiaro volto a l'aria imbruna;
e di ridente gelo
spargendo l'erbe e i fiori,
nel suo ridente ciel ride la luna.
Per l'ombra azzurra e bruna
nel notturno seren spiegan le stelle
ridenti i crini d'oro,
ridenti i raggi loro;
e con le rose sue ridenti e belle
fa l'alba in ciel ritorno,
tutta ridente dal balcon del giorno.
　　Scopre ridendo il sole,
quando al ciel splende e s'erge,
di ridenti fiammelle il crine ornato;
e pur ridendo sòle,
quando nel mar s'immerge,
tuffar tutto ridente il carro aurato.

All that is locked from the heavens, and all that is welcomed to the heavens, laughs, and shows itself lovely in the laugh. The green bosom and face of the earth is laughing, and adorns and dresses itself with laughing flowers. In its gloomy enclosure, with its wrinkled face, the sea laughs, and checks the wind as it shrieks and groans, checks the wave as it weeps and quivers. The serene air laughs at the laugh of the sea, and in the aerial fields the clouds laugh, and lightning is their laughter.

The veil [of night] laughs as it unfurls, and night darkens the clear face of the air with laughing horrors; and, scattering laughing frost over grass and flowers, the moon laughs in its laughing heaven. Through the brown and azure shade of serene midnight, the stars laughing scatter their golden hair, laughing [scatter] their rays; and dawn returns to the heaven with lovely laughing roses, all laughing from the balcony of day.

The sun appears laughing when he shines and rises to the sky, his hair adorned with little laughing flames; and he still laughs when he plunges into the sea, to sink his golden chariot all in laughter. Laugh, blessed laugh, you have so

Riso, riso beato,
tanto hai di bello in te, tanto in me puoi,
che, sciolto il fren tenace
a la favella audace,
omai dirò ch'un sol de' raggi tuoi
faria, tra 'l pianto eterno,
quasi sereno ciel rider l'inferno.
   Canzon, figlia del riso, indegna figlia
di padre sì gentile,
sol tu resti al suo lume oscura e vile.

Fleming

ER VERWUNDERT SICH SEINER GLUECKSELIGKEIT
SONETT

Wie mir es gestern ging und wie ich ward empfangen
In meiner Freundin Schoss, weiss sie nur und nur ich.
Das allerliebste Kind, das herzt' und grüsste mich,
Sie hielte feste mich, wie ich sie hart umfangen.

Auf meinem lag ihr Mund, auf ihren meine Wangen.
Oft sagte sie mir auch, was nicht lässt sagen sich,
Darum du, Momus, nicht hast zu bekümmern dich,
Bei ihr ist noch mein Sinn, bei mir noch ihr Verlangen;

O wohl mir, der ich weiss, was nur die Götter wissen,
Die sich auch, wie wir uns, in reiner Keuschheit küssen,
O wohl mir, der ich weiss, was kein Verliebter weiss.

much beauty in you, so much power over me, that, with my daring tongue
released from its reins, I will yet say that a single one of your rays would make
hell laugh across its eternal grief like a serene heaven.
   Canzone, daughter of a laugh, unworthy daughter of such a gentle father,
you alone remain dark and unworthy in his light.

HE MARVELS AT HIS BLISS
What happened to me yesterday, and how I was received in my mistress's lap,
that only she and I know. The darling child hugged me and saluted me, she held
me tight, as I put my arms round her tightly.
   Her mouth lay on mine, my cheek touched hers. Often, too, she said to me
things that cannot be repeated, and which are no business of yours, Momus.
My mind is still with her, her desire still with me.
   O lucky me who knows what only the gods know, who, like us, kiss in chaste
purity, O lucky me, who knows what no lover knows.

Wird meiner Seelen Trost mich allzeit also laben,
Mir allzeit also tun, so werd ich an ihr haben
Ein weltlichs Himmelreich, ein sterblichs Paradeiss.

Hofmann von Hofmannswaldau

AUF DEN MUND

Mund! der die Seelen kann durch Lust zusammen hetzen,
Mund! der viel süsser ist als starker Himmelswein,
Mund! der du Alikant des Lebens schenkest ein,
Mund! den ich vorziehn muss der Inden reichen Schätzen,
Mund! dessen Balsam uns kann stärken und verletzen,
Mund! der vergnügter blüht als aller Rosen Schein,
Mund! welchem kein Rubin kann gleich und ähnlich sein,
Mund! den die Gratien mit ihren Quellen netzen;
Mund! auch Korallenmund, mein einziges Ergetzen!
Mund! lass mich einen Kuss auf deinen Purpur setzen.

Góngora

SONNET

La dulce boca que a gustar convida
un humor entre perlas distilado
y a no invidiar aquel licor sagrado
que a Júpiter ministra el garzón de Ida,

If my soul's solace is going to regale me thus at all times, if she will treat me in this fashion always, I shall have in her heaven on earth, a mortal paradise.

TO A MOUTH

Mouth! which can cause souls to rush together through desire. Mouth! which is much sweeter than strong wine from heaven. Mouth! which pours out life-giving wine from Alicante. Mouth! which I prefer to the rich treasures of the Indies. Mouth! whose balm can fortify or hurt us. Mouth! which blooms more cheerfully than the splendour of all the roses. Mouth! like which and resembling which there is no ruby. Mouth! which the Graces moisten with their springs. Mouth! coral mouth, my only delight! Mouth! let me place one kiss on your ruby [lips].

The sweet mouth which invites to taste a liquid distilled between pearls, and not to covet that sacred liquor which the boy of Ida ministers to Jove,

amantes, no toquéis, si queréis vida;
porque entre un labio y otro colorado
Amor está, de su veneno armado,
cual entre flor y flor sierpe escondida.

No os engañen las rosas que a la Aurora
diréis que aljofaradas y olorosas
se le cayeron del purpúreo seno;

manzanas son de Tántalo, y no rosas,
que después huyen del que incitan hora
y sólo del Amor queda el veneno.

De un caminante enfermo que se enamoró donde fue hospedado

Descaminado, enfermo, peregrino,
en tenebrosa noche, con pie incierto,
la confusión pisando del desierto,
voces en vano dio, pasos sin tino.

Repetido latir, si no vecino,
distincto oyó de can siempre despierto,
y en pastoral albergue mal cubierto
piedad halló, si no halló camino.

Salió el Sol, y entre armiños escondida,
soñolienta beldad con dulce saña
salteó al no bien sano pasajero.

Pagará el hospedaje con la vida;
más le valiera errar en la montaña
que morir de la suerte que yo muero.

do not touch, lovers, if you want to remain alive, for between one crimson lip
and another stands love, armed with his poison, like a snake hidden between
flower and flower.

Let not roses deceive, which you will say that dawn let fall from her purple
bosom encrusted with pearls, and perfumed;

they are the apples of Tantalus, and not roses, which afterwards escape what
now they invite, and leave only the poison of love.

Of a sick traveller, who fell in love where he was sheltered
Lost, sick, in a strange land, in the shades of night, with infirm steps, treading
on the confusion of the desert, he uttered shouts in vain, took aimless steps.

He heard the repeated barking, distinctly if not close by, of the ever-wakeful
dog, and he found piety, if not his way, in a humble shepherd dwelling.

The sun came out, and wrapped in ermines, sleepy beauty with sweet fury
waylaid the not quite recovered traveller.

He will pay for his lodging with his life; it would have been a better bargain
to wander on the mountain than to die the way I die.

Love

Gryphius

AN EUGENIEN

Gleich als ein Wandersmann, dafern die trübe Nacht,
  Mit dicker Finsternis, Luft, Erd, und See verdecket,
  Betrübt irrt hin und her, und mit viel Furcht erschrecket,
Nicht weiss wohin er geht, noch was er lässt und macht:
So eben ists mit mir: doch wenn der Mond erwacht
  Und seiner Strahlen Kerz im Wolkenhaus anstecket;
  Bald find't er Weg' und Rat: so wird mein Geist erwecket;
Nun mich der neue Trost aus eurem Brief anlacht.
Doch, darum heisst ihr mich dies schöne Pfand verbrennen?
  Wollt ihr in meiner Nacht mich bei der Glut' erkennen?
  Dies, meines Herzens Feu'r entdeckt ja wer ich sei.
Soll Schönste, dies Papier nur meine Brust berühren:
  So wird es alsobald in Aschen sich verlieren,
  Wo von der Flamm' es nicht wird durch mein Weinen frei.

Carew

Song MURDR'ING BEAUTY

I'll gaze no more on her bewitching face,
Since ruin harbours there in every place;
For my enchanted soul alike she drowns
With calms and tempests of her smiles and frowns.
I'll love no more those cruel eyes of hers,
Which, pleas'd or anger'd, still are murderers:
For if she dart, like lightning, through the air
Her beams of wrath, she kills me with despair:
If she behold me with a pleasing eye,
I surfeit with excess of joy, and die.

TO EUGENIE

Like a traveller who, when overcast night conceals air, earth and sea in dense darkness, sadly roams hither and thither, terrified and not knowing where to go nor what to do:

exactly so it is with me: but when the moon awakes and lights the candle of his rays in his cloud-house; he quickly finds a way out: thus my spirit is woken now that fresh consolation smiles at me from your letter.

But why do you command me to burn this fair token? Is it that you would recognize me in my night by the flames? This, the fire in my heart, reveals who I am.

If this sheet of paper should but touch my breast, it will swiftly be burned to ashes, unlesy the flames are extinguished by my tears.

INGRATEFUL BEAUTY THREAT'NED

Know, Celia, since thou art so proud,
   'Twas I that gave thee thy renown:
Thou hadst in the forgotten crowd
   Of common beauties liv'd unknown,
Had not my verse exhal'd thy name,
And with it imp'd the wings of Fame.

That killing power is none of thine:
   I gave it to thy voice and eyes;
Thy sweets, thy graces, all are mine;
   Thou art my star, shin'st in my skies:
Then dart not from thy borrow'd sphere
Lightning on him that fix'd thee there.

Tempt me with such affrights no more,
   Lest what I made I uncreate;
Let fools thy mystic forms adore,
   I'll know thee in thy mortal state.
Wise poets that wrapp'd Truth in tales
Knew her themselves through all her veils.

Günther

DIE VERWORF'NE LIEBE

Ich habe genug!
Lust, Flammen und Küsse
Sind giftig und süsse
Und machen nicht klug:
Komm selige Freiheit und dämpfe den Brand,
Der meinem Gemüte die Weisheit entwandt.

Was hab ich getan!
Jetzt seh ich die Triebe
Der törichten Liebe
Vernünftiger an:

SCORNED LOVE

I have had enough! Sensuality, flames and kisses are poisonous and sweet and do not make one wise: come blessed freedom and quench the conflagration which has taken all wisdom from my mind.

   What have I done! Now I see the desires of foolish love more reasonably: I

Love

Ich breche die Fessel, ich löse mein Herz,
Und hasse mit Vorsatz den zärtlichen Schmerz.

Was quält mich vor Reu!
Was stört mit vor Kummer
Den nächtlichen Schlummer!
Die Zeit ist vorbei,
O köstliches Kleinod! o teurer Verlust!
O hätt' ich die Falschheit nur eher gewusst!

Geh Schönheit und fleuch!
Die artigsten Blicke
Sind schmerzliche Stricke:
Ich merke den Streich.
Es lodern die Briefe, der Ring bricht entzwei,
Und zeigt meiner Schönen: nun leb ich recht frei.

Nun leb ich recht frei,
Und schwöre von Herzen,
Dass Küssen und Scherzen
Ein Narren-Spiel sei,
Denn wer sich verliebet, der ist wohl nicht klug,
Geh! falsche Sirene! ich habe genug.

Waller

GO, LOVELY ROSE!

Go, lovely Rose!
   Tell her that wastes her time and me,
That now she knows,
    When I resemble her to thee,
    How sweet and fair she seems to be.

break my fetters, I detach my heart, and deliberately I hate the tender pain.
    What remorse torments me! What sorrow disturbs my sleep at night! Gone is the time, O splendid jewel! O precious loss! O if only I had realized her falseness earlier!
    Begone, my beauty and flee hence! The prettiest looks are painful bonds: I have noticed the trick. Her letters are in flames, her ring breaks in two and shows my mistress that now I am quite free.
    Now I am quite free and swear from my heart that kissing and flirting are tomfooleries, for whoever falls in love is not a wise man. Begone! False siren! I have had enough!

Tell her that's young,
    And shuns to have her graces spied,
That hadst thou sprung
    In deserts, where no men abide,
    Thou must have uncommended died.

Small is the worth
    Of beauty from the light retired;
Bid her come forth,
Suffer herself to be desired,
And not blush so to be admired.

Then die! that she
    The common fate of all things rare
May read in thee;
    How small a part of time they share
    That are so wondrous sweet and fair!

Saint-Amant

STANCES

Quand tu me vois baiser tes bras,
Que tu poses nuds sur tes draps,
Bien plus blancs que le linge mesme:
Quand tu sens ma bruslante main
Se pourmener dessus ton sein
Tu sens bien, Cloris, que je t'ayme.

Comme un devot devers les cieux
Mes yeux tournez devers tes yeux,
A genoux auprès de ta couche
Pressé de mille ardens desirs
Je laisse sans ouvrir ma bouche
Avec toy dormir mes plaisirs.

STANZAS

When you see me kiss your arms which whitely appear over your sheets, your arms which are whiter than the linen itself: when you feel my burning hand fluttering over your breast, you know well, Cloris, that I love you.

My eyes turned towards yours like a devotee towards the heavens, and kneeling beside your bed, urged by a thousand burning desires, I, without opening my mouth, leave my pleasures to sleep with you.

Love

Le sommeil, aisé de t'avoir
Empesche tes yeux de me voir
Et te retient dans son empire
Avec si peu de liberté
Que ton esprit tout arresté
Ne murmure ny ne respire.

La rose en rendant son odeur,
Le Soleil donnant son ardeur,
Diane et le char qui la traine.
Une Naiade dedans l'eau,
Et les Graces dans un tableau,
Font plus de bruict que ton haleine.

Là, je souspire auprès de toy
Et, considerant comme quoy
Ton oeil si doucement repose,
Je me'escrie: O Ciel! peux-tu bien
Tirer d'une si belle chose
Un si cruel mal que le mien!

Sor Juana

Que demuestran decoroso esfuerzo de la razón contra la vil tiranía de un amor violento

Dime vencedor rapaz,
vencido de mi constancia,
¿qué ha sacado tu arrogancia
de alterar mi firme paz

Sleep, happy to have you, prevents your eyes from seeing me and keeps you in his empire with so little liberty, your arrested spirit neither murmurs nor breathes.

The rose in offering up her perfume, the sun in giving its heat, Diana in the chariot which draws her, a naiad in water, and the Graces in a picture, make more noise than your breath.

There I sigh by your side, and seeing how your eye sleeps so sweetly, I cry: 'Oh, Heaven! can you really derive such a cruel ill as mine from such a lovely thing!'

Verses describing the decorous effort of reason against the vile tyranny of a violent love

Tell me, rapacious conqueror, conquered by my constancy, what has your arrogance achieved in altering my firm peace—although the point of your dart

136

—que aunque de vencer capaz
es la punta de tu arpón
el más duro corazón—
qué importa el tiro violento
si a pesar del vencimiento
queda viva la razón?

    Tienes grande señorío;
pero tu jurisdicción
domina la inclinación
mas no pasa al albedrío.
Y así librarme confío
de tu loco atrevimiento,
pues, aunque rendida siento
y presa la libertad,
se rinde la voluntad
pero no el consentimiento.

    En dos partes dividida
tengo el alma en confusión:
una, esclava a la pasión,
y otra, a la razón medida.
Guerra civil encendida
aflige el pecho importuna,
quiere vencer cada una,
y entre fortunas tan varias
morirán ambas contrarias
pero vencerá ninguna.

    Cuando fuera, amor, te vía
no merecí de tí, palma;
y hoy que estás dentro del alma
es resistir valentía.

is capable of defeating the hardest heart—what does your violent shot matter, if despite having been conquered, reason is still alive?

You have an enormous domain; but your jurisdiction dominates [simple] inclination, but does not extend to the [free] will. And thus I trust to free myself from your mad insolence, for when I feel that my liberty is conceded and captured, volition surrenders, but consent does not.

My confused soul is split into two; one is the slave of passion, the other controlled by reason. A blazing civil war, inopportune, afflicts my breast, and each side strives to win, but, caught between conflicting fortunes, both contrary forces will die, and neither will conquer.

When, love, I saw you from the outside, I deserved no palm of victory over you; and now that you are within my soul, to resist is bravery. Away then with

137

Love

Córrase, pues, tu porfía
de los triunfos que te gano,
pues cuando ocupas, tirano,
el alma sin resistillo
tienes vencido el castillo
e invencible el castellano.

Invicta razón alienta
armas contra tu vil saña
y el pecho es corta campaña
a batalla tan sangrienta.
Y así, amor, en vano intenta
tu esfuerzo loco ofenderme,
pues podré decir, al verme
espirar sin entregarme,
que conseguiste matarme
mas no pudiste vencerme.

Donne

THE AUTUMNALL

No *Spring*, nor *Summer* Beauty hath such grace,
    As I have seen in one *Autumnall* face.
Yong *Beauties* force our love, and that's a *Rape*,
    This doth but *counsaile*, yet you cannot scape.
If t'were a *shame* to love, here t'were no *shame*,
    Affection here take *Reverences* name.
Were her first yeares the *Golden Age*; That's true,
    But now she's *gold* oft tried, and ever new.
That was her torrid and inflaming time,
    This is her tolerable *Tropique clyme*.
Faire eyes, who askes more heate than comes from hence,
    He in a fever wishes pestilence.
Call not these wrinkles, *graves*; If *graves* they were,
    They were *Loves graves;* for else he is no where.
Yet lies not Love *dead* here, but here doth sit
    Vow'd to this trench, like an *Anachorit*.

your importunity, for I gain victories over you, since when, tyrant, you occupy the unresisting soul, you find the keep defeated, the keeper undefeatable.

Undefeated reason encourages arms against your wicked ferocity, and the breast is a little battlefield for such a bloody battle. And so, love, your mad efforts try in vain to assail me, for I will be able to say, when I see myself expire without submitting, that you succeeded in killing me, but could not conquer me.

And here, till hers, which must be his *death*, come,
   He doth not digge a *Grave*, but build a *Tombe*.
Here dwells he, though he sojourne ev'ry where,
   In *Progresse*, yet his standing house is here.
Here, where still *Evening* is; not *noone*, nor *night;*
   Where no *voluptuousnesse*, yet all *delight*.
In all her words, unto all hearers fit,
   You may at *Revels*, you at *Counsaile*, sit.
This is loves timber, youth his under-wood;
   There he, as wine in *June*, enrages blood,
Which then comes seasonabliest, when our tast
   And appetite to other things, is past.
Xerxes strange *Lydian* love, the *Platane* tree,
   Was lov'd for age, none being so large as shee,
Or else because, being yong, nature did blesse
   Her youth with ages glory, *Barrennesse*.
If we love things long sought, *Age* is a thing
   Which we are fifty yeares in compassing.
If transitory things, which soone decay,
   Age must be lovelyest at the latest day.
But name not *Winter-faces*, whose skin's slacke;
   Lanke, as an unthrifts purse; but a soules sacke;
Whose *Eyes* seeke light within, for all here's shade;
   Whose *mouthes* are holes, rather worne out, than made,
Whose every tooth to a severall place is gone,
   To vexe their soules at *Resurrection;*
Name not these living *Deaths-heads* unto mee,
   For these, not *Ancient*, but *Antique* be.
I hate extreames; yet I had rather stay
   With *Tombs*, than *Cradles*, to weare out a day.
Since such loves naturall lation is, may still
   My love descend, and journey downe the hill,
Not panting after growing beauties, so,
   I shall ebbe out with them, who home-ward goe.

Stigliani

RIMEMBRANZA D'AMOR PUERILE

Essendo Lidia ed io
già fanciulli ambeduo,
io scrissi il nome suo
ne' tronchi de' più piccoli arboscelli;

REMEMBRANCE OF A BOYHOOD LOVE

When Lidia and I were still both children together, I wrote her name on the trunks of the smallest little trees, and then, as they grew, the letters I carved

139

Love

e poi, crescendo quelli,
son cresciute le note e i segni impressi,
e cresciuti noi stessi.
Così fusser cresciuti anco gli affetti
in ambi i nostri petti!
Ma, lasso!, in me s'è fatto
giovane Amor, ch'era fanciullo avante,
ed in lei di fanciul s'è fatto infante.

Scudéry

POUR UNE INCONSTANTE

Elle aime, et n'aime plus, et puis elle aime encore,
La volage beauté que je serts constamment;
L'on voit ma fermeté; l'on voit son changement;
Et nous aurions besoin, elle et moy, d'ellebore.

Cent fois elle brusla du feu qui me devore;
Cent fois elle esteignit ce foible embrazement;
Et semblable à l'Egipte, en mon aveuglement,
C'est un cameleon que mon esprit adore.

Puissant maistre des sens, escoute un mal-heureux;
Amour, sois alchimiste, et sers toy de tes feux,
A faire que son coeur prenne une autre nature;

grew, and we ourselves grew also. Would that the affections in both our breasts had grown thus! But, alas, in me Love, who was then a boy, has become a young man, and in her, the boy has become a baby.

FOR HIS FAITHLESS MISTRESS

She loves, and loves no more, and then she loves again, the inconstant beauty I serve constantly; my firmness and her faithlessness are clear, and both of us will need hellebore [thought to cure madness].

A hundred times she burned with the fire which devours me, a hundred times she quenched the feeble blaze, and, like Egypt in my blindness, it is a chameleon which my heart adores.

Great master of the senses, listen to an unfortunate; love, be my alchemist, use your fires to make her heart assume another nature;

140

Comme ce coeur constant me seroit un thresor,
Je ne demande point que tu faces de l'or,
Travaille seulement, à fixer ce mercure.

Carew

Song TO MY INCONSTANT MISTRESS

When thou, poor excommunicate
  From all the joys of love, shalt see
The full reward and glorious fate
  Which my strong faith shall purchase me,
  Then curse thine own inconstancy.

A fairer hand than thine shall cure
  That heart which thy false oaths did wound;
And to my soul a soul more pure
  Than thine shall by Love's hand be bound
  And both with equal glory crown'd.

Then shalt thou weep, entreat, complain
  To love, as I did once to thee;
When all thy tears shall be as vain
  As mine were then, for thou shalt be
  Damn'd for thy false apostacy.

Lord Herbert of Cherbury

INCONSTANCY

Inconstancy's the greatest of sins,
It neither ends well nor begins;
All other faults we simply do:
This, 'tis the same fault and next too.

Inconstancy no sin will prove,
If we consider that we love
But the same beauty in another face,
Like the same body in another place.

  since this constant heart would be a treasure to me, I no longer ask that you
make gold, work only to fix this mercury.

Love

Sor Juana

Consuelos seguros en el desengaño

Ya, desengaño mío,
llegasteis al extremo
que pudo en vuestro ser
verificar el serlo.

Todo lo habéis perdido.
Mas no todo, pues creo
que aun a costa es de todo
barato el escarmiento.

No envidiaréis de amor
los gustos lisonjeros
que está un escarmentado
muy remoto del riesgo.

El no esperar alguno
me sirve de consuelo,
que también es alivio
el no buscar remedio.

En la pérdida misma
los alivios encuentro;
pues si perdí el tesoro
también se perdió el miedo.

No tener qué perder
me sirve de sosiego,
que no teme ladrones,
desnudo, el pasajero.

Sure counsels against disillusion

Already, my disillusion, you have reached the extreme [of disillusionment] which can be verified in your existence.

You have destroyed everything. But not everything, for I believe that even at the price of everything, the lesson I have learned is cheap.

You do not covet the deceitful pleasures of love. He who has learned his lesson is very remote from risk.

To expect nothing consoles me, for to seek no remedy is still a relief.

In loss itself I find relief; for if I have lost the treasure, I have also lost the fear [that goes with it].

To have nothing to lose gives me rest, for the naked traveller fears no thieves.

142

Ni aun la libertad misma
tenerla por bien quiero,
que luego será daño
si por tal la poseo.

No quiero más cuidados
de bienes tan inciertos
sino tener el alma
como que no la tengo.

Carew

Song MEDIOCRITY IN LOVE REJECTED

Give me more love, or more disdain;
 The torrid or the frozen zone
Bring equal ease unto my pain,
 The temperate affords me none:
Either extreme of love or hate
Is sweeter than a calm estate.

Give me a storm; if it be love,
 Like Danaë in that golden shower,
I swim in pleasure; if it prove
 Disdain, that torrent will devour
My vulture-hopes; and he's possess'd
Of heaven, that's but from hell releas'd.
 Then crown my joys, or cure my pain:
 Give me more love, or more disdain.

Cleveland

THE ANTIPLATONICK

For shame, thou everlasting Woer,
Still saying Grace and ne're fall to her!
Love that's in Contemplation plac't,
Is *Venus* drawn but to the Wast.
Unlesse your Flame confesse its Gender,
And your Parley cause surrender,

I do not even want to see liberty as a blessing, for once I have defined it as such, it will come to grief.
I want no other worries from such uncertain blessings, except to possess my soul as if I did not possess it.

143

Love

Y'are Salamanders of a cold desire,
That live untouch't amid the hottest fire.

What though she be a Dame of stone,
The Widow of *Pigmalion*;
As hard and un-relenting She,
As the new-crusted *Niobe*;
Or what doth more of Statue carry
A Nunne of the Platonick Quarrey?
Love melts the rigor which the rocks have bred,
A Flint will break upon a Feather-bed.

For shame you pretty Female Elves,
Cease for to Candy up your selves;
No more, you Sectaries of the Game,
No more of your calcining flame.
Women Commence by *Cupids* Dart,
As a Kings Hunting dubs a Hart.
Loves Votaries inthrall each others soul,
Till both of them live but upon Paroll.

Vertue's no more in Woman-kind
But the green-sicknesse of the mind.
Philosophy, their new delight,
A kind of Charcoal Appetite.
There is no Sophistry prevails,
Where all-convincing Love assails,
But the disputing Petticoat will Warp,
As skilfull Gamesters are to seek at Sharp.

The souldier, that man of Iron,
Whom Ribs of *Horror* all inviron,
That's strung with Wire, in stead of Veins,
In whose imbraces you're in chains,
Let a Magnetick Girle appear,
Straight he turns *Cupids* Cuiraseer.
Love storms his lips, and takes the Fortresse in,
For all the Brisled Turn-pikes of his chin.

Since Loves Artillery then checks
The Breast-works of the firmest Sex,
Come let us in Affections Riot,
Th' are sickly pleasures keep a Diet.
Give me a Lover bold and free,
Not Eunuch't with Formality;
Like an Embassador that beds a Queen,
With the Nice Caution of a sword between.

144

Errico

CONTRA L'AMOR PLATONICO

Baciami, o Clori, e fa' ch'io goda a pieno
tua leggiadra beltà, tuoi pregi tanti,
e de le grazie tue nel prato ameno
fa' che appaghi a mia voglia i sensi erranti.

    Fa' che nel molle tuo nettareo seno
gli spirti appaghi languidi e tremanti,
e con l'opre da noi scherniti sieno
quei che dan legge ai desïosi amanti.

    Non vuol filosofia de l'amar l'arte,
perché il fanciullo Amor non ha costume
molto internarsi ne le dotte carte.

    Ceda al tatto la vista, al labro il lume;
il guatar, l'affissar vada in disparte,
perché tocca e non mira il cieco nume.

Cartwright

NO PLATONIQUE LOVE

Tell me no more of Minds embracing Minds,
    And hearts exchang'd for hearts;
That Spirits Spirits meet, as Winds do winds,
    And mix their subt'lest parts;
That two unbodi'd Essences may kiss,
And then like Angels, twist and feel one Bliss.

AGAINST PLATONIC LOVE

Kiss me, Chloris, and let me fully enjoy your delicious beauty, your so many charms, and let me satisfy at my will my errant desires with your graces in this lovely meadow.

    Let me quench my languishing and trembling spirits in your sweet and nectared breast, and let those who give laws to lustful lovers be mocked by our actions.

    I don't want a philosophy of the art of love, because it isn't the custom of the boy Love to pore over learned pages.

    Let sight surrender to touch, the eye to the lip; away with staring and gazing, because the blind God touches, he doesn't look.

145

Love

I was that silly thing that once was wrought
   To Practise this thin Love;
I climb'd from Sex to Soul, from Soul to Thought;
   But thinking there to move,
Headlong I rowl'd from Thought to Soul, and then
From Soul I lighted at the Sex agen.

As some strict down-look'd Men pretend to fast,
   Who yet in Closets Eat;
So Lovers who profess they Spirits taste,
   Feed yet on grosser meat;
I know they boast they Soules to Souls Convey,
How e'er they meet, the Body is the Way.

Come, I will undeceive thee, they that tread
   Those vain Aëriall waies,
Are like young Heyrs, and Alchymists misled
   To waste their Wealth and Daies,
For searching thus to be for ever Rich,
They only find a Med'cine for the Itch.

Sor Juana

Porque la tiene en su pensamiento, desprecia, como inútil, la vista de los ojos

   Aunque cegué de mirarte
¿qué importa cegar o ver,
si gozos que son del alma,
también un ciego los ve?

   Cuando el amor intentó
hacer tuyos mis despojos,
Lisi, y la luz me privó,
me dió en el alma los ojos
que en el alma me quitó.

Because she has sight in her mind she despises as useless the sight of her eyes
Although I went blind from looking on you, what is the difference between sight
and blindness, when a blind man can see the joys which come from the soul?
   Lisi, when love set out to make my treasures yours, and deprived me of light,
he gave my soul the eyes which he had taken from it [your eyes reached my
soul hence enlightening it although blinding my actual eyes]. He gave me, to

146

Dióme, para que a adorarte
con más atención asista,
ojos con que contemplarte,
y así cobré mejor vista
aunque cegué de mirarte.

  Y antes los ojos en mí
fueron estorbos penosos,
que no teniéndote aquí
claro está que eran ociosos
no pudiendo verte a tí.
Con que el cegar, a mi ver,
fué providencia más alta
por no poderte tener,
porque ¿a quién la luz le falta
qué importa cegar o ver?

  Pero es gloria tan sin par
la que de adorarte siento
que llegándome a matar
viene a acabar el contento
lo que no pudo el pesar.
¿Mas qué importa que la palma
no lleven de mí, violentos,
en esta amorosa calma,
no del cuerpo los tormentos
si gozos que son del alma?

  Así tendré, en el violento
rigor de no verte aquí,
por alivio del tormento
siempre el pensamiento en tí,
siempre a tí en el pensamiento.

adore you with a more rapt attention, eyes to contemplate you with, and so I gained a better sight although I went blind from looking on you.

And before the eyes in me were clumsy impediments, for when you were not here, it is clear they were useless in not being able to see you. Therefore, in my eyes [opinion], blindness was a higher providence, because I couldn't have you, and to the man in darkness, what is the difference between sight and blindness?

But it is an unequalled glory which I feel by adoring you, which almost killing me, comes to kill the content which sorrow couldn't kill. What does it matter, in this amorous calm, that those violent things, which are not the torments of the body but the joys of the soul, do not defeat me?

So, in the violent cruelty of not seeing you here, I will have as a relief from torment always my thoughts in you, always you in my thoughts. So in my heart

Love

Acá en el alma veré
el centro de mis cuidados
con los ojos de mi fe,
que gustos imaginados
también un ciego los ve.

Donne

THE DREAME

Deare love, for nothing lesse than thee
Would I have broke this happy dreame,
   It was a theame
For reason, much too strong for phantasie,
Therefore thou wakd'st me wisely; yet
My Dreame thou brok'st not, but continued'st it,
Thou art so truth, that thoughts of thee suffice,
To make dreames truths; and fables histories;
Enter these armes, for since thou thoughtst it best,
Not to dreame all my dreame, let's act the rest.

As lightning, or a Tapers light,
Thine eyes, and not thy noise wak'd mee;
   Yet I thought thee
(For thou lovest truth) an Angell, at first sight,
But when I saw thou sawest my heart,
And knew'st my thoughts, beyond an Angels art,
When thou knew'st what I dreamt, when thou knew'st when
Excesse of joy would wake me, and cam'st then,
I must confesse, it could not chuse but bee
Prophane, to thinke thee any thing but thee.

Comming and staying show'd thee, thee,
But rising makes me doubt, that now,
   Thou art not thou.
That love is weake, where feare's as strong as hee;
'Tis not all spirit, pure, and brave,
If mixture it of *Feare, Shame, Honor,* have.
Perchance as torches which must ready bee,
Men light and put out, so thou deal'st with mee,
Thou cam'st to kindle, goest to come; Then I
Will dreame that hope againe, but else would die.

I will see the centre of my cares with the eyes of my faith, for these imagined
pleasures are also seen by the blind.

148

De Viau

From LA SOLITUDE

Dans ce val solitaire et sombre
Le cerf qui brame au bruict de l'eau,
Panchant ses yeux dans un ruisseau,
S'amuse à regarder son ombre.

De ceste source une Naïade
Tous les soirs ouvre le portal
De sa demeure de crystal,
Et nous chante une serenade.

Les Nymphes que la chasse attire
A l'ombrage de ces forests
Cherchent les cabinets secrets
Loing de l'embusche du satyre.

Jadis au pied de ce grand chesne,
Presque aussi vieux que le Soleil,
Bacchus, l'Amour et le Sommeil,
Feirent la fosse de Silene.

Un froid et tenebreux silence
Dort à l'ombre de ces ormeaux,
Et les vents battent les rameaux
D'une amoureuse violence.

. . . .

SOLITUDE

In this dark and solitary valley, the stag who bells at the noise of the water, staring down into a stream, delights in looking at his shadow.

In this stream a Naïad every evening opens the gates of her crystal dwelling and sings us a serenade.

The nymphs lured by the hunt to the shade of these forests, seek secret alcoves, far from the snares of the Satyr.

Once, at the foot of this great oak, almost as old as the sun, Bacchus, Love and Sleep made the den of Silenus.

A cold and darkening silence sleeps in the shadow of his elms, and the winds beat the boughs with an amorous violence. . . .

Love

Approche, approche, ma Driade!
Icy murmureront les eaux;
Icy les amoureux oyseaux
Chanteront une serenade.

Preste-moy ton sein pour y boire
Des odeurs qui m'embasmeront;
Ainsi mes sens se pasmeront
Dans les lacs de tes bras d'yvoire.

Je baigneray mes mains folastres
Dans les ondes de tes cheveux,
Et ta beauté prendra les vœux
De mes œillades idolatres.

Ne crains rien, Cupidon nous garde.
Mon petit Ange, es tu pas mien?
Ha! je voy que tu m'aymes bien:
Tu rougis quand je te regarde.

Dieux! que ceste façon timide
Est puissante sur mes esprits!
Regnauld ne fut pas mieux espris
Par les charmes de son Armide.

Ma Corine, que je t'embrasse!
Personne ne nous voit qu'Amour;
Voy que mesme les yeux du jour
Ne trouvent point icy de place.

Come near, come near, my Dryad, here the waters will murmur, here the amorous birds will sing a serenade.

Grant me your bosom, that I may drink there of perfumes that will embalm me, and so my senses will swoon in the lakes of your ivory arms.

I will bathe my playful hands in the waves of your hair, and your beauty will capture the vows of my idolatrous glances.

Fear nothing, Cupid is watching over us, my little angel, are you not mine? Ha! I see you love me well, you blush when I look at you.

Gods, how this timid bearing is master of my feelings. Rinaldo was not better held by the charms of his Armida.

My Corinna, let me embrace you, no-one can see us but Love; see, even the eyes of the day cannot come here.

Les vents, que ne se peuvent taire,
Ne peuvent escouter aussy,
Et ce que nous ferons icy
Leur est un incogneu mystere.

Marvell

TO HIS COY MISTRESS

Had we but World enough, and Time,
This coyness Lady were no crime.
We would sit down, and think which way
To walk, and pass our long Loves Day.
Thou by the *Indian Ganges* side
Should'st Rubies find: I by the Tide
Of *Humber* would complain. I would
Love you ten years before the Flood:
And you should if you please refuse
Till the Conversion of the *Jews*.
My vegetable Love should grow
Vaster then Empires, and more slow.
An hundred years should go to praise
Thine Eyes, and on thy Forehead Gaze.
Two hundred to adore each Breast:
But thirty thousand to the rest.
An Age at least to every part,
And the last Age should show your Heart.
For Lady you deserve this State;
Nor would I love at lower rate.
    But at my back I alwaies hear
Times winged Charriot hurrying near:
And yonder all before us lye
Desarts of vast Eternity.
Thy Beauty shall no more be found;
Nor, in thy marble Vault, shall sound
My ecchoing Song: then Worms shall try
That long preserv'd Virginity:
And your quaint Honour turn to dust;
And into ashes all my Lust.
The Grave's a fine and private place,
But none I think do there embrace.

The winds which cannot be silent, neither can hear, and what we are about to do here is an unknown mystery to them.

Love

Now therefore, while the youthful hew
Sits on thy skin like morning dew,
And while thy willing Soul transpires
At every pore with instant Fires,
Now let us sport us while we may;
And now, like am'rous birds of prey,
Rather at once our Time devour,
Than languish in his slow-chapt pow'r.
Let us roll all our Strength, and all
Our sweetness, up into one Ball:
And tear our Pleasures with rough strife,
Thorough the Iron gates of Life.
Thus, though we cannot make our Sun
Stand still, yet we will make him run.

Opitz

ACH LIEBSTE, LASS UNS EILEN

Ach Liebste, lass uns eilen,
  Wir haben Zeit:
Es schadet das Verweilen
  Uns beiderseit.
Der schönen Schönheit Gaben
  Fliehn Fuss für Fuss,
Das alles, was wir haben,
  Verschwinden muss.
Der Wangen Zier verbleichet,
  Das Haar wird greis,
Der Aeuglein Feuer weichet,
  Die Flamm wird Eis.
Das Mündlein von Korallen
  Wird ungestalt,
Die Händ als Schnee verfallen,
  Und du wirst alt.

AH, DEAREST LOVE, LET'S HURRY

Ah, dearest love, let's hurry, time's running out fast: tarrying will do harm to both of us. The gifts of fair beauty flee step by step, all we possess must vanish. Pretty cheeks will grow pale, hair will become grey, the fire in your eyes will go out, flame will turn to ice. Your coral mouth will grow misshapen, your snowy hands gnarled, and you'll grow old. Therefore let us enjoy youth's fruits now,

Drum lass uns jetzt geniessen
   Der Jugend Frucht,
Eh dann wir folgen müssen
   Der Jahre Flucht.
Wo du dich selber liebest,
   So liebe mich,
Gib mir, das, wann du gibest,
   Verlier auch ich.

Weckherlin

DIE LIEB IST LEBEN UND TOD

Das Leben, so ich führ, ist wie der wahre Tod,
Ja über den Tod selbs ist mein trostloses Leben.
Es endet ja der Tod des Menschen Pein und Leben,
Mein Leben aber kann nicht enden dieser Tod.

Bald kann ein Anblick mich verletzen auf den Tod,
Ein andrer Anblick bald kann mich wiedrum beleben,
Dass ich von Blicken muss dann sterben und dann leben,
Und bin in einer Stund bald lebendig bald tot.

Ach, Lieb! Verleih mir doch nunmehr ein anders Leben,
Wenn ich ja leben soll, oder den andern Tod:
Denn weder diesen Tod lieb ich, noch dieses Leben.

Verzeih mir, Lieb, ich bin dein lebendig und tot.
Und ist der Tod mit dir ein köstlich süsses Leben,
Und Leben, von dir fern, ist ein ganz bittrer Tod.

before we must follow the flight of the years. Love me as you love yourself, give me that which, given, I thereby lose.

LOVE IS LIFE AND DEATH

The life I lead is like very death, indeed beyond death is my desolate life. Thus death ends man's pain and life, but my life cannot be ended by this death.

   At times, some sight can hurt me to the death, then again, another sight can bring me back to life, so that on account of glances I must now die, now live, and within an hour I am now alive, now dead.

   Ah, beloved! Bestow upon me now another life, if I am to live, or another death: for I love neither this death, nor this life.

   Forgive me, beloved, I am yours alive and dead. And death with you is deliciously sweet life, and life, apart from you, is a most bitter death.

153

Love

ABWESENHEIT

Auf, auf, fleug bald mein junges Herz,
Zu deren, die dich allein nähret,
Sag ihr, wie übergrosser Schmerz
Ihrethalb' meine Seel' betöret.

Sag ihr, wie mein Geist Tag und Nacht
Von ihr nichts dann Klagwort erdichtet,
Und wie Amors zu grosse Macht
Alle meine Vernunft vernichtet.

Sag ihr, wie die Abwesenheit
Mein Gesicht unablässig netzet
Und wie ihr' süsse Freundlichkeit
Mich leider! jetzt tödlich verletzet.

Doch sag auch, dass wann in der Pein,
Not, Angst, Trübsal, Elend und Klagen,
Sie meiner eingedenk wird sein,
Ich selig solches zu ertragen.

Fleming

AUF IHR ABWESEN

Ich irrte hin und her und suchte mich in mir,
Und wusste dieses nicht, dass ich ganz war in dir.
Ach! tu dich mir doch auf, du Wohnhaus meiner Seelen!
Komm, Schöne, gib mich mir, benimm mir dieses Quälen!

ABSENCE

Arise, arise, my young heart and presently fly to her who alone sustains you, tell her how intolerable pain for her sake has bewitched my soul.

Tell her how day and night my spirit writes nothing but lamenting poetry about her, and how Amor's infinite power has destroyed all my reason.

Tell her how her absence makes my face wet [with tears] and how, alas, her sweet friendliness causes me mortal hurt now.

But say also that if in all this pain, anguish, sadness, misery and lamentation she will think of me, I shall be delighted to bear it all.

ON HER ABSENCE

I was roaming hither and thither, searching for myself in myself. And I did not know that I was wholly contained in you. Ah, open yourself to me, you dwelling house of my soul! Come, dearest, give me to myself, set me free from this

Schau wie er sich betrübt, mein Geist, der in dir lebt!
Tötst du den, der dich liebt? Itzt hat er ausgelebt.
Doch gib mich mir nicht aus dir! Ich mag nicht in mich kehren.
Kein Tod hat Macht an mir, du kannst mich leben lehren.
Ich sei auch, wo ich sei, bin ich, Schatz nicht bei dir,
So bin ich nimmermehr selbest in und bei mir.

King

AN EXEQUY TO HIS MATCHLESSE NEVER TO BE FORGOTTEN FREIND

Accept, thou Shrine of my Dead Saint!
Instead of Dirges this Complaint;
And, for sweet flowres to crowne thy Hearse,
Receive a strew of weeping verse
From thy griev'd Friend; whome Thou might'st see
Quite melted into Teares for Thee.
    Dear Losse! since thy untimely fate
My task hath beene to meditate
On Thee, on Thee: Thou art the Book,
The Library whereon I look
Though almost blind. For Thee (Lov'd Clay!)
I Languish out, not Live the Day,
Using no other Exercise
But what I practise with mine Eyes.
By which wett glasses I find out
How lazily Time creepes about
To one that mournes: This, only This
My Exercise and bus'nes is:
So I compute the weary howres
With Sighes dissolved into Showres.
    Nor wonder if my time goe thus
Backward and most præposterous;
Thou hast Benighted mee. Thy Sett
This Eve of blacknes did begett,

torment! Look how dejected is this my spirit which lives in you! Are you going
to kill him who loves you? Now he has already passed away. And yet, do not
return me from yourself to myself. I do not want to go back to myself. There is
no death that has any power over me, provided you can teach me how to live.
Wherever I might be, my darling, if I am not with you, I am not in and with
myself either.

Love

Who wast my Day, (though overcast
Before thou hadst thy Noon-tide past)
And I remember must in teares,
Thou scarce hadst seene so many Yeeres
As Day tells Howres. By thy cleere Sunne
My Love and Fortune first did run;
But Thou wilt never more appeare
Folded within my Hemispheare:
Since both thy Light and Motion
Like a fledd Starr is fall'n and gone;
And 'twixt mee and my Soule's deare wish
The Earth now interposed is,
Which such a straunge Ecclipse doth make
As ne're was read in Almanake.

    I could allow Thee for a time
To darken mee and my sad Clime,
Were it a Month, a Yeere, or Ten,
I would thy Exile live till then;
And all that space my mirth adjourne,
So Thou wouldst promise to returne,
And putting off thy ashy Shrowd
At length disperse this Sorrowe's Cloud.

    But woe is mee! the longest date
Too narrowe is to calculate
These empty hopes. Never shall I
Be so much blest, as to descry
A glympse of Thee, till that Day come
Which shall the Earth to cinders doome,
And a fierce Feaver must calcine
The Body of this World, like Thine,
(My Little World!) That fitt of Fire
Once off, our Bodyes shall aspire
To our Soules' blisse: Then wee shall rise,
And view our selves with cleerer eyes
In that calme Region, where no Night
Can hide us from each other's sight.

    Meane time, thou hast Hir Earth: Much good
May my harme doe thee. Since it stood
With Heaven's will I might not call
Hir longer Mine; I give thee all
My short liv'd right and Interest
In Hir, whome living I lov'd best:
With a most free and bounteous grief,
I give thee what I could not keep.
Be kind to Hir: and prethee look
Thou write into thy Doomsday book

156

Each parcell of this Rarity,
Which in thy Caskett shrin'd doth ly:
See that thou make thy reck'ning streight,
And yeeld Hir back againe by weight;
For thou must Auditt on thy trust
Each Grane and Atome of this Dust:
As thou wilt answere Him, that leant,
Not gave thee, my deare Monument.

    So close the ground, and 'bout hir shade
Black Curtaines draw, My Bride is lay'd.

    Sleep on (my Love!) in thy cold bed
Never to be disquieted.
My last Good-night! Thou wilt not wake
Till I Thy Fate shall overtake:
Till age, or grief, or sicknes must
Marry my Body to that Dust
It so much loves; and fill the roome
My heart keepes empty in Thy Tomb.
Stay for mee there: I will not faile
To meet Thee in that hollow Vale.
And think not much of my delay;
I am already on the way,
And follow Thee with all the speed
Desire can make, or Sorrowes breed.
Each Minute is a short Degree
And e'ry Howre a stepp towards Thee.
At Night when I betake to rest,
Next Morne I rise neerer my West
Of Life, almost by eight Howres' sayle,
Then when Sleep breath'd his drowsy gale.

    Thus from the Sunne my Bottome steares,
And my Daye's Compasse downward beares.
Nor labour I to stemme the Tide,
Through which to Thee I swiftly glide.

    'Tis true; with shame and grief I yeild
Thou, like the Vann, first took'st the Field,
And gotten hast the Victory
In thus adventuring to Dy
Before Mee; whose more yeeres might crave
A just præcedence in the Grave.
But hark! My Pulse, like a soft Drum
Beates my Approach, Tells Thee I come;
And, slowe howe're my Marches bee,
I shall at last sitt downe by Thee.

    The thought of this bids mee goe on,
And wait my dissolution

With Hope and Comfort. Deare! (forgive
The Crime) I am content to live
Divided, with but half a Heart,
Till wee shall Meet and Never part.

THE SURRENDER

My once Deare Love; Happlesse that I no more
Must call thee so: The rich affection's store
That fed our hopes, lyes now exhawst and spent,
Like Summes of Treasure unto Bankerupts lent.
    Wee that did nothing study but the way
To love each other, with which thoughts the Day
Rose with delight to us, and with them sett,
Must learne the hatefull Art, how to forgett.
    Wee that did nothing wish that Heav'n could give
Beyond our selves, nor did desire to live
Beyond that Wish, all these now cancell must,
As if not writt in faith, but Words, and Dust.
    Yet witnes those cleere Vowes which Lovers make!
Witnes the chast Desires, that never brake
Into unruly heates; Witnes that breast
Which in thy bosome anchor'd his whole rest,
Tis no default in us. I dare acquite
Thy Mayden-faith, thy purpose faire and white
As thy pure self. Crosse Plannets did envy
Us to each other, and Heav'n did unty
Faster then Vowes could bind. O that the Starrs
When Lovers meet, should stand oppos'd in Warrs!
    Since then some higher Destinyes command
Let us not strive, nor labour to withstand
What is past help. The longest date of grief
Can never yeild a hope of our releife.
And though wee wast our selves in moist laments,
Teares may drowne us, but not our discontents.
    Fold back our armes, take home our fruitlesse Loves,
That must new fortunes try, like Turtle Doves
Dislodged from their hauntes. Wee must in teares
Unwind a Love knitt up in many Yeares.
In this last kisse I here surrender thee
Back to Thyself. Lo thou againe art free.
Thou in another, sad as that, resend
The truest heart that Lover e're did lend.
    Now turne from each. So fare our sever'd Hearts
As the Divorc't Soule from her Body parts.

Anonymous

L'œil flambeau de mes jours s'éteignant en l'oubli
Et mon cœur périssant en une même Sirte
O ciel disais-je hélas d'un accent affaibli
Foudroie mes lauriers et pardonne à mon myrte

Mais l'avare nocher ne fléchit à ma voix
Et volant mon trésor aborda son Rivage
Où fermant ce bel œil pour la dernière fois
Ne fit d'elle et d'amour et de moi qu'un naufrage

Dieux jaloux de mon heur que ne fit votre sort
Ravir à vos destins ma vie pour la sienne?
M'ouvrant mille tombeaux pour sauver de la mort
La vie dont la mort est la mort de la mienne

O bel œil obscurci qui du Ciel de l'Amour
As fait dedans mon cœur tant de flammes descendre
Si tu fus mon soleil et si tu fus mon jour
Ou revis en mes feux ou m'éteins en ta cendre

A que ne puis-je encor rempourprer en mourant
Du vermeil de mon sang la pâleur de sa face
Mais au trompeur esprit je faux en espérant
Mon tour étant défait que mon rien le refasse

The eye, torch of my days, being darkened in forgetfulness, and my heart perishing in a similar quicksand, O Heaven, alas, I cried with feeble voice, strike my laurels with lightning, and pardon my myrtles.

But the miserly pilot did not bend to my voice, and, stealing my treasure, landed on her shore, where closing that lovely eye for the last time made one shipwreck out of her, and love, and me.

Gods, envious of my fortune, why did not your lot, according to the destiny [you planned], ravish my life instead of hers? Opening a thousand tombs for me to save from death the life whose death is the death of my own [life]?

Oh, beautiful darkened eye, which has made so many flames descend from the Heaven of love upon my heart, if you were my sun, if you were my day, either relive in my fires, or extinguish me in your dust.

Ah, that I cannot in dying re-colour the pallor of her face with the crimson of my blood; but in the deceiving spirit, I fail in hoping, when my whole being is destroyed, that my nothingness can remake it.

Love

Hélas triste départ plein de pleurs et d'effroi
Funèbre messager d'une Parque si fière
Tu ne pouvais faillir ton augure est trop vrai
En lieu du lit d'amour je la trouve en la bière

Que n'est le ciel ouvert aux courages parfaits
Pour mourir à la mort j'emploierais les armes
Mais je veux sans pouvoir et venant aux effets
L'éclair de mes fureurs dément l'eau de mes larmes

Ployons donc sous le faix et vivant malgré nous
Que son doux souvenir soit l'âme de mon âme
Puisqu'étant empêchés par les astres jaloux
Les glaçons de sa mort ne fondent à ma flamme

Mais en vain les destins mon bel ange ont ravi
Notre parfaite amour d'une même aile vole
Et par tout l'Univers l'un de l'autre est suivi
Sa mémoire est mon jour mon cœur est son mausole

De Saint-Luc

Vers de Mr. de Saint Luc sur les Cheveux de sa Femme morte

Doux cheveux mes liens, l'ornement et pareure
Du beau chef honoré objet de mes desirs,
Tesmoin de mon ennuy, non plus de mes plaisirs,
Comment seuls estes vous privez de sepulture?

Alas, sad departure, full of tears and terror, funereal harbinger of so proud a fate, you could not fail, your augury is too true, instead of in a bed of love, I find her in the bier.

Ah, that heaven is not open for perfect courage! I would take up arms against death to die, but my wish is powerless, and the result is that the lightning of my ravings belies the water of my tears.

Let us then bow beneath the burden, and living in spite of ourselves, let her sweet memory be the soul of my soul, since, hindered by the jealous stars, the ice of her death does not melt in my flame.

But in vain have the fates snatched away my beautiful angel: our perfect love flies on one and the same wing, and throughout the entire Universe one is followed by the other: her memory is my day, my heart is her mausoleum.

Verses of Mr de Saint Luc on the hair of his dead wife
Sweet hairs my bonds, the ornament and embellishment of the beautiful head, honoured object of my desires, witness of my emptiness, no longer of my pleasures, how is it that you alone are deprived of burial?

160

Hors de luy pensez-vous vous conserver la vie?
Vous estes vous disjoints pour craindre le trespas?
Seuls avez vous vescu pour seuls ne mourir pas?
Et sans luy pensez-vous en conservez l'envie?

Beaux cheveux de vos noeuds encor la forme dure
Lustrez et collorez vous estes à mes yeux:
Mais ainsi séparez vous ne vivez pas mieux
Que des branches sans tronc qui meurent en verdure.

Hé quoy! doncquez privez du beau chef de Madame
Encore vous luisez encor estes vous beaux!
Et ses beaux yeux aimez gisent dans les tombeaux,
Amortis, mais bruslans et vivans en mon ame.

Hé! que vous m'estez chers parmi ma triste vie,
Bien que trop faux amis: car lors de son depart
Vous qui d'elle restez rare et certaine part
Ingrats dites pourquoi vous ne l'avez suivie?

Brignole Sale

PER LA MORTE DI EMILIA ADORNI RAGGI

De l'arrabbiato Can sotto i latrati,
sotto il ruggir de l'anelante fiera,
io t'ho visto esalare, o primavera,
di moribondo odor gli ultimi fiati.

Do you expect to conserve your life away from her? Did you cut yourselves off through fear of death? Have you alone lived so that you alone should not die? And without her do you expect to keep the wish to go on living?

Lovely hairs the form of your knots still remains, you are still lustrous and colourful in my eyes, but thus separated you live no better than trunkless branches which die in leaf.

But then! although deprived of the lovely head of Milady still you shine, still you are beautiful! And her beautiful beloved eyes lie in the tomb, dimmed, but still burning and living in my soul.

Ah, how dear to me you are in my sad life, although you are such false friends: for after her departure, you, who remain the precious, tangible part of her, ungrateful ones, tell why you didn't follow her?

SONNET ON THE DEATH OF EMILIA ADORNI RAGGI
Beneath the barking of the frenzied Dog[-star], beneath the roarings of the panting beast [the constellation of Leo] I saw you, O Spring, exhale your last breaths with the odour of death.

E pur sorgi di nuovo, e i pregi usati
teco hai di molli fior, d'aura leggiera;
rinascer tosto entro la guancia altera
miro di rose iblee gli ostri beati.

Ma d'Emilia gentil che si morio
più non vedrò le belle guance e i rai,
done un april rilusse, un sol fiorio.

De gli anni tuoi, mia vita, or che farai?
Vengan pur rose, escan pur gigli, oh Dio,
ch'un aprile per me non fia più mai!

D'Ambillou

L'Astre de mon Printemps qui faisait mes beaux jours
Eclipse pour jamais J'ai vu sa flamme éteindre
L'hiver a pris les fleurs de nos jeunes amours
Et le fruit en est mort en commençant à poindre

Rien ne m'est demeuré de ma belle saison
Voilà ma vie aux vents et aux pluies rangée
Le désir de la mort possède ma raison
Et toute ma mémoire en la tombe est plongée

Mémoire ton objet me fut jadis si cher
Que j'en adore en toi le fantôme et l'idole
Rien ne m'est si plaisant mais c'est comme un éclair
Qui nous gâte la nuit les yeux et les console

And then you rise again, and with you you have the customary prizes of soft flowers, and gentle breeze; I see the blessed purples of Hyblaean roses born again soon in the proud cheek.

But I shall see no more the beautiful cheeks of gentle Emily, who is dead, or her rays [eyes] where an April shone, a sun blossomed.

What will you do now, O my life, with your years? Let the roses come then, let the lilies appear, O God, but there will be no more April for me.

The Star of my Spring, which made my happy days, is eclipsed forever. I have seen its flame go out. Winter has taken the flowers of our young loves and the fruit of them is dead as it begins to sprout.

Nothing remains to me of my lovely season; see my life ranged between winds and rains; desire for death possesses my reason, and all my memory is plunged into the tomb.

Memory, your object was formerly so dear to me that now I adore in you the phantom and image of her. Nothing is so pleasing to me [as you] but it is like a flash of lightning which destroys our night and eyes, and consoles them.

162

Sous la nuit de mon deuil ta prompte illusion
Vient donner à mon âme un sursaut de sa gloire
Mais tu portes hélas dans ta condition
Le désespoir du bien dont tu es la mémoire

Mémoire tu retiens comme un miroir ardent
De notre ardent Amour la flamme non-mortelle
Tu échauffes mon cœur de loin te regardant
Et ta glace de près en éteint l'étincelle

Je te devrais haïr Mémoire et supplier
La mort qui serait seule à mon mal secourable
Mais je n'ose mourir de peur de t'oublier
Et ta vaine beauté rend mon deuil perdurable

Ombre de mon bien mort triste et sensible attrait
De mon malheur présent tu me combles de peine
Je ressemble Ixion j'embrasse un feint portrait
Et tire un vrai tourment d'une apparence vaine

Mais rien ne m'est si doux Mon cœur dans ce tourment
Trouve tout son plaisir d'autre joie incapable
Et mon âme constante aime ainsi loyaument
Le cendres dont le feu me fut tant agréable

Mon cœur malgré la Mort ne cessant point d'aimer
Remporte du Destin une gloire immortelle
Laurier bien précieux s'il porte un fruit amer
Sa feuille glorieuse au moins est toujours belle

Under the night of my mourning, your sudden illusion comes to startle my soul with her glory, but you carry, alas, in your condition, despair for the good of which you are the memory.

Memory, you retain like a burning mirror the non-mortal flame of our ardent Love; seeing you from afar, you warm my heart, but when you come close, your ice puts out its spark.

I ought to hate you, Memory, and crave Death, which alone could aid my disease, but I dare not die from fear of forgetting you, and your useless beauty makes my mourning everlasting.

Shadow of my good, sad death, and feeling enticement in my present unhappiness, you overwhelm me with pain. I resemble Ixion, I embrace a feigned portrait, and extract a real torment from an unreal appearance.

But nothing is so sweet to me, My Heart, in this torment, finds all its pleasure incapable of any other joy, and my constant soul still loyally loves the ashes whose fire was so dear to me.

My heart, in spite of Death, never ceasing its love, carries off from Destiny an immortal glory, a truly precious laurel, if it bears a bitter fruit, but its glorious leaf at least is always beautiful.

Günther

ALS ER DER PHYLLIS EINEN RING MIT EINEN TOTENKOPF UEBERREICHTE

Erschrick nicht vor dem Liebeszeichen,
Es träget unser künftig Bild,
Vor dem nur die allein erbleichen,
Bei welchen die Vernunft nichts gilt.
Wie schickt sich aber Eis und Flammen?
Wie reimt sich Lieb und Tod zusammen?
Es schickt und reimt sich gar zu schön,
Denn beide sind von gleicher Stärke
Und spielen ihre Wunderwerke
Mit allen, die auf Erden geht.

Ich gebe dir dies Pfand zur Lehre;
Das Gold bedeutet feste Treu,
Der Ring, dass uns die Zeit verehre,
Die Täubchen, wie vergnügt man sei,
Der Kopf erinnert dich des Lebens;
Im Grab ist aller Wunsch vergebens,
Drum lieb und lebe, weil man kann,
Wer weiss, wie bald wir wandern müssen!
Das Leben steckt im treuen Küssen.
Ach! fang den Augenblick noch an!

Lovelace

Song TO AMARANTHA, THAT SHE WOULD DISHEVEL HER HAIR

Amarantha sweet and fair
Ah braid no more that shining hair!
As my curious hand or eye,
Hovering round thee let it fly.

UPON GIVING TO PHYLLIS A RING WITH A DEATH'S HEAD

Do not be frightened at this token of love, it bears the image of what we are to become, at the sight of which only those who do not believe in reason grow pale. How, though, do ice and flames go together? How do love and death rhyme? They go together and rhyme beautifully, for both are equally strong, and both display their strange deeds to all who live on earth.

I am giving you this pledge as a lesson: the gold means steadfast faithfulness, the ring that time should favour us, the little dove how happy we might be, the head is to remind you of life; in the grave all desires are vain, therefore love and live while you may, who knows how soon we may have to be on our way! There is life in true kisses, ah, quickly let the moment begin.

Let it fly as unconfin'd
As its calm ravisher, the wind,
   Who hath left his darling, th'East,
To wanton o'er that spicy nest.

   Ev'ry tress must be confess'd
But neatly tangled at the best;
   Like a clew of golden thread
Most excellently ravelled.

   No not then wind up that light
In ribbands, and o'ercloud in night;
   Like the sun in's early ray,
But shake your head and scatter day.

   See, 'tis broke! Within this grove,
The bower and the walks of love
   Weary lie we down and rest,
And fan each other's panting breast.

   Here we'll strip and cool our fire
In cream below, in milk-baths higher;
   And when all wells are drawn dry,
I'll drink a tear out of thine eye

   Which our very joys shall leave,
That sorrows thus we can deceive;
   Or our very sorrows weep
That joys so ripe so little keep.

Sor Juana

*Arguye de inconsecuentes el gusto y la censura de los hombres que en las
mujeres acusan lo que causan*

   Hombres necios que acusáis
a la mujer sin razón,
sin ver que sois la ocasión
de lo mismo que culpáis,

*Which argues the inconsistency of men's taste in, and attacks on, women, whom
they accuse of that which they cause*

Foolish men, who accuse women without cause, not seeing that you are the
occasion of what you condemn,

165

si con ansia sin igual
solicitáis su desdén
¿por qué queréis que obren bien
si las incitáis al mal?

Combatís su resistencia
y luego, con gravedad,
decís que fué liviandad
lo que hizo la diligencia.

Parecer quiere el denuedo
de vuestro parecer loco,
al niño que pone el coco,
y luego le tiene miedo.

Queréis, con presumpción necia,
hallar a la que buscáis,
para pretendida, Thais,
y en la posesión, Lucrecia.

¿Qué humor puede ser más raro
que el que, falto de consejo,
él mismo empaña el espejo
y siente que no esté claro?

Con el favor y el desdén
tenéis condición igual:
quejándos si os tratan mal;
burlándoos si os quieren bien.

if you solicit their disdain with unequalled yearning, why do you want them
to act well if you incite them to ill?

You combat her resistance, and then, heavily, you say it was her own lightness which did the trick.

[The line could also be translated 'You say it was her lightness when it was your
diligence.' The double meaning of *diligencia* (diligence and trick) is untrans-
latable.]

In their mad appearance your efforts look like those of the child who makes
ugly faces and then is frightened of them.

In your blind presumption, you want to find in her whom you woo, while
you are soliciting her, a Thais, and when you possess her, a Lucretia.

What cast of mind can be odder than that which, lacking sense, first breathes
on the glass, and then complains it isn't clear?

Her favour and her disdain you treat the same, complaining if you are treated
badly, mocking if you are treated well.

Opinión ninguna gana,
pues la que más se recata,
si no os admite, es ingrata,
y si os admite, es liviana.

Siempre tan necios andáis
que con desigual nivel
a una culpáis por cruel
y a otra por fácil culpáis.

¿Pues cómo ha de estar templada
la que vuestro amor pretende,
si la que es ingrata ofende
y la que es fácil enfada?

Mas entre el enfado y pena
que vuestro gusto refiere
bien haya la que no os quiere
y quejáos en hora buena.

Dan vuestras amantes penas
a sus libertades alas,
y después de hacerlas malas
las queréis hallar muy buenas.

¿Cuál mayor culpa ha tenido,
en una pasión errada,
la que cae de rogada,
o el que ruega de caído?

No one gains your respect, for the most modest of women, if she doesn't accept you, is cruel, but, if she does, is loose.

You are always so foolish in that you, with unfair censure, blame one for being cruel, and the other for being easy.

What should be the temperament of the woman who aspires to your love, if she who is obdurate offends, and she who is easy angers?

But in the anger and sorrow that your pleasure brings about, good luck to her who doesn't want you, and though you complain, it serves you right.

Your lovers' complaints give wings to women's liberty, and after making them bad, you want them to be good.

Who commits the greater fault in a sinful passion, the women who falls through being entreated, or the man who, fallen, entreats?

167

Love

¿O cuál es más de culpar,
aunque cualquiera mal haga,
la que peca por la paga
o el que paga por pecar?

Pues ¿para qué os espantáis
de la culpa que tenéis?
Queredlas cuál las hacéis
o hacedlas cual las buscáis.

Dejad de solicitar
y después, con más razón,
acusaréis la afición
de la que os fuere a rogar.

Bien con muchas armas fundo
que lidia vuestra arrogancia,
pues, en promesa e instancia
juntáis diablo, carne y mundo.

En que describe racionalmente los efectos irracionales del amor

Este amoroso tormento
que en mi corazón se ve,
sé que lo siento y no sé
la causa porque lo siento.

Siento una grave agonía
por lograr un devaneo
que empieza como deseo
y pára en melancolía.

Who is more to blame, even if each is guilty, the women who sins for pay, or the man who pays for sin?

Why do you seem shocked by the guilt of your own making? Take them as you make them, or make them what you want them to be.

Stop entreating, and then you'll have more right to blame the fondness of she who comes to entreat you.

And I maintain that your arrogance fights with many weapons since, in both promise and performance, you combine the world, the flesh, and the devil.

In which she describes rationally the irrational effects of love

This amorous torment which is seen in my heart, I know that I feel, but do not know the cause of my feeling it.

I feel a great agony to obtain a madness which begins in desire and ends in melancholy.

Y cuando con más terneza
mi infeliz estado lloro
sé que estoy triste e ignoro
la causa de mi tristeza.

Siento un anhelo tirano
por la ocasión a que aspiro,
y cuando cerca la miro
yo mismo aparto la mano.

Porque, si acaso se ofrece,
después de tanto desvelo
la desazona el recelo
o el susto la desvanece.

Y si alguna vez sin susto
consigo tal posesión
[cualquiera] leve ocasión
me malogra todo el gusto.

Siento mal del mismo bien
con receloso temor
y me obliga el mismo amor
tal vez a mostrar desdén.

Cualquier leve ocasión labra
en mi pecho, de manera
que el que imposibles venciera
se irrita de una palabra.

And when with greater softheartedness I bewail my unhappy state I know that I am sad, and do not know the cause of my sadness.

I feel a tyrannic yearning for the event I crave, but when it comes close, I myself withdraw my hand.

For if, after so much weary waiting, the opportunity offers itself, distrust turns it sour or fear makes it vanish.

And if, sometime, without fear, I reach such possession, any trivial little thing spoils all the pleasure for me.

With distrustful fear I feel evil [coming] from the same good, and perhaps the love itself compels me to show disdain.

Any trivial occasion leaves a mark on my breast in such a way that that which can vanquish impossibles is hurt by a mere word.

Love

Con poca causa ofendida
suelo, en mitad de mi amor,
negar un leve favor
a quien le diera la vida.

Ya sufrida, ya irritada,
con contrarias penas lucho:
que por él sufriré mucho,
y con él sufriré nada.

No sé en qué lógica cabe
el que tal cuestión se pruebe:
que por él lo grave es leve,
y con él lo leve es grave.

Sin bastantes fundamentos
forman mis tristes cuidados,
de conceptos engañados
un monte de sentimientos.

Y en aquel fiero conjunto
hallo, cuando se derriba,
que aquella máquina altiva
sólo estrivaba en un punto.

Tal vez el dolor me engaña
y presumo sin razón,
que no habrá satisfacción
que pueda templar mi saña.

Offended by some little thing, in the midst of my love I often deny a trivial
favour to him for whom I would lay down my life.

Sometimes suffering, sometimes angrily, I struggle between opposing pains,
since *for* him I'll suffer much, but *with* him I'll suffer nothing.

I do not know what logic can resolve this dilemma: that *for* him the serious is
trivial, but *with* him the trivial is serious.

Without adequate foundations, my sad cares make a mountain of feelings
out of contradictory concepts.

And in that wild mass I find, when it collapses, that the lofty edifice was only
balanced upon a point.

Perhaps grief deceives me, and I assume, without reason, that there will be no
satisfaction to alleviate my fury.

Y cuando a averiguar llego
el agravio porque riño
es como espanto de niño
que pára en burlas y juego.

Y aunque el desengaño toco
con la misma pena lucho
de ver que padezco mucho
padeciendo por tan poco.

A vengarse se avalanza
tal vez el alma ofendida
y después, arrepentida,
toma de mí otra venganza.

Y si al desdén satisfago
con tan ambiguo error
que yo pienso que es rigor
y se remata en halago.

Hasta el labio desatento
suele, equívoco, tal vez,
por usar de la altivez
encontrar el rendimiento.

Cuando por soñada culpa
con más enojo me incito
yo le acrimino el delito
y le busco la disculpa.

But when I come to examine the wound which hurts me it turns out to be a child's fright, which goes away in laughter and playfulness.

And even when I reach disillusionment I struggle with the same pain when I see that I suffer greatly when I suffer for so little.

Perhaps my offended soul rushes for vengeance, and afterwards, when I have repented, it takes a second vengeance on me.

And if I give in to disdain, [I do it] with such an ambiguous error that I take it to be strictness, and it ends up in flattery.

And then the equivocal, inattentive lip, perhaps, while using haughtiness, discovers submission.

Even when I work myself up to anger for some imagined fault, at one and the same time I accuse him of the guilt, and seek excuses for him.

Love

No huyo el mal, ni busco el bien:
porque, en mi confuso error,
ni me asegura el amor
ni me despecha el desdén.

En mi ciego devaneo
bien hallada con mi engaño
solicito el desengaño
y no encontrarlo deseo.

Si alguno mis quejas oye
más a decirlas me obliga,
porque me las contradiga
que no porque las apoye.

Porque si con la pasión
algo contra mi amor digo,
es mi mayor enemigo
quien me concede razón.

Y si acaso en mi provecho
hallo la razón propicia,
me embaraza la justicia
y ando cediendo el derecho.

Nunca hallo gusto cumplido,
porque entre alivio y dolor
hallo culpa en el amor
y disculpa en el olvido.

I neither flee the bad, nor search for the good, for, in my confused error, neither does love reassure me, nor disdain exacerbate me.

In my blind ravings, in the middle of my deceit, I seek disillusionment but do not wish to find it.

If anyone hears me in my complaints, I am driven to tell them for them to be contradicted, more than for them to be approved.

For if in passion I say anything against my love my worst enemy becomes he who concedes that I am right.

And if, perhaps, I find reason convenient to my cause, justice then embarrasses me and I begin to concede my case.

Never can I find enough pleasure for between relief and grief, I find guilt in love and pardon in forgetfulness.

Esto de mi pena dura
es algo del dolor fiero
y mucho más no refiero
porque pasa de locura.

Si acaso me contradigo
en este confuso error
aquél que tuviere amor
entenderá lo que digo.

Davenant

Song PHILOSOPHER AND THE LOVER; TO A MISTRESS DYING

LOVER.

Your Beauty, ripe, and calm, and fresh,
　As Eastern Summers are,
Must now, forsaking Time and Flesh,
　Add light to some small Star.

PHILOSOPHER.

Whilst she yet lives, were Stars decay'd,
　Their light by hers, relief might find:
But Death will lead her to a shade
　Where Love is cold, and Beauty blinde.

LOVER.

Lovers (whose Priests all Poets are)
　Think ev'ry Mistress, when she dies,
Is chang'd at least into a Starr:
　And who dares doubt the Poets wise?

PHILOSOPHER.

But ask not Bodies doom'd to die,
　To what abode they go;
Since Knowledge is but sorrows Spy,
　It is not safe to know.

That is something of my hard pain and a part of my savage grief and I do not mention more because it is more than madness.

If perhaps I contradict myself in my confused error, he who has been in love will understand what I say.

173

On Life, Time and Death

There is some consolation, in a life one thinks to be painful or incomprehensible, in asserting that one's existence is only a dream from which one will, perhaps, awake. Many baroque poets, used as they were to 'proving' that their sense-experiences were no more valid or real than their imagination and art, found it easy to transfer a similar series of proofs to the speculation of life itself. And a whole tradition of Christian thought reinforced them in their declarations that what appears to be 'real life' is no more than an illusion, and what seems in this life to be illusory is in fact the truth. Hence we find poems which almost lovingly describe the power of death as the killer of the body, and its illusions, poems which assert the dreamlike quality of life itself, and poems which try to face the nature of the reality to which their authors will awake.

> . . . solamente
> lo fugitivo permanece y dura.   ('A Roma', Quevedo [1])

Awareness of that central paradox is the first, and most important, stage in the baroque analysis of life and time. The process of flux being the only reliable process in the world, the poets are continually aware that all their experiences, however powerful and attractive, are volatile and unreliable. What they know is as short-lived and deceptive as a dream, and from there it is a short and necessary step to seeing all human life as itself merely a dream:

> Qué es la vida? Un frenesí,
> Qué es la vida? Una ilusión,
> Una sombra, una ficción,
> Y el mayor bien es pequeño
> Que toda la vida es sueño,
> Y los sueños, sueños son.   (Calderón [2])

Several common poetic themes emerge from this basic awareness of the possible unreality of life. Study, retirement, stoicism, quietude offer a defence: many poets declare that a simple country existence, removed

[1] See p. 179.   [2] See p. 185.

from the greater unrealities of courts, power, and career-seeking can alone offer some basis, some solidity.[1] Quevedo draws a distinction between the hours wasted trying to get money and position and the hours profitably used in studious poverty, contrasting petty arithmetic of the world with the greater arithmetic of learning and piety:

> En fuga irrevocable huye la hora;
> pero aquella el mejor cálculo cuenta,
> que en la lección y estudios nos mejora.[2]

Gryphius, far away from the court and the desires of the rabble ('fern von dem Palast; weit von des Pöbels Lüsten') discovers the power of a landscape seen in solitude to endow him with some spiritual tranquillity:

> Der Mauern alter Graus, dies unbebaute Land
> Ist schön und fruchtbar mir, der eigentlich erkannt,
> Dass alles, ohn ein Geist, den Gott selbst hält, muss wanken.[3]

Such defences seem to be small oases of tranquillity in a desert of anguish, for even piety and study are subject to all-devouring time, slaves to the hours. The passage of the years, the documentation of the decay of physique, awareness of all that is represented by such symbols as the clock, the sundial, the hourglass, these are the subjects which seem most to have fired the imagination, and even a minor poet like Fontanella can, in addressing Time, communicate the depth of his fear:

> Tu corri, sì; ma col tuo corso, edace,
> ogni cosa qua giù che giova o nòce
> consumi e rompi, involator rapace.
> Ah, m'insegna nel cor celeste voce
> che non sei tu che fuggi: io son fugace,
> ch'innanzi al corso tuo corro veloce.[4]

But just as in some of the wittiest and finest love-poems the reader senses a core of doubt, even revulsion, in some of the most bizarre and striking poems about death he senses its attractiveness. If death is a glutton, he is at least a reliable one, perhaps the only reliable thing in a world of noisy, destructive change:

> Come then, YOUTH, BEAUTY, & blood!
>   All ye soft powres,
> Whose sylken flatteryes swell a few fond howres
> Into a false aeternity. Come man;
> Hyperbolized NOTHING! know thy span;

[1] See p. 189.   [2] See p. 193.   [3] See p. 191.
[4] See p. 208.

> Take thine own measure here: down, down, & bow
> Before thy self in thine idaea; thou
> Huge emptynes! contract thy self! & shrinke
> All thy Wild circle to a point. O sink
> Lower & lower yet; till thy leane size
> Call heavn to look on thee with narrow eyes.
> . . . .
> All-daring dust & ashes! only you
> Of all interpreters read Nature true.   (Crashaw [1])

Man may be born to unhappiness, live only to die; yet still one possibility of existence outside Time, beyond Death, remained: God. Many poems are built around a contrast between powerful description of the forces which destroy man and final expression of faith in the One who can destroy those forces. A fine example of this contrast is Sponde's sonnet:

> Tout s'enfle contre moy, tout m'assaut, tout me tente,
> Et le Monde et la Chair, et l'Ange révolté,
> Dont l'onde, dont l'effort, dont le charme inventé
> Et m'abysme, Seigneur, et m'esbranle, et m'enchante.
>
> Quelle nef, quel appuy, quelle oreille dormante,
> Sans péril, sans tomber, et sans estre enchanté,
> Me donras-tu? Ton Temple où vit ta Saincteté,
> Ton invincible main et ta voix si constante.
>
> Et quoy? mon Dieu, je sens combattre maintesfois
> Encore avec ton Temple, et ta main, et ta voix,
> Cest Ange revolté, ceste Chair, et ce Monde.
>
> Mais ton Temple pourtant, ta main, ta voix sera
> La nef, l'appuy, l'oreille, où ce charme perdra
> Où mourra cest effort, où se rompra ceste Onde. [2]

In three English poems, Donne, Herbert, and Marvell present three different views of the continuous battle between the time-dominated fragility of the body and the timeless aspirations of the soul: Marvell in his 'Dialogue between the Soul and the Body' allows the debate between the two to remain unsolved, so creating an impression of the perpetual and painful balance between the two sides, a balance never to be upset as the soul continues to torture the body, the body continues to imprison the

---

[1] See p. 216.   [2] See p. 196.

soul; [1] Herbert sees how the death of the Saviour has changed the face of mortality:

> Therefore we can go die as sleep, and trust
> Half that we have
> Unto an honest faithfull grave;
> Making our pillows either down or dust. [2]

and Donne in famous lines asserts the answer to Quevedo's 'Solamente/lo fugitivo permanece y dura':

> One short sleepe past, wee wake eternally,
> And death shall be no more, Death thou shalt die. [3]

See p. 194.   [2] See p. 201.   [3] See p. 220.

Du Bellay

SONNET

Nouveau venu, qui cherches Rome en Rome
  Et rien de Rome en Rome n'apperçois,
  Ces vieux palais, ces vieux arcz que tu vois,
  Et ces vieux murs, c'est ce que Rome on nomme.
Voy quel orgueil, quelle ruine, & comme
  Celle qui mist le monde sous ses loix,
  Pour donter tout, se donta quelquefois,
  Et devint proye au temps, qui tout consomme.
Rome de Rome es le seul monument,
  Et Rome Rome a vancu seulement,
  Le Tybre seul, qui vers la mer s'enfuit,
Reste de Rome. O mondaine inconstance!
  Ce qui est ferme est par le temps destruit,
  Et ce qui fuit, au temps fait resistance.

Quevedo

A ROMA SEPULTADA EN SUS RUINAS

Buscas en Roma a Roma ¡oh peregrino!
y en Roma misma a Roma no la hallas:
cadáver son las que ostentó murallas,
y, tumba de sí propio, el Aventino.

Newcomer, who seeks for Rome in Rome and sees nothing of Rome in Rome, these old palaces, these old arches you see, and these old walls are what men call Rome.

See that pride, that ruin and [see] how she who subdued the world to her laws in order to conquer everything finally defeated herself and became a prey to all-consuming time.

Rome is the sole monument of Rome and Rome has only conquered Rome, only the Tiber rushing to the sea

remains of Rome. O inconstancy of this world! That which is solid is destroyed by time, and that which is fugitive resists time.

TO ROME BURIED IN ITS RUINS

In Rome you seek for Rome, O traveller, and in Rome itself you cannot find Rome: the walls she displayed are a corpse, and the Aventine its own tomb.

Yace, donde reinaba, el Palatino;
y limadas del tiempo las medallas,
más se muestran destrozo, a las batallas
de las edades, que blasón latino.

Sólo el Tíber quedó; cuya corriente,
si ciudad la regó, ya sepoltura
la llora con funesto son doliente.

¡Oh Roma!, en tu grandeza, en tu hermosura
huyó lo que era firme, y solamente
lo fugitivo permanece y dura.

EL SUEÑO

¿Con qué culpa tan grave
sueño blando y suave,
pude en largo destierro merecerte,
que se aparte de mí tu olvido manso?
pues no te busco yo por ser descanso
si no por muda imágen de la muerte.
Cuidados veladores
hacen inobedientes mis dos ojos
a la ley de las horas;
no hab podido vencer a mis dolores
las noches, ni dar paz a mis enojos.
Madrugan más en mí que en las auroras
lágrimas a este llano,
que amanece a mi mal siempre temprano;

The Palatine lies where it once reigned; and the medals filed down by time
seem more like the remains of the battles of the ages than a Latin crest.

Only the Tiber remains: whose current, which once washed her when she was
a city, now weeps for her as a tomb with funereal, grieving sound.

O Rome, in your greatness, in your beauty, what was solid has gone and
only the transient remains and lasts.

SLEEP

Through what grave crime, O soft, gentle sleep, have I merited from you so long
an exile that your sweet oblivion should leave me? for I do not seek you as a
refuge, but as a silent image of death. Ever-wakeful cares make my two eyes
disobedient to the law of the hours; the nights have left my griefs undefeated,
my troubles without peace. Tears rise earlier in me than [they do] at dawn, upon
this plain which wakens always too soon to my misfortune, and with such force

y tanto, que persuade la tristeza
a mis dos ojos, que nacieron antes
para llorar, que para verse sueño.
De sosiego los tienes ignorantes,
de tal manera, que al morir el día
con luz enferma vi que permitía
el sol que le mirasen en Poniente.

Con pies torpes al punto, ciega y fría,
cayó de las estrellas blandamente
la noche, tras las pardas sombras mudas
que el sueño persuadieron a la gente.
Escondieron las galas a los prados,
estas laderas y sus peñas solas:
duermen ya entre sus montes recostados
los mares y las olas.
Si con algun acento
ofenden las orejas,
es que entre sueños dan el cielo quejas
del yerto lecho y duro acogimiento,
que blandos hallan en los cerros duros.
Los arroyuelos puros
se adormecen al son del llanto mío,
y a su modo también se duerme el río.

Con sosiego agradable
se dejan poseer de tí las flores;
mudos están los males,
no hay cuidado que hable,
faltan lenguas y voz a los dolores,
y en todos los mortales
yace la vida envuelta en alto olvido.

that sadness persuades my two eyes that they were rather born for tears than
dreams. They know not peace, so that when day died in its sick light I saw that
the sun allowed them to look at it as it set.

Then slow-footed, blind and frozen, night fell softly from the stars across the
grey silent shadows which usher sleep towards mankind. These slopes and their
solitary rocks cover the flowers of the field; the oceans and their waves sleep
between their reclining mountains. If with some sound they offend ears, it is
because in dreams they utter complaints about their rigid bed and the hard
shelter which their softness finds in the hard mountains. The pure streams are
lulled to sleep by the sound of my weeping, and the river also sleeps in its way.

In pleasant peace the flowers give themselves to you; evils are stilled, no care
alarms, pains lose their tongues and voice, and in all mortals life lies wrapped in

Tan sólo mi gemido
pierde el respeto a tu silencio santo:
yo tu quietud molesto con mi llanto,
y te desacredito
el nombre de callado, con mi grito.
Dame, cortés mancebo, algún reposo:
no seas digno del nombre de avariento,
en el más desdichado y firme amante,
que lo merece ser por dueño hermoso.

Débate alguna pausa mi tormento;
gozante en las cabañas,
y debajo del cielo
los ásperos villanos:
Hállate en el rigor de los pantanos,
y encuéntrate en las nieves y en el hielo
el soldado valiente,
y yo no puedo hallarte aunque lo intente
entre mi pensamiento y mi deseo.
Ya, pues, con dolor creo
que eres más riguroso que la tierra,
más duro que la roca,
pues te alcanza el soldado envuelto en guerra;
y en ella mi alma
por jamás te toca.
Mira que es gran rigor: dame siquiera
lo que de ti desprecia tanto avaro,
por el oro en que alegre considera,
hasta que da la vuelta el tiempo claro.
Lo que había de dormir en blando lecho,
y da el enamorado a su señora,
y a ti se te debía de derecho.

deep oblivion. Only my groans lack respect for your holy silence; I disturb your quiet with my weeping, I with my groans cheapen your reputation for tranquillity. Kind boy, give me some rest; do not be worthy of the name of miser in my eyes, the most faithful and unfortunate lover, who, as such, deserves a beautiful master.

Give my torments some pause; crude peasants enjoy you in their huts, or under the sky; the valiant soldier finds you in the severity of mud, meets you in snow and frost; but I cannot find you, however I try, in my thought or my desire. Now, then, sadly, I believe you are crueller than the earth, harder than the rock, for the soldier wrapped in war reaches you, while my soul, wrapped in her, never touches you. Lo, a harsh cruelty; give me at least that little bit of you which many a miser despises in favour of the gold he joyfully counts till daylight returns. [Give me] that which should sleep in a soft bed, which the lover gives his lady and which is rightly owed to you.

181

On Life, Time and Death

Dame lo que desprecia de ti agora
por robar el ladrón; lo que deshecha
el que invidiosos celos tuvo y llora.
Quede en parte mi queja satisfecha,
tócame con el cuento de tu vara,
oirán siquiera el ruido de tus plumas
mis desventuras sumas;
que yo no quiero verte cara a cara,
ni que hagas más caso
de mí, que hasta pasar por mí de paso;
o que a tu sombra negra por lo menos,
si fueres a otra parte peregrino,
se le haga camino
por estos ojos de sosiego ajenos.
Quítame blando sueño este desvelo,
o de él alguna parte,
y te prometo, mientras viere el cielo,
de desvelarme sólo en celebrarte.

Calderón

Two soliloquies from *La vida es sueño*

Segismundo

Tu voz pudo enternecerme,
Tu presencia suspenderme
Y tu respeto turbarme.
¿Quién eres? Que aunque yo aquí
Tan poco del mundo sé,
Que cuna y sepulcro fué
Esta torre para mí;

Give me that which the robber despises in order to rob; that which is rejected by him who has and weeps over transports of envy. Let my complaints be partially satisfied, touch me with the fairy-tale of your wand, let my unhappy calculations hear something of the sound of your feathers. For I do not want to see you face to face, nor that you pay more attention to me than to pass me in passing; or that your black shadow, at least, if visiting some other place, should find its way through these eyes, strangers to peace. Sweet sleep, free me from this wakefulness, or from a little of it, and I promise you, as long as I can see the sky, only to stay awake in order to celebrate you.

Your voice could arouse tenderness in me, your presence keep me in suspense, and your respect disturb me. Who are you? Although I know so little of the world, for this tower was both my cradle and my sepulchre, and ever since I was

Y aunque desde que nací
(Si esto es nacer) sólo advierto
Este rústico desierto
Donde miserable vivo,
Siendo un esqueleto vivo,
Siendo un animado muerto;
Y aunque nunca vi ni hablé,
Sino a un hombre solamente
Que aquí mis desdichas siente,
Por quien las noticias sé
De cielo y tierra, y aunque
Aquí, por que más te asombres
Y monstruo humano me nombres,
Entre asombros y quimeras,
Soy un hombre de las fieras
Y una fiera de los hombres;
Y aunque en desdichas tan graves
La política he estudiado,
De los brutos enseñado,
Advertido de las aves,
Y de los astros süaves
Los círculos he medido;
Tú sólo, tú has suspendido
La pasión a mis enojos,
La suspensión a mis ojos,
La admiración a mi oído.
Con cada vez que te veo
Nueva admiración me das,
Y cuando te miro más,
Aun más mirarte deseo.
Ojos hidrópicos creo
Que mis ojos deben ser;

born (if this is to have been born) I have only seen this rural wilderness where I live as a living skeleton, an animated corpse; and although I never saw or spoke save to one man only who knows of my sufferings here, through whom I receive news from heaven and earth, and although here, although this surprises you more, and you call me a human monster, between marvels and chimaeras, I am a man among beasts, and a beast among men; and even in the midst of such great sufferings, I have studied politics, taught by the beasts, advised by the birds, and I have measured the orbits of the sweet stars; you only have quieted the passion of my hatreds, the blind stare of my eyes, the wonder in my ears. Each time I see you, you create a new wonder in me, and the more I see you the more I want to see you. I believe that my eyes must be hydroptic [insatiable] for

On Life, Time and Death

Pues, cuando es muerte el beber,
Beben más, y desta suerte,
Viendo que el ver me da muerte,
Estoy muriendo por ver.
Pero véate yo y muera;
Que no sé, rendido ya,
Si el verte muerte me da,
El no verte qué me diera.
Fuera más que muerte fiera,
Ira, rabia y dolor fuerte;
Fuera muerte: desta suerte
Su rigor he ponderado,
Pues dar vida a un desdichado
Es dar a un dichoso muerte.

Segismundo

Es verdad; pues reprimamos
Esta fiera condición,
Esta furia, esta ambición,
Por si alguna vez soñamos;
Y sí haremos, pues estamos
En mundo tan singular,
Que el vivir sólo es soñar;
Y la experiencia me enseña
Que el hombre que vive, sueña
Lo que es, hasta dispertar.
Sueña el rey que es rey, y vive
Con este engaño mandando,
Disponiendo y gobernando;

although to drink is to die they still drink more, and in such a way that seeing that to see gives me death, I am still dying to see. So I would see you and die; because, having already surrendered to you, I do not know, since seeing you gives me death, what not seeing you would give me. It would be more than brutal death, wrath, fury, and great pain; it would be death, and I have considered its rigour in this way, since to give life to a desperate man is to give death to a happy one.

It is true, so let us master this wild condition, this fury, this ambition, in case we have dreams; and we will succeed, for we are in such a peculiar world that living is only dreaming; and experience teaches me that the man who lives dreams what he is, till he awakes. The king dreams he is a king, and rules while he lives in this delusion, ordering and governing, and the applause which he

184

Y este aplauso, que recibe
Prestado, en el viento escribe,
Y en cenizas le convierte
La muerte (¡desdicha fuerte!).
¿Que hay quien intente reinar,
Viendo que ha de dispertar
En el sueño de la muerte?
Sueña el rico en su riqueza,
Que más cuidados le ofrece;
Sueña el pobre que padece
Su miseria y su pobreza;
Sueña el que a medrar empieza,
Sueña el que afana y pretende,
Sueña el que agravia y ofende,
Y en el mundo, en conclusión,
Todos sueñan lo que son,
Aunque ninguno lo entiende.
Yo sueño que estoy aquí
Destas prisiones cargado,
Y soñé que en otro estado
Más lisonjero me vi.
¿Qué es la vida? Un frenesí.
¿Qué es la vida? Una ilusión,
Una sombra, una ficción,
Y el mayor bien es pequeño,
Que toda la vida es sueño,
Y los sueños, sueños son.

receives on loan, is written on the wind and turned to ashes by death (unhappy fate!). Who is he that tries to be king, seeing that he has to awake in the dream of death? The rich man dreams in his riches, which give him more cares; the pauper dreams that he is suffering his misery and poverty; the man beginning to prosper is dreaming; the man labouring, and aspiring is dreaming; the man annoying and insulting is dreaming, and in the world, in conclusion, all men dream what they are, even if no-one knows [what they are]. I dream that I am here weighted down by fetters and I dreamed that I saw myself in another more flattering state. What is life? A frenzy. What is life? An illusion, a shadow, a fiction, and the greatest blessing [in life] is tiny, for all life is a dream, and dreams are only dreams.

Lubrano

IL SONNO

Antipode del senno, oppio de' sensi,
benché di mezzo l'essere ci privi
ed a dazii di morte astringa i vivi,
esige il sonno volontari censi.

Rende cimmeria l'alma, e ciò che pensi,
sposando a lazie muse i plettri argivi,
larva è di sogni or mesti ed or festivi,
delirio di vapori or radi or densi.

Di piacevole oblio vesta l'orrore,
di sibarite rose il letto impiumi,
sepolcro è pur de l'uom che a tempo mòre.

Tobido il viso e 'l sen d'umidi fumi,
per non farsi veder che ruba l'ore,
adulato ladron ci chiude i lumi.

George Herbert

LIFE

I made a posie, while the day ran by:
Here will I smell my remnant out, and tie
    My life within this band.
But Time did beckon to the flowers, and they
By noon most cunningly did steal away,
    And wither'd in my hand.

SLEEP

Antipodes of sense, opium of the senses, although it deprives us of half our being and forces the living to pay customs duties to death, sleep exacts its voluntary taxes.

It makes the soul Cimmerian, and the brain marrying Argive strings to Latin muses, is a mask for dreams now sad now happy, the delirium of vapours now tenuous now thick.

It clothes horror in pleasant oblivion, it fills the bed with feathers of sybaritic roses, it is the pure sepulchre of the man who can die there for a time.

With a clouded face and a bosom of moistened smoke you close our eyes, adored thief, to make yourself invisible as you steal our hours away.

186

My hand was next to them, and then my heart:
I took, without more thinking, in good part
    Times gentle admonition:
Who did so sweetly deaths sad taste convey,
 Making my minde to smell my fatall day;
    Yet sugring the suspicion.

Farewell deare flowers, sweetly your time ye spent,
Fit, while ye liv'd, for smell or ornament,
    And after death for cures.
I follow straight without complaints or grief,
Since if my sent be good, I care not if
    It be as short as yours.

Gryphius

ES IST ALLES EITEL

Du siehst, wohin du siehst nur Eitelkeit auf Erden.
  Was dieser heute baut, reisst jener morgen ein:
  Wo itzund Städte stehn, wird eine Wiesen sein,
Auf der ein Schäferskind wird spielen mit den Herden:
Was itzund prächtig blüht, soll bald zertreten werden.
  Was itzt so pocht und trotzt ist Morgen Asch und Bein,
  Nichts ist, das ewig sei, kein Erz, kein Marmorstein.
Itzt lacht das Glück uns an, bald donnern die Beschwerden.
  Der hohen Taten Ruhm muss wie ein Traum vergehn.
  Soll denn das Spiel der Zeit, der leichte Mensch bestehn?
Ach! was ist alles dies, was wir vor köstlich achten,
  Als schlechte Nichtigkeit, als Schatten, Staub und Wind;
  Als eine Wiesenblum, die man nicht wieder find't.
Noch will was ewig ist kein einig Mensch betrachten!

ALL IS VANITY

Wherever you look, you see nothing but vanity on earth. What this one builds today, that one will pull down tomorrow. Where now there are towns, there will be a meadow tomorrow, where a shepherd's child will play with the flocks.

What at this moment is blossoming so splendidly, will soon be trampled underfoot. What is boastful and defiant today, will turn to dry bones tomorrow. There is nothing which lasts forever, neither metal nor marble. Now fortune smiles on us, soon troubles will thunder down on us.

The glory of lofty deeds must vanish like a dream. And is then slight man, that plaything of time, to endure?

Ah, what is all this that we regard as splendid other than base vanity, shadow, dust and wind; a flower blooming in a meadow which we cannot find again. And yet not one man is willing to contemplate what is eternal.

Donne

SONNET

This is my playes last scene, here heavens appoint
My pilgrimages last mile; and my race
Idly, yet quickly runne, hath this last pace,
My spans last inch, my minutes last point,
And gluttonous death, will instantly unjoynt
My body, and soule, and I shall sleepe a space,
But my'ever-waking part shall see that face,
Whose feare already shakes my every joynt:
Then, as my soule, to' heaven her first seate, takes flight,
And earth-borne body, in the earth shall dwell,
So, fall my sinnes, that all may have their right,
To where they'are bred, and would presse me, to hell.
Impute me righteous, thus purg'd of evill,
For thus I leave the world, the flesh, and devill.

Sponde

SONNET

Tandis que dedans l'air un autre air je respire,
Et qu'à l'envy du feu j'allume mon désir,
Que j'enfle contre l'eau les eaux de mon plaisir,
Et que me colle à Terre un importun martyre,

Cest air tousjours m'anime, et le désir m'attire,
Je recerche à monceaux les plaisirs a choisir,
Mon martyre eslevé me vient encor saisir
Et de tous mes travaux le dernier est le pire.

While I breathe another air in the air, while I kindle my desire to compete with the fire, while I swell out the waters of my pleasure against water, and while an importunate martyrdom binds me to Earth,

this air always vivifies me, and desire allures me, I seek to pick piles of pleasures, my exalted martyrdom still comes to capture me, and of all my toils the last is the worst.

A la fin je me trouve en un estrange esmoy,
Car ces divers effets ne sont que contre moy;
C'est mourir que de vivre en ceste peine extrême.

Voilà comme la vie à l'abandon s'espard,
Chaque part de ce Monde en emporte sa part,
Et la moindre à la fin est celle de nous mesme.

Quevedo

A un amigo que retirado de la corte pasó su edad

Dichoso tú, que alegre en tu cabaña,
mozo y viejo espiraste la aura pura,
y te sirven de cuna y sepoltura,
de paja el techo, el suelo de espadaña.
     En esa soledad, que libre baña
callado sol con lumbre más segura,
la vida al día más espacio dura,
y la hora sin voz te desengaña.
     No cuentas por los cónsules los años,
hacen tu calendario tus cosechas,
pisas todo tu mundo sin engaños.
     De todo lo que ignoras te aprovechas;
ni anhelas premios, ni padeces daños,
y te dilatas cuanto más te estrechas.

In the end I find myself strangely disturbed, for all these different effects only work against me: it is to die to live in this great pain.

See how life is poured out in abandon, each part of this world carries away its share, and the smallest share left in the end is ours.

~ *To a friend who passed his life in retirement from court*
How fortunate you are, who, happy in your cottage, have breathed pure air from boyhood to age, and the straw roof and reed floor serve you both as cradle and grave.

In this solitude which the quiet sun freely bathes in a more secure light, life in daytime endures for a greater space and the voiceless hour teaches you to shed illusions.

You do not count the years by consuls, but your calendar is made by harvests, and you can walk your whole world without lies.

You profit by everything you don't know; you neither covet rewards nor suffer losses, and the more you contract the more you expand.

On Life, Time and Death

Conveniencia de no usar de los ojos, de los oídos y de la lengua

Oír, ver y callar, remedio fuera
en tiempo que la vista y el oído
y la lengua, pudieran ser sentido,
y no delito que ofender pudiera.

Hoy, sordos los remeros con la cera,
golfo navegaré, que (encanecido
de huesos no de espumas) con bramido
sepulta a quien oyó voz lisonjera.

Sin ser oído y sin oír, ociosos
ojos y orejas, viviré olvidado
del ceño de los hombres poderosos.

Si es delito saber quien ha pecado,
los vicios escudriñen los curiosos,
y viva yo ignorante, y ignorado.

Góngora

Determinado a dejar sus pretensiones y volverse a Córdoba

De la merced, señores, despedido,
pues lo ha querido así la suerte mía,
de mis deudos iré a la compañía,
no poco de mis deudas oprimido.

Si haber sido del Carmen culpa ha sido,
sobra el que se me dio hábito un día:
huélgome que es templada Andalucía,
ya que vuelvo descalzo al patrio nido.

The convenience of not using one's eyes, ears, and tongue

To hear, to see, and to keep silent would be a remedy in a time when sight, hearing and speech would be simply senses, not [become] crimes which might offend.

Today, with the oarsmen's ears stopped by wax I will sail the gulf, which (bleached with bones, not foam) buries with a roar the man who hears the flattering voice [of the siren].

Unheard, unhearing, with ears and eyes unused, I will live forgotten by the frown of the mighty.

If it is a crime to know who has sinned, let the curious examine vices, and let me live ignoring and ignored.

Determined to abandon his ambitions and return to Córdoba

Señores, deprived of favours for so has my luck decreed, I will go back to the company of my departed kindred, not a little oppressed by debts.

If it was a sin to devote myself to poetry, the habit I was once given is superfluous; I am pleased that Andalucia is warm, because I am returning barefooted to my home-nest.

Mínimo, pues, si capellán indino
del mayor Rey, monarca al fin de cuanto
pisa el Sol, lamen ambos oceanos,
    la fuerza obedeciendo del destino,
el cuadragesimal voto en tus manos,
desengaño haré, corrector santo.

Gryphius

EINSAMKEIT

In dieser Einsamkeit, der mehr denn öden Wüsten,
    Gestreckt auf wildes Kraut, an die bemooste See:
    Beschau' ich jenes Tal und dieser Felsen Höh'
Auf welchem Eulen nur und stille Vögel nisten.
Hier, fern von dem Palast; weit von des Pöbels Lüsten,
    Betracht ich: wie der Mensch in Eitelkeit vergeh'
    Wie, auf nicht festem Grund' all unser Hoffen steh'
Wie die vor Abend schmähn, die vor dem Tag uns grüssten.
    Die Höl', der rauhe Wald, der Totenkopf, der Stein,
    Den auch die Zeit auffrisst, die abgezehrten Bein,
Entwerfen in dem Mut unzählige Gedanken.
    Der Mauern alter Graus, dies unbebaute Land
    Ist schön und fruchtbar mir, der eigentlich erkannt,
Dass alles, ohn ein Geist, den Gott selbst hält, muss wanken.

The smallest, if unworthy chaplain of the greatest King, monarch of whatever is trodden by the sun, or licked by both oceans,
    obeying the force of destiny will perform, disillusioned, his forty day vow, offered to your hands, O holy corrector.

SOLITUDE

In this solitude, in this more than desolate wasteland, stretched out on wild-growing grass by the mossy [banks of the] water, I gaze upon the valley yonder and upon these rocks rising up, on which only owls and silent birds make their nests.

Here, far from the palace, away from the desires of the rabble, I ponder on how man wastes [his life] in vanity, how all our hopes are based on unsafe foundations, how those who earlier in the day had saluted us, will insult us before nightfall.

This cave, this rugged forest, this death's head, this stone which time will devour too, those wasted bones, arouse in my mind innumerable thoughts.

The dread of these old ruins, this untilled land, is beautiful and fertile to me who have realized that intrinsically nothing can be stable without a spirit which is in the hands of God Himself.

191

Greville

From *Mustapha* CHORUS SACERDOTUM

Oh wearisome condition of humanity!
Born under one law, to another bound:
Vainly begot, and yet forbidden vanity,
Created sick, commanded to be sound:
What meaneth Nature by these diverse laws?
Passion and reason, self-division cause:
Is it the mark, or majesty of power
To make offences that it may forgive?
Nature herself, doth her own self deflower,
To hate those errors she herself doth give.
For how should man think that, he may not do
If Nature did not fail, and punish too?
Tyrant to others, to herself unjust,
Only commands things difficult and hard.
Forbids us all things, which it knows is lust,
Makes easy pains, unpossible reward.
If Nature did not take delight in blood,
She would have made more easy ways to good.
We that are bound by vows, and by promotion,
With pomp of holy sacrifice and rites,
To teach belief in good and still devotion,
To preach of Heaven's wonders, and delights:
Yet when each of us, in his own heart looks,
He finds the God there, far unlike his books.

Quevedo

Gustoso el autor con la soledad y sus estudios, escribió este soneto

Retirado en la paz de estos desiertos,
con pocos, pero doctos libros juntos,
vivo en conversación con los difuntos,
y escucho con mis ojos a los muertos.

The author delighting in his solitude and studies, wrote this sonnet

Having retired into the peace of these deserts, with a few but learned books, I exist in conversation with the dead, and with my eyes I listen to the departed.

Sino siempre entendidos, siempre abiertos,
o enmiendan, o secundan mis asuntos;
y en músicos callados contrapuntos
al sueño de la vida hablan despiertos.

Las grandes almas, que la muerte ausenta,
de injurias de los años vengadora,
libra, ¡oh gran don Joseph! docta la emprenta.

En fuga irrevocable huye la hora;
pero aquella el mejor cálculo cuenta,
que en la lección y estudios nos mejora.

En vano busca la tranquilidad

A fugitivas sombras doy abrazos,
en los sueños se cansa el alma mía;
paso luchando á solas noche y día,
con un trasgo que traigo entre mis brazos.

Cuando le quiero más ceñir con lazos,
y viendo mi sudor se me desvia,
vuelvo con nueva fuerza a mi porfía,
y temas con amor me hacen pedazos.

Voime a vengar en una imagen vana,
que no se aparta de los ojos míos;
búrlame, y de burlarme corre ufana.

Empiézola a seguir, fáltanme bríos,
y como de alcanzarla tengo gana,
hago correr tras ella el llanto en ríos.

If not eternally heard, eternally open they amend or assist my labours and in silent musical counterpoint speak wakefully to the dream of life.

O great Don Joseph! Learned print frees the great spirits taken away by death, the avenger of the insults of the years.

The hour flies in irrevocable flight but that hour which improves us in reading and studies makes up the best reckoning.

In vain he seeks for peace

I embrace fugitive shadows. My soul is wearied in its dreams; wrestling on my own I pass the days and nights with the phantom I hug within my arms.

When I seek to hold him firmer in my toils, and, as I sweat, he eludes me, I turn with a new strength to my obstinacy and with love my struggles break me in pieces.

I go to avenge myself on a vain image, which is always before my eyes. It mocks me and joyfully runs from mocking me.

I start to follow it, my courage fails me and as I desire to reach it I make my tears run in rivers after it.

193

On Life, Time and Death

Describe el apetito exquisito de pecar

No agradan a Polycles los pecados,
con el uso plebeyo repetidos;
ni delitos por otro introducidos,
sí los mayores, y por sí inventados.

Cual si fueran virtud, los moderados
vicios Polycles tiene aborrecidos;
y los templadamente distraídos
yacen de su privanza desterrados.

De puro pecador le son ingratos
los pecados tal vez, pues al pequeño,
o desprecia, o le admite con recatos.

De vicios hace escrupuloso empeño,
ni los quiere ordinarios ni baratos;
si tú le imitas, tú serás su dueño.

Marvell

A DIALOGUE BETWEEN THE SOUL AND BODY

Soul

O who shall, from this Dungeon, raise
A Soul inslav'd so many wayes?
With bolts of Bones, that fetter'd stands
In Feet; and manacled in Hands.
Here blinded with an Eye; and there
Deaf with the drumming of an Ear.
A Soul hung up, as 'twere, in Chains
Of Nerves, and Arteries, and Veins.
Tortur'd, besides each other part,
In a vain Head, and double Heart.

Concerning an exquisite appetite for sin

Sins repeated in a plebeian manner do not please Polycles, nor crimes introduced by someone else—only the greatest ones, contrived by himself.

Polycles holds the moderate vices in as much abhorrence as if they were virtues and the moderately dissolute are exited from his favour.

He is so wholly sinful that at times sins are unwelcome to him, for he either despises the small sin or admits it with misgivings.

He makes a scrupulous punctiliousness out of vices and doesn't bother with the ordinary cheap ones; if you imitate him you'll be his master.

Body

O who shall me deliver whole,
From bonds of this Tyrannic Soul?
Which, stretcht upright, impales me so,
That mine own Precipice I go;
And warms and moves this needless Frame:
(A Fever could but do the same.)
And, wanting where its spight to try,
Has made me live to let me dye.
A Body that could never rest,
Since this ill Spirit it possest.

Soul

What Magick could me thus confine
Within anothers Grief to pine?
Where whatsoever it complain,
I feel, that cannot feel, the pain.
And all my Care its self employes,
That to preserve, which me destroys:
Constrain'd not only to indure
Diseases, but, whats worse, the Cure:
And ready oft the Port to gain,
Am Shipwrackt into Health again.

Body

But Physick yet could never reach
The Maladies Thou me dost teach;
Whom first the Cramp of Hope does Tear:
And then the Palsie Shakes of Fear.
The Pestilence of Love does heat:
Or Hatred's hidden Ulcer eat.
Joy's chearful Madness does perplex:
Or Sorrow's other Madness vex.
Which Knowledge forces me to know;
And Memory will not foregoe.
What but a Soul could have the wit
To build me up for Sin so fit?
So Architects do square and hew,
Green Trees that in the Forest grew.

195

Donne

SONNET

Oh my blacke Soule! now thou art summoned
By sicknesse, deaths herald, and champion;
Thou art like a pilgrim, which abroad hath done
Treason, and durst not turne to whence hee is fled,
Or like a thiefe, which till deaths doome be read,
Wisheth himselfe delivered from prison;
But damn'd and hal'd to execution,
Wisheth that still he might be imprisoned;
Yet grace, if thou repent, thou canst not lacke;
But who shall give thee that grace to beginne?
Oh make thy selfe with holy mourning blacke,
And red with blushing, as thou art with sinne;
Or wash thee in Christs blood, which hath this might
That being red, it dyes red soules to white.

Sponde

SONNET

Tout s'enfle contre moy, tout m'assaut, tout me tente,
Et le Monde et la Chair, et l'Ange révolté,
Dont l'onde, dont l'effort, dont le charme inventé
Et m'abysme, Seigneur, et m'esbranle, et m'enchante.

Quelle nef, quel appuy, quelle oreille dormante,
Sans péril, sans tomber, et sans estre enchanté,
Me donras-tu? Ton Temple où vit ta Saincteté,
Ton invincible main et ta voix si constante.

Et quoy? mon Dieu, je sens combattre maintesfois
Encore avec ton Temple, et ta main, et ta voix,
Cest Ange revolté, ceste Chair, et ce Monde.

Everything swells up against me, everything assaults me, everything tempts me,
and the world, the flesh, and the rebellious angel whose wave, whose effort,
whose contrived spell engulfs me, Lord, and weakens me, and enchants me.

What ship, what support, what sleeping ear will you give me without peril,
without falling, without being enchanted? Your temple where your sanctity
lives, your invincible hand, and your so constant voice?

And then? My God, I often feel this rebellious angel, this flesh, and this
world combatting still your temple, and your hand, and your voice.

Mais ton Temple pourtant, ta main, ta voix sera
La nef, l'appuy, l'oreille, où ce charme perdra
Où mourra cest effort, où se rompra ceste Onde.

Marino

ALLA PROPRIA COSCIENZA

Verme immortal, che con secreto dente
i mordaci pensier sempre rimordi;
interno can, che de la pigra mente
con perpetuo latrar l'orecchie assordi;

sollecito avoltor, che avidamente
intendi a divorar gli affetti ingordi;
vespa sottil, ch'a stimulo pungente
susurro acuto entro 'l mio petto accordi;

lima, che rodi l'anima; martello,
che l'incude del cor batti sì spesso;
spina del peccator, sferza e flagello;

voce di Dio, che con parlar sommesso
mi sgridi e chiami; ahi! qual tentato è quello,
che non faccia di te freno a se stesso?

Fontanella

INFELICITÀ

Piange l'uomo infelice, allor che viene
fanciullino a spirar l'aura vitale;
e per mostrar che varca un mar di pene
celebra con le lagrime il natale.

But yet your temple, your hand, and your voice will be the ship, the support, the ear where the enchantment will fade where this effort [against me] will die, and this wave break.

TO HIS OWN CONSCIENCE

Immortal worm, forever gnawing my gnawing thoughts with your secret tooth; internal dog, deafening with your perpetual barking the ears of the black mind; industrious vulture avidly intent on devouring the gluttonous affections; subtle wasp suiting your sharp buzzing to the stinging goad within my breast; file, rasping down the soul; hammer battering so often on the anvil of the heart; thorn, whip, and lash of the sinner; voice of God, calling and rebuking me with your submissive voice; ah, what temptation is his who does not make you a restraint upon himself.

UNHAPPINESS

Unhappy man weeps, when, as a little child, he comes to breathe the vital air; and to show he sails a sea of griefs, he celebrates his birthday with tears.

197

Piange, quando in età più ferma sale,
sotto maestra man ch'a freno il tiene;
e piange punto d'amoroso strale
quando al regno d'Amor servo diviene.

Piange, poiché l'età vede fornita,
sotto il freddo de gli anni aspro rigore;
quando ecco in un sospir chiude la vita.

Così fra pianto e duol passando l'ore,
senza aver mai felicità compita,
piangendo nasce e sospirando muore.

MEDITAZIONE DELLA SUA MORTE

Verrà la Parca, e di pallor gelato
l'insegna spanderà spora il mio volto,
e dentro un letto di miserie accolto
con angoscia trarrò l'ultimo fiato.

Il mio duro aversario avrò da lato
ad accusarmi innanzi a Dio rivolto;
posto di qua di là fra dubbio stato,
sarò fra téma e fra speranza involto.

Deh tu, Vergine Donna, alta reina,
da quell'empiree e luminose squadre
ver' me le luci tue pietosa inchina.

Sarà ver' me sdegnato il Sommo Padre;
ma tu, ch'in grembo hai la Pietà divina,
vogli al soccorso mio mostrarti madre.

He weeps when he enters on a firmer state, beneath a master hand which holds him to the reins; and, pierced by an amorous arrow, he weeps when he becomes a slave to the kingdom of Love.

He weeps, as he sees his life weighed down with the cold harsh rigour of the years; even when he closes his life with a sigh.

Thus, passing the hours between grief and mourning, never having reached happiness, he is born in tears, and, sighing, dies.

MEDITATION UPON HIS DEATH

The Fate will come, and will scatter her insignia of frozen whiteness across my face, and, gathered into a bed of miseries, I will with anguish draw my last breath.

My hard adversary will be at my side to accuse me of rebellion before God; pushed to and fro through a state of doubt, I will be whelmed between hope and fear.

O Thou, Blessed Virgin, queen of heaven, bend your eyes in pity upon me from those empyrean and luminous hosts.

The Almighty Father will be hard on me; but Thou, who nursed the divine Piety upon your bosom, wilt want to show Thyself as a mother, to help me.

Chassignet

SONNET

Mortel, pense quel est dessous la couverture
D'un charnier mortuaire un cors mangé de vers,
Descharné, desnervé, où les os descouvers,
Depoulpez, desnouez, delaissent leur jointure;

Icy l'une des mains tombe de pourriture,
Les yeux d'autre costé destournez à l'envers
Se distillent en glaire, et les muscles divers
Servent aux vers goulus d'ordinaire pasture;

Le ventre deschiré cornant de puanteur
Infecte l'air voisin de mauvaise senteur,
Et le né my-rongé difforme le visage;

Puis connoissant l'estat de ta fragilité,
Fonde en Dieu seulement, estimant vanité
Tout ce qui ne te rend plus scavant et plus sage.

Sponde

SONNET

Tout le monde se plainct de la cruelle envie
Que la Nature porte aux longueurs de noz jours;
Hommes, vous vous trompez, ils ne sont pas trop cours
Si vous vous mesurez au pied de vostre vie.

Mortal, think that there lies beneath the roof of a charnel-house a body eaten
by worms, defleshed, denerved, where the revealed bones, marrowless and
untied, abandon their joints;
   here one of the hands falls as it rots, the eyes roll back, liquefy into phlegm,
and the various muscles form the usual fodder for the greedy worms;
   the torn belly, bursting with putrescence, infects the neighbouring air with a
foul stench, and the half-gnawed nose deforms the face;
   then, knowing the condition of your fragility, rely on God alone, deeming
vanity all which makes you no more knowledgeable, no wiser.

Everyone complains of the cruel jealousy which Nature has for the length of our
days: men, you are deceived, they are not too short, if you match yourselves
against the basis of your life.

On Life, Time and Death

Mais quoy? Je n'entens point quelqu'un de vous qui die:
Je me veux despestrer de ces fascheux destours,
Il faut que je revole à ces plus beaux sejours,
Où sejourne des Temps l'entresuitte infinie.

Beaux sejours, loin de l'œil, prez de l'entendement,
Au prix de qui ce temps ne monte qu'un moment,
Au prix de qui le jour est un ombrage sombre,

Vous estes mon desir; et ce jour, et ce Temps,
Où le Monde s'aveugle, et prend son passetemps,
Ne me seront jamais qu'un moment, et qu'une ombre.

George Herbert

DEATH

Death, thou wast once an uncouth hideous thing,
    Nothing but bones,
  The sad effect of sadder grones:
Thy mouth was open, but thou couldst not sing.

For we consider'd thee as at some six
    Or ten yeares hence,
  After the losse of life and sense,
Flesh being turn'd to dust, and bones to sticks.

We lookt on this side of thee, shooting short;
    Where we did finde
  The shells of fledge souls left behinde,
Dry dust, which sheds no tears, but may extort.

But since our Saviours death did put some bloud
    Into thy face;
  Thou art grown fair and full of grace,
Much in request, much sought for as a good.

But what? I hear none of you say: I want to extricate myself from these
wearisome winding ways, I must fly back to the places of beauty where dwells the
infinite succession of Time.

Places of beauty, far from the eye, but near to the understanding, beside the
value of which this time amounts to only a moment, beside the value of which
day is a dark shadow,

you are my desire, and this day and this Time in which the world goes blind,
and makes its pastime, will never be for me more than a moment, a shadow.

For we do now behold thee gay and glad,
    As at dooms-day;
  When souls shall wear their new array,
And all thy bones with beautie shall be clad.

Therefore we can go die as sleep, and trust
    Half that we have
  Unto an honest faithfull grave;
Making our pillows either down, or dust.

Di Pers

TERREMOTO

Deh, qual possente man con forze ignote
il terreno a crollar sì spesso riede?
Non è chiuso vapor, come altri crede,
né sognato tridente il suol percuote.

  Certo, la terra si risente e scuote
perché del peccator l'aggrava il piede;
e i nostri corpi impazïente chiede
per rïempir le sue spelonche vòte.

  È linguaggio del Ciel che ne riprende
il turbo, il tuono, il fulmine, il baleno;
or parla anco la terra in note orrende,

  perché l'uom, ch'esser vuol tutto terreno,
né del cielo il parlar straniero intende,
il parlar della terra intenda almeno.

EARTHQUAKE

Lo, what powerful hand with unknown forces, returns so often to shake the earth? It is not imprisoned gas as some believe, nor does a dreamed-of trident strike the ground.

Surely the earth resents and shakes because the foot of the sinner weighs upon her: and she impatiently claims our bodies to re-fill her empty caves.

It is the language of Heaven which again takes up the whirlwind, the thunder, the thunderbolt and the lightning, and now also the earth speaks in terrible notes

because Man wishing to be wholly of earth does not listen to the foreign speech of the sky, but listens at least to the speech from the earth.

On Life, Time and Death

Gryphius

AN EUGENIEN

Was wundert ihr euch noch, Ihr Rose der Jungfrauen,
Dass dieses Spiel der Zeit, die Ros in Eurer Hand,
Die alle Rosen trotzt, so unversehns verschwand?
Eugenie! so gehts, so schwindet was wir schauen.

Sobald des Todes Sens wird diesen Leib abhauen,
Schaut man den Hals, die Stirn, die Augen, dieses Pfand
Der Liebe, diese Brust in nicht zu reinstem Sand,
Und dem, der euch mit Lieb itzt ehrt, wird für euch grauen.

Der Seufzer ist umsonst, nichts ist, das auf der Welt,
Wie schön es immer sei, Bestand und Farbe hält.
Wir sind von Mutterleib zum Untergang erkoren.

Mag auch an Schönheit was der Rosen gleiche sein,
Doch ehe sie recht blüht, verwelkt und fällt sie ein;
Nicht anders gehn wir fort, sobald wir sind geboren.

Quevedo

Con ejemplos muestra a Flora la brevedad de la hermosura, para no malograrla

La mocedad del año, la ambiciosa
vergüenza del jardín, el encarnado
oloroso rubí, tiro abreviado,
también del año presunción hermosa:

TO EUGENIE

Are you then still surprised, O rose among maidens, that that plaything of time, the rose in your hand, which defies all roses, has vanished so suddenly? Eugenie, that's how it goes, thus vanishes what we behold.

Once death's scythe has mown down your body, one will see your neck, forehead, eyes, and that pledge of love, your breast, lie in earth that is none too clean, and he who now loves and reveres you, will be filled with dread of you.

The sigh is vain, there is nothing, however beautiful, that in this world retains its shape or colour. From the moment we are in our mother's womb, we are destined to perish.

Though there may be one who is fair like a rose, yet even before she has come into full flower, she will wilt and collapse; in the same way we depart as soon as we are born.

With examples he demonstrates to Flora the brevity of beauty, so that she does not waste it

The youth of the year, the ambitious shame of the garden, the scarlet, scented ruby, brief arrow-shot, which is yet the lovely vainglory of the year:

La ostentación lozana de la rosa,
deidad del campo, estrella del cercado,
el almendro en su propria flor nevado,
que anticiparse a los calores osa:

Reprensiones son, ¡oh Flora! mudas
de la hermosura y la soberbia humana,
que a las leyes de flor está sujeta.

Tu edad se pasará mientras lo dudas,
de ayer te habrás de arrepentir mañana,
y tarde, y con dolor, serás discreta.

Represéntase la brevedad de lo que se vive, y cuán nada parece lo que se vivió

¡Há de la vida! ¿Nadie me responde?
Aquí de los antaños que he vivido;
la fortuna mis tiempos ha mordido,
las horas mi locura las esconde.

¡Qué sin poder saber cómo ni a dónde,
la salud y la edad se hayan huído!
Falta la vida, asiste lo vivido,
y no hay calamidad que no me ronde.

Ayer se fué, mañana no ha llegado,
hoy se está yendo sin parar un punto,
soy un fué, y un será y un es cansado.

the fresh ostentation of the rose, deity of the field, star of the garden, the almond tree snowy with white blossom, daring to anticipate the heats of summer;

are dumb reminders, O Flora, of beauty and human pride, which are subject to the laws of flowers.

While you are doubting it, your youth will pass away, tomorrow you will have to repent your yesterdays, and too late, and sorrowfully, you will be discreet.

Depicting the brevity of the living and how that which lived seems nothing

Life, are you there? Does no one answer me? Come back, past years I've lived; fortune has eaten through my times, and my madness hides the hours away.

Not to know how or where health and years have fled! Life is absent, what I've lived through stands round me, and there is no calamity which doesn't hunt me down.

Yesterday is gone, tomorrow is not yet here, today is leaving and won't stay for a moment, I am a *was*, a *will-be*, and a weary *is*.

En el hoy, y mañana, y ayer, junto
pañales y mortaja, y he quedado
presentes sucesiones de difunto.

Fleming

GEDANKEN UEBER DER ZEIT

Ihr lebet in der Zeit und kennt doch keine Zeit;
So wisst ihr Menschen nicht, von und in was ihr seid.
Dies wisst ihr, dass ihr seid in einer Zeit geboren
Und dass ihr werdet auch in einer Zeit verloren.
Was aber war die Zeit, die euch in sich gebracht?
Und was wird diese sein, die euch zu nichts mehr macht?
Die Zeit ist was und nichts, der Mensch in gleichem Falle,
Doch was dasselbe was und nichts sei, zweifeln alle.
Die Zeit, die stirbt in sich und zeugt sich auch aus sich.
Dies kömmt aus mir und dir, von dem du bist und ich.
Der Mensch ist in der Zeit; sie ist in ihm ingleichen,
Doch aber muss der Mensch, wenn sie noch bleibet, weichen.
Die Zeit ist was ihr seid, und ihr seid, was die Zeit,
Nur dass ihr wen'ger noch, als was die Zeit ist, seid.
Ach dass doch jene Zeit, die ohne Zeit ist, käme
Und uns aus dieser Zeit in ihre Zeiten nähme,
Und aus uns selbsten uns, dass wir gleich könnten sein
Wie *der* itzt jener Zeit, die keine Zeit geht ein!

In today, tomorrow, and yesterday, joining nappies to shrouds, I have
remained present successions of the dead.

THOUGHTS ON TIME

You live in time and yet know no time; thus you men are not aware of your
origin and your present state. All you know is that you were born in time and
that you will die in time. But of what essence was that time which brought you
into itself? And of what essence will be the time which will change you into
nothing? Time is something and nothing, and so is man. But all have doubts as
to what that something-and-nothing is. Time dies within itself and creates itself
out of itself. What you and I are created out of, comes out of you and me. Man
exists in time; and similarly time exists in him. And yet man must depart, while it
remains behind. Time is what you are, and you are what time is, except that you
are still less than time. Ah, if only that time which is without [the limits of] time
would come and remove us from this time to its [timeless] time [i.e. eternity] and
from our own selves so that we might be as He is now, like that time which has
no temporal beginning.

Gryphius

BETRACHTUNG DER ZEIT

Mein sind die Jahre nicht, die mir die Zeit genommen;
Mein sind die Jahre nicht, die etwa möchten kommen;
Der Augenblick ist mein, und nehm ich den in Acht,
So ist der mein, der Zeit und Ewigkeit gemacht.

DIE ZEIT

Kein höher Schatz ist in der grossen Welt
Als nur die Zeit; wer die nach Würden hält,
Wer die recht braucht, trotzt Tod und Not und Neid
Und baut ihm selbst den Thron der Ewigkeit.

Di Pers

OROLOGIO DA ROTE

Mobile ordigno di dentate rote
lacera il giorno e lo divide in ore,
ed ha scritto di fuor con fosche note
a chi legger le sa: SEMPRE SI MORE.

A MEDITATION UPON TIME

Not mine are the years which time has taken from me; not mine are the years which might still come; the moment is mine, and if I grasp that, He will be mine who made time and eternity.

TIME

In this great world there is no treasure more sublime than time. Whoever honours it, whoever uses it well, defies death, anguish and envy, and builds for himself a throne in eternity.

A CLOCK

The moving engine, with its cog wheels, tears up the day and divides it into hours, and on its case in black letters, it has written for whoever can read: WE ALL DIE.

Mentre il metallo concavo percuote,
voce funesta mi risuona al core;
né del fato spiegar meglio si puote
che con voce di bronzo il rio tenore.

Perch'io non speri mai riposo o pace,
questo, che sembra in un timpano e tromba,
mi sfida ognor contro all'età vorace.

E con que' colpi, onde il metal rimbomba,
affretta il corso al secolo fugace,
e perché s'apra, ognor picchia a la tomba.

OROLOGIO DA SOLE

Con l'ombra sua del sole i giri immensi
misura un lieve stile al sole esposto;
e ben di questo dì, che muor sì tosto,
l'ore con l'ombra misurar conviensi.

Di quell'ombra al girar forza è ch'io pensi
che co' suoi passi al tumulo m'accosto;
né m'è il tenor di quelle note ascosto:
parlan del mio morir con chiari sensi.

Saette son, ch'avventa arco di Morte,
quelle linee ch'io miro; e 'n van riparo
di tempra oppongo adamantina e forte.

A lo splendor del sol veggo pur chiaro
che del giorno vital l'ore son corte;
e ch'io son vanità da l'ombra imparo.

While the concave metal ticks, a funereal voice resounds in my heart nor can destiny be better signified than by the cruel tenor of its brazen voice.

Because I never hope for rest or peace this, seeming at once a drum and trumpet, always dares me to confront voracious age.

And with those beats from which the metal resounds the pace to the fugitive death quickens, and it always taps at the tomb to open it.

SUNDIAL

A little needle, exposed in the sun, measures the immense circles of the sun with its shade, and it is truly fitting to measure with a shadow the hours of today which dies so quickly.

In the turning of that shadow I am forced to think that I approach the tomb with its footsteps, nor is the tenor of those notes hidden from me: they clearly speak of my death.

Those lines that I stare at are arrows fired by the bow of death and in vain do I oppose the strong adamantine temper of my resistance.

In the splendour of the sun I see more clearly that the hours of vital day are short and I learn from the shadows that I am but vanity.

Auvray

From *Grâces rendues en l'année 1608*

....

Non, non, cercher du ferme au mouvant de ce monde,
C'est appuyer ses pieds sur une boule ronde,
Traverser l'occean dans un batteau percé
Se tenir a la mousse, et luitter sur la planche,
Se suspendre au filet, voltiger sur la branche,
Et courir (indiscret) sur un pendant glacé.

Le soleil des honneurs souffre tousjours eclypse,
Au miel des voluptez, le fiel du mal se glisse,
L'endroit de la Fortune a tousjours son envers;
L'on ne trouve jamais de calme sans tourmente,
De roze sans espine, et de mont sans descente,
Ny de medaille encor qui n'aye son revers.

....

Fontanella

AL TEMPO

Tu voli, o Tempo, e dibattendo i vanni
tosto al fine de l'uom giungi ed arrivi;
e col giro che fai di mesi e d'anni
termine angusto ai giorni suoi prescrivi.

No, no, to look for stability in the motion of this world is to set one's feet on a round ball, to cross the ocean in a leaky boat, to walk on foam, to wrestle on a plank, to hang by a thread, to dance on a branch, and to run (reckless) on an icy cliff.

The sun of honour always suffers eclipse, the gall of evil always slides into the honey of pleasure, the place of fortune always has its opposite, where one never finds calm without torment, a rose without thorn, a mountain without descent, and never a medal without its reverse.

TO TIME

You fly, O Time, and, beating your wings, quickly come and meet the end of man; and you prescribe a narrow span for his days in the circle you make from months and years.

Tu fuggi, sì; ma col fuggir n'inganni,
come ingannano altrui correndo i rivi;
n'empi di cure e di gravosi affanni,
ma di bellezza e di vigor ne privi.

Tu corri, sì; ma col tuo corso, edace,
ogni cosa qua giù che giova o nòce
consumi e rompi, involator rapace.

Ah, m'insegna nel cor celeste voce
che non sei tu che fuggi: io son fugace,
ch'innanzi al corso tuo corro veloce.

Quevedo

EL RELOX DE ARENA

¿Qué tienes que contar, relox molesto,
en un soplo de vida desdichada
que se pasa tan presto?
¿En un camino que es una jornada
breve y estrecha de este al otro polo,
siendo jornada que es un paso solo?
Que si son mis trabajos y mis penas,
no alcanzarás allá, si capaz vaso
fueses de las arenas,
en donde el alto mar detiene el paso.
Deja pasar las horas sin sentirlas,
que no quiero medirlas,
ni que me notifiques de esa suerte
los términos forzosos de la muerte.

Yes, you flee, but in your flight you do not deceive, as rivers in their courses deceive some, for you fill us with cares and great worries, but you empty us of vigour and beauty.

Yes, you run; but in your course, hungry, you consume and break everything in this world which either delights or hurts, rapacious robber.

Ah, the celestial voice tells my heart that it is not you who flees; I am the fugitive, I who run fast ahead of your running.

THE HOUR-GLASS

What do you have to tell, troublesome hour-glass, in a breath of unhappy life that passes so quickly? On a road which is a brief and narrow day's march from pole to pole, a day's march is but a single step? Even if you were a vessel big enough to contain all the sands where the mighty ocean holds back its footstep it would not be equal to my griefs and pains. Let the hours pass unfelt, for I do not wish to count them, nor do I wish you to inform me of the binding

No me hagas más guerra,
déjame, y nombre de piadosa cobra,
que harto tiempo me sobra
para dormir debajo de la tierra.
Pero si acaso por oficio tienes
el contarme la vida,
presto descansarás, que los cuidados
mal acondicionados
que alimenta lloroso
el corazón cuitado y lastimoso,
y la llama atrevida
que amor ¡triste de mí! arde en mis venas
(menos de sangre que de fuego llenas),
no sólo me apresura
la muerte pero abréviame el camino:
pues con pie doloroso,
mísero peregrino,
doy cercos a la negra sepultura.
Bien sé que soy aliento fugitivo:
ya sé, ya temo, ya también espero
que he de ser polvo, como tú, si muero;
y que soy vidro, come tú, si vivo.

Stigliani

OROLOGIO DA POLVERE

Questa in duo vetri imprigionata arena,
che l'ore addita e la fugace etade,
mentr'ognor giù, quasi filata, cade
rapidamente per angusta vena,

conditions of death. Stop troubling me, leave me alone, let yourself be called merciful, for there is more than enough time for me to sleep under the earth. But if it is your business to count out my life, you will soon rest, for the ill-disposed cares, fed by the weeping, grieving, and piteous heart, and the bold flame which Love, woe is me, burns in my veins (fuller of fire than blood), not only speeds me to death, but shortens my road; for, with grieving footsteps, a miserable pilgrim, I circle the black tomb. I know well enough that I am but a fleeting breath; I know, I am afraid, and yet I hope that I will be dust, like you, if I die, and glass, like you, if I live.

THE HOUR-GLASS

This sand, imprisoned in two glasses, counting up hours and fugitive time, as it always falls like a thread, rapidly through the narrow vein,

era un tempo Aristeo, ch'amò Tirrena,
Tirrena, che, com'angelo in beltade,
così parve in orgoglio o 'n crudeltade
libica serpe o fera tigre armena.

Amolla e n'era il misero deluso,
fin che, dall'aspro incendio addutto a morte,
si fece in polve a fu da lei qui chiuso.

Oh crudel degli amanti e dura sorte!
Serban l'arse reliquie anco il prim'uso:
travaglian vive, e non riposan morte.

Hall

ON AN HOUR-GLASS

My life is measur'd by this glass, this glass
By all those little sands that thorough pass.
See how they press, see how they strive, which shall
With greatest speed and greatest quickness fall.
See how they raise a little mount, and then
With their own weight do level it again.
But when th' have all got thorough, they give o'er
Their nimble sliding down, and move no more.
Just such is man, whose hours still forward run,
Being almost finish'd ere they are begun;
So perfect nothings, such light blasts are we,
That ere we're aught at all, we cease to be.
Do what we will, our hasty minutes fly,
And while we sleep, what do we else but die?
How transient are our joys, how short their day!
They creep on towards us, but fly away.
How stinging are our sorrows! where they gain
But the least footing, there they will remain.
How groundless are our hopes, how they deceive
Our childless thoughts, and only sorrow leave!

was once Aristeo, who loved Tirrena, Tirrena, who, like an angel in beauty,
yet seemed in her pride and cruelty to be a Libyan serpent, or a savage Ar-
menian tigress.

He lost his form [literally 'softened'], and through his love the miserable man
went mad, until, brought to death by the bitter fire, he turned to dust, and was
shut in the hour-glass by her.

O cruel and harsh fate of lovers! The burned remains are used again as they
were used before: in life they suffered, and in death they do not rest.

210

How real are our fears! they blast us still,
Still rend us, still with gnawing passions fill;
How senseless are our wishes, yet how great!
With what toil we pursue them, with what sweat!
Yet most times for our hurts, so small we see,
Like children crying for some Mercury.
This gapes for marriage, yet his fickle head
Knows not what cares wait on a marriage bed:
This vows virginity, yet knows not what
Loneness, grief, discontent, attends that state.
Desires of wealth another's wishes hold,
And yet how many have been chok'd with gold?
This only hunts for honour, yet who shall
Ascend the higher, shall more wretched fall.
This thirsts for knowledge, yet how is it bought?
With many a sleepless night, and racking thought.
This needs will travel, yet how dangers lay
Most secret ambuscados in tho way?
These triumph in their beauty, though it shall
Like a pluck'd rose or fading lily fall.
Another boasts strong arms: 'las! giants have
By silly dwarfs been dragg'd unto their grave.
These ruffle in rich silk: though ne'er so gay,
A well-plum'd peacock is more gay than they.
Poor man! what art? A tennis-ball of error,
A ship of glass toss'd in a sea of terror;
Issuing in blood and sorrow from the womb,
Crawling in tears and mourning to the tomb:
How slippery are thy paths! How sure thy fall!
How art thou nothing, when th' art most of all!

Sponde

SONNET

Helas! contez vos jours: les jours qui sont passez
Sont desjà morts pour vous, ceux qui viennent encore
Mourront tous sur le point de leur naissante Aurore,
Et moytie de la vie est moytie du décez.

Alas, count your days: the days which have passed are already dead for you,
those which still come will all die at the break of their nascent Dawn, and half of
life is half of death.

On Life, Time and Death

Ces désirs orgueilleux pesle-mesle entassez,
Ce coeur outrecuidé que vostre bras implore,
Cest indomptable bras que vostre coeur adore,
La Mort les met en geine, et leur fait le procez.

Mille flots, mille escueils, font teste à vostre route,
Vous rompez à travers, mais à la fin sans doubte
Vous serez le butin des escueils, et des flots.

Une heure vous attend, un moment vous espie,
Bourreaux desnaturez de vostre propre vie,
Qui vit avec la peine, et meurt sans le repos.

Góngora

De la brevedad engañosa de la vida

Menos solicitó veloz saeta
destinada señal, que mordió aguda;
agonal carro por la arena muda
no coronó con más silencio meta,
    que presurosa corre, que secreta
a su fin nuestra edad. A quien lo duda,
fiera que sea de razón desnuda,
cada sol repetido es un cometa.

These proud desires pell-mell piled together, this presumptuous heart which your arm implores, this indomitable arm which your heart adores, Death puts them in jeopardy, and then condemns them.

A thousand waves, a thousand reefs, frown on your journey, you break through, but in the end without doubt you will be the prize of the reefs and waves.

The hour waits for you, a moment spies on you, the unnatural executioners of your own life, which lives with pain, and dies without repose.

Of the deceitful brevity of life

No sooner sped the fast arrow to its destined target than it bit deep into it; the agonistic chariot [in the funeral games] did not round the mark through the mute sand with more silence

than our age swiftly and stealthily rushes to its end. Whoever doubts it would be a wild beast stripped of reason—every dawning sun is a comet [of ill-omen].

¿Confiésalo Cartago, y tú lo ignoras?
Peligro corres, Licio, si porfías
en seguir sombras y abrazar engaños.
　Mal te perdonarán a ti las horas;
las horas que limando están los días,
los días que royendo están los años.

Sponde

SONNET

　Mortels, qui des mortels avez prins vostre vie,
Vie qui meurt encor dans le tombeau du Corps:
Vous qui rammoncelez vos thrésors des thrésors
De ceux dont par la mort la vie fust ravie:

　Vous qui voyant de morts leur mort entresuyvie,
N'avez point de maisons que les maisons des morts,
Et ne sentez pourtant de la mort un remors,
D'ou vient qu'au souvenir son souvenir s'oublie?

　Est-ce que vostre vie adorant ses douceurs,
Déteste des pensers de la mort les horreurs,
Et ne puisse envier une contraire envie?

　Mortels, chacun accuse, et j'excuse le tort
Qu'on forge en vostre oubly. Un oubly d'une mort
Vous montre un souvenir d'une éternelle vie.

Does Carthage confess it, and you remain unaware of it? Licio, you are taking a risk, if you keep on chasing shadows and embracing deceptions.

The hours will scarcely forgive you, the hours which file down the days, the days which gnaw at the years.

Mortals, who have taken your life from [other] mortals, life always dying in the tomb of the body: you who pile up your treasures again from the treasures of those whose life was ravished by death:

You who seeing their death followed by [other deaths] have as your only houses the houses of the dead, and still do not feel remorse for death, how does it happen that in your memory memory of it is forgotten?

Is it that your life, in adoring its own sweetnesses, detests the horrors of the thoughts of death, and cannot covet a different kind of covetousness?

Mortals, everyone accuses, but I excuse the charge that is fabricated from your forgetfulness. A forgetfulness of one death offers you the memory of one eternal life.

Góngora

SONNET

En este occidental, en este, oh Licio,
climatérico lustro de tu vida,
todo mal afirmado pie es caída,
toda fácil caída es precipicio.
    ¿Caduca el paso? Ilústrese el juicio.
Desatándose va la tierra unida.
¿Qué prudencia, del polvo prevenida,
la rüina aguardó del edificio?
    La piel, no sólo sierpe venenosa,
mas con la piel los años se desnuda,
y el hombre no. ¡Ciego discurso humano!
    ¡Oh aquel dichoso, que, la ponderosa
porción depuesta en una piedra muda,
la leve da al zafiro soberano!

Carew

MARIA WENTWORTH

THOMAE COMITIS CLEVELAND FILIA PRAEMORTUA PRIMA VIRGINEAM
ANIMAM EXHALAVIT: ANNO DOMINI (1632). AETATIS SUAE

And here the precious dust is laid,
Whose purely temper'd clay was made
So fine, that it the guest betray'd.

In this occident, in this, O Licio, climacteric lustrum of your life, every badly placed footstep is a fall, every easy fall is a precipice.

Does the foot become weaker? Let the judgment become clearer. The unity of the world comes apart. What kind of prudence forewarned by dust waited for the ruin of the building?

A poisonous snake casts off not only its skin but, with its skin its years; not so man. Blind discourse of man!

Happy the man who, having resigned the weighty part of a life to a dumb stone, gives the lighter part to the sovereign sapphire!

Else the soul grew so fast within
It broke the outward shell of sin,
And so was hatch'd a cherubin.

In heighth it soar'd to God above;
In depth it did to knowledge move,
And spread in breadth to general love.

Before a pious duty shin'd
To parents; courtesy behind;
On either side, an equal mind.

Good to the poor, to kindred dear,
To servants kind, to friendship clear:
To nothing but herself severe.

So though a virgin, yet a bride
To every grace, she justifi'd
A chaste polygamy, and di'd.

Learn from hence, Reader, what small trust
We owe this world, where virtue must,
Frail as our flesh, crumble to dust.

Gryphius

GRABSCHRIFT MARIANAE GRYPHIAE
seines Bruders Pauli Töchterlein

Geboren in der Flucht, umringt mit Schwert und Brand,
Schier in dem Rauch erstickt, der Mutter herbes Pfand,
Des Vatern höchste Furcht, die an das Licht gedrungen,
Als die ergrimmte Glut mein Vaterland verschlungen—

EPITAPH ON MARIANA GRYPHIUS, HIS BROTHER PAUL'S SMALL DAUGHTER

Born during flight, surrounded by fire and sword, almost suffocated by smoke, my mother's bitter pledge, my father's greatest concern, I came into the world, as the grim conflagration had devoured my country. I looked upon this world

On Life, Time and Death

Ich habe diese Welt beschaut und bald gesegnet,
Weil mir auf einen Tag all Angst der Welt begegnet.
Wo ihr die Tage zählt, so bin ich jung verschwunden;
Sehr alt, wofern ihr schätzt, was ich für Angst empfunden.

Opitz

EINER JUNGFRAU GRABUEBERSCHRIFT

Du wurdest aus Befehl der Venus umgebracht,
Weil deine Zierlichkeit sie schamrot hat gemacht.

Crashaw

DEATH'S LECTURE AT THE FUNERAL OF A YOUNG
GENTLEMAN

Dear Reliques of a dislodg'd SOUL, whose lack
Makes many a mourning paper put on black!
O stay a while, ere thou draw in thy head
And wind thyself up close in thy cold bed.
Stay but a little while, untill I call
A summons worthy of thy funerall.
Come then, YOUTH, BEAUTY, & blood!
    All ye soft powres,
Whose sylken flatteryes swell a few fond howres
Into a false aeternity. Come man;
Hyperbolized NOTHING! know thy span;
Take thine own measure here: down, down, & bow
Before thy self in thine idaea; thou
Huge emptynes! contract thy self; & shrinke
All thy Wild circle to a point. O sink
Lower & lower yet; till thy leane size
Call heavn to look on thee with narrow eyes.

and soon bade it farewell, because in one day I encountered all the anguish of
the world. If you count days, I died young; and yet [I was] very old if you
consider the anguish I had felt.
[Mariana Gryphius was born on July 8, 1637, i.e. during the Thirty Years War,
at Freystadt. During the following night, Freystadt was completely destroyed
by a conflagration.]

A MAIDEN'S EPITAPH

You had to die at the command of Venus, because your charms had made her
blush with shame.

Lesser & lesser yet; till thou begin
To show a face, fitt to confesse thy Kin,
Thy neighbourhood to NOTHING.
Proud lookes, & lofty eyliddes, here putt on
Your selves in your unfaign'd reflexion,
Here, gallant ladyes! this unpartiall glasse
(Though you be painted) showes you your true face.
These death-seal'd lippes are they dare give the lie
To the lowd Boasts of poor Mortality;
These curtain'd windows, this retired eye
Outstares the liddes of larg-look't tyranny.
This posture is the brave one, this that lyes
Thus low, stands up (me thinkes) thus & defies
The world. All-daring dust & ashes! only you
Of all interpreters read Nature true.

Von Logau

EPIGRAMS

DER TOD

Der sich nicht zu sterben fürchtet, der sich nicht zu leben schämet,
Dieser sorgt nicht, wie und wanne sich sein Sterben ihm bequemet.

DAS BESTE VON DER WELT

Weist du, was in dieser Welt
Mir am meisten wohlgefällt?
Dass die Zeit sich selbst verzehret
Und die Welt nicht ewig währet.

DEATH

He who is not afraid to die and not ashamed to live, does not worry how and
when it will suit death to come to him.

THE BEST THING IN THE WORLD

Do you know what I like best in this world? That time consumes itself, and that
the world is not going to last forever.

Sponde

SONNET

Et quel bien de la Mort? où la vermine ronge
Tous ces nerfs, tous ces os? où l'Ame se depart
De ceste orde charogne, et se tient à l'escart
Et laisse un souvenir de nous comme d'un songe?

Ce Corps, qui dans la vie en ses grandeurs se plonge,
Si soudain dans la mort estouffera sa part,
Et sera ce beau Nom, qui tant partout s'espard,
Borné de Vanité, couronné de Mensonge.

A quoy ceste Ame, hélas! et ce corps désunis
Du commerce du monde hors du monde bannis?
A quoy ces noeuds si beaux que le Trespas deslie?

Pour vivre au Ciel il faut mourir plustost ici:
Ce n'en est pas pourtant le sentier raccourcy,
Mais quoy? nous n'avons plus ny d'Hénoch, ni d'Elie.

Gombauld

JE VOGUE SUR LA MER

Je vogue sur la mer où mon ame craintive,
Aux jours les plus sereins, void les vents se lever.
Pour vaincre leurs efforts, j'ay beau les observer,
Ma force, ou ma prudence, est ou foible, ou tardive.

And what good comes of death? where vermin gnaw all these nerves and bones?
where the Soul leaves this carcass of dirt, stands apart, and leaves a memory of
us like [a memory] of a dream.

This Body, which in life plunges into its greatnesses, will have its function so
quickly stifled in death, and this good Name, so much acclaimed everywhere,
will be bounded by Vanity, crowned with Lies.

Why should this Soul, alas, and this body, disunited by the commerce of the
world, be banished from the world? To what end are these beautiful knots
which Death unties?

To live in Heaven, one has first to die here: but still the road is no shorter for
that, but why? we have no more Enochs or Elijahs. [These prophets were
elevated to Heaven without having undergone physical death.]

I SAIL ON THE SEA

I sail on the sea where my fearful soul, on the most serene days, [still] sees the
winds rising. To defeat their attacks, in spite of all my watching, my strength, or
my wisdom, is either feeble or late.

Je me laisse emporter à l'onde fugitive,
Parmy tous les dangers qui peuvent arriver,
Où tant d'hommes divers se vont perdre, ou sauver,
Et dont la seule mort est le fonds, ou la rive.

Le monde est cette mer, où pour me divertir,
Dans un calme incertain, j'escoute retentir
Les accens enchanteurs des perfides sirenes.

C'est lors que la frayeur me fait tout redouter;
Que je voy les escueils, que je voy les arenes,
Et le gouffre où le Ciel me va precipiter.

Southwell

SINNES HEAVIE LOADE

O Lord my sinne doth over-charge thy brest,
    The poyse thereof doth force thy knees to bow;
Yea flat thou fallest with my faults opprest,
    And bloody sweat runs trickling from thy brow:
But had they not to earth thus pressed thee,
Much more they would in hell have pestred mee.

This Globe of earth doth thy one finger prop,
    The world thou doo'st within thy hand embrace;
Yet all this waight of sweat drew not a drop,
    Ne made thee bow, much lesse fall on thy face:
But now thou hast a loade so heavy found,
That makes thee bow, yea flat fall to the ground.

O sinne, how huge and heavie is thy waight,
    Thou wayest more then all the world beside,
Of which when Christ had taken in his fraight
    The poyse thereof his flesh could not abide;
Alas, if God himselfe sinke under sinne,
What will become of man that dies therein?

I let myself be carried by the fugitive wave, among all the dangers that may chance, where so many divers men go to death or to safety, and of which death alone is the bottom, or shore.

The world is that sea, where to amuse me, in an uncertain calm, I hear re-echo the enchanting accents of perfidious sirens.

It is then that terror makes me dread everything, when I see the rocks, when I see the sands, and the abyss where heaven is going to throw me.

First, flat thou fel'st, when earth did thee receave,
    In closet pure of Maries virgin brest;
And now thou fall'st of earth to take thy leave,
    Thou kissest it as cause of thy unrest:
O loving Lorde that so doost love thy foe,
As thus to kisse the ground where he doth goe.

Thou minded in thy heaven our earth to weare,
    Doo'st prostrate now thy heaven our earth to blisse;
As God, to earth thou often wert severe,
    As man, thou seal'st a peace with bleeding kisse:
For as of soules thou common Father art,
So is she Mother of mans other part.

She shortly was to drink thy dearest blood,
    And yeeld thy soule a way to sathans cave;
She shortly was thy corse in tombe to shrowd,
    And with them all thy deitie to have:
Now then in one thou joyntly yeeldest all,
That severally to earth should shortly fall.

O prostrate Christ, erect my crooked minde,
    Lord let thy fall my flight from earth obtaine;
Or if I still in earth must needes be shrinde,
    Then Lord on earth come fall yet once againe:
And eyther yeeld with me in earth to lie,
Or else with thee to take me to the skie.

Donne

SONNET

Death be not proud, though some have called thee
Mighty and dreadfull, for, thou art not soe,
For, those, whom thou think'st, thou dost overthrow,
Die not, poore death, nor yet canst thou kill mee;
From rest and sleepe, which but thy pictures bee,
Much pleasure, then from thee, much more must flow,
And soonest our best men with thee doe goe,
Rest of their bones, and soules deliverie.
Thou art slave to Fate, Chance, kings, and desperate men,
And dost with poyson, warre, and sicknesse dwell,
And poppie, or charmes can make us sleepe as well,
And better then thy stroake; why swell'st thou then?
One short sleepe past, wee wake eternally,
And death shall be no more, Death thou shalt die.

The Love of God

> O sacred Fire come shewe thy force on me
> That sacrifice to Christe I maye retorne,
> If withered wood for fuell fittest bee,
> If stones and dust, if fleshe and blood will burne,
> I withered am and stonye to all good,
> A sacke of dust, a masse of flesh and bloode.[1]

In these words Southwell prays for the fire of the Lord to come and relieve his sufferings. He can hope for no salvation arising from his own actions, and can see no value or creativity in the virtues of others ('I withered am and stonye to *all* good'); however he knows that the whole body of earth is combustible by the fire of God's power, will one day be burned by God the Judge, and therefore, since he too is earth ('a sacke of dust') and body ('a *masse* of flesh and bloode') he too can implore release from the terrible emptiness of human time and life.

> Esta vida que yo vivo
> Es privación de vivir;
> Y así, es contino morir
> Hasta que vivo contigo.
> Oye, mi Dios, lo que digo,
> Que esta vida no la quiero;
> Que muero porque no muero.[2]

San Juan's paradox ('muero porque no muero') defines the major cause of his awareness of the emptiness of his existence: so great is his yearning for God that life separated from Him is a form of death, and death alone can give him life. God, though always present, is absent from *this* world, exists in a timeless perfection to which the poet aspires, and which the poem itself may partly help him to reach.

> fosti sempre e sarai; ma propriamente
> l'infinito esser tuo no fu, né fia:
> sempre, astratto dai secoli, presente.

[1] See p. 264.   [2] See p. 226.

The Love of God

> Se tenta il volo inaccessibil via,
> tu le forze avvalora, e si sostente
> su lo spirito tuo la penna mia.[1]

Gaudiosi's confidence and trust cope with the fact of God's being *astratto dai secoli* (absent from the centuries) and his clear elegance lacks the urgency and drama of San Juan. Of all the poets represented here only two, George Herbert and Sor Juana, can maintain a poetic style sufficiently versatile to encompass the two tones, the dramatic, questioning, agonized turbulence of the flesh and emotion, and the trust that such painful energy can be turned into harmonious love:

> I know the wayes of Pleasure, the sweet strains,
> The lullings and the relishes of it;
> The propositions of hot bloud and brains;
> What mirth and music mean; what love and wit
> Have done these twentie hundred yeares, and more;
> I know the projects of unbridled store:
> My stuffe is flesh, not brasse; my senses live
> And grumble oft, that they have more in me
> Than he that curbs them, being but one to five:
>   Yet I love thee.[2]

and:

> Muero ¿quién lo creerá?, a manos
> de la cosa que más quiero,
> y el motivo de matarme
> es el amor que le tengo.
>   Así alimentando, triste,
> la vida con el veneno,
> la misma muerte que vivo,
> es la vida con que muero.
>   Pero valor, corazón:
> porque en tan dulce tormento,
> en medio de cualquier suerte
> no dejar de amar protesto.[3]

The use of paradox, often a mere cleverness in the love-poetry of the period, is an integral part of the religious verse. Many of the poems deal either directly or indirectly with the central paradoxes of the Christian religion, the Incarnation, that blissful moment when God became man and man God, and the Passion, when by suffering and dying Jesus conquered suffering and death. Gryphius in his sonnet on the birth of Jesus calls the

[1] See p. 240. [2] See pp. 237–8. [3] See p. 236.

night of His birth brighter than day, for through this night the nights of ignorance and pain are conquered, and our normal time of nights and days has become infinity:

> Der Zeit und Nächte schuf, ist diese Nacht ankommen
> Und hat das Recht der Zeit und Fleisch an sich genommen
> Und unser Fleisch und Zeit der Ewigkeit vermacht.
> Die jammertrübe Nacht, die schwarze Nacht der Sünden,
> Des Grabes Dunkelheit muss durch die Nacht verschwinden.
> Nacht, lichter als der Tag! Nacht, mehr denn lichte Nacht![1]

and, more extravagantly still, Crashaw combines the symbols of crucifix and flood to prove that the deluge of Christ's blood will save us from drowning in our own sins, and then adds the further refinement that the flood-water (blood) is a new creation, a baptism:

> Rain-swoln rivers may rise proud,
> Bent all to drown and overflow.
> But when indeed all's overflow'd
> They themselves are drowned too.
>
> This thy blood's deluge, a dire chance
> Dear Lord to thee, to us is found
> A deluge of Deliverance;
> A deluge lest we should be drown'd.
>
> N'ere was thou in a sense so sadly true,
> The WELL of living WATERS, Lord till now.[2]

Such ingenuity strives to present a vision of human nature transformed, enlarged into an other-world of eternal significance. Each action of man, finite, contingent, limited, may, by the operation of God, become infinite, essential, boundless; every human emotion may be touched by God, turned into its obverse, its other and deeper meaning; and awareness of these oppositions, together with awareness of the limitations of human freedom and love, drive Donne to ask God to imprison him into liberty, rape him into chastity,

> Take mee to you, imprison mee, for I
> Except you'enthrall mee, never shall be free,
> Nor even chaste, except you ravish me.[3]

Milton's 'At a Solemn Music'[4] hymns the great state of universal concord before sin, praying for that concord to return and drive out the

[1] See p. 243. [2] See p. 263. [3] See p. 265.
[4] See p. 247.

oppositions and paradoxes of fallen man; Sor Juana's 'Romance on the Nativity' explores the perfect interdependence of Christ and Mary through the symbols of the bee and the lily [1]; Le Moyne rhapsodizes on the operation of Divine Love which orders the universe [2]; and Vaughan ecstatically visualizes the moment when a 'vision of nature' and 'the love of God' become the same:

> In what Rings,
> And *Hymning Circulations* the quick world
> Awakes and sings,
> The rising winds
> And fallen springs,
> Birds, beasts, all things
> Adore him in their kinds.
> Thus all is hurl'd
> In sacred *Hymnes* and *Order*, The great *Chime*
> And Symphony of nature.[3]

What we know (our historical present) may be illusory, and what we believe (our faith) may be painful to understand, difficult to grasp, impossible to live up to, and certainly in perpetual conflict with our desires, but the possibility of a harmony between the two, and hence of a harmony between ourselves and nature, is the final theme of the baroque poets. But the last poem in the book sombrely rejects ecstasy and hope. In stoic vein Fulke Greville proffers advice and warning, and, along with them, a vision of nature which is much closer to the visions of succeeding ages, and even to our own:

> Man should make much of life, as Nature's table,
> Wherein she writes the cypher of her glory.
> Forsake not Nature, nor misunderstand her:
> Her mysteries are read without faith's eyesight:
> She speaketh in our flesh; and from our senses,
> Delivers down her wisdoms to our reason.
> If any man would break her laws to kill,
> Nature doth, for defence, allow offences.
> She neither taught the father to destroy:
> Nor promis'd any man, by dying, joy.[4]

[1] See p. 247.   [2] See p. 252.   [3] See p. 270.
[4] See p. 273.

La Ceppède

BLANC

Blanc est le vestement du grand Pere sans âge,
Blancs sont les courtisans de sa blanche maison,
Blanc est de son esprit l'étincelant pennage;
Blanche est de son agneau la brillante toison.

Blanc est le crespe sainct dont (pour son cher blason)
Aux nopces de L'Agneau L'Espouse s'advantage.
Blanc est or' le manteau dont par mesme raison
Cet innocent Espous se pare en son nopçage.

Blanc estoit l'ornement, dont le pontife vieux
S'affeubloit pour devot offrir ses vœux aux cieux;
Blanc est le parement de ce nouveau grand Prestre.

Blanche est la robe deüe au fort victorieux.
Ce vainqueur (bien qu'il aille à la mort se souzmettre)
Blanc, sur la dure mort triomphe glorieux.

Von Grimmelshausen

DAS FINSTRE LICHT

Ach allerhöchstes Gut! du wohnest so im finstern Licht!
Dass man vor Klarheit gross den grossen Glanz kann sehen nicht.

WHITE

White is the raiment of the almighty and ageless Father; white are the courtiers of his white house, white is the shining plumage of his spirit, white is the brilliant fleece of his lamb.

White is the holy robe with which (as her precious emblem) the Spouse adorns herself on her marriage to the Lamb. White is now the cloak with which for the same reason this innocent Husband appears on his nuptials.

White was the adornment with which the old pontiff grew weak to offer, devout, his prayers to the heavens; white is the attire of our new High Priest.

White is the robe owed to him who is mighty and victorious. This victor (although he goes to submit himself to death), white, triumphs in glory over harsh death.

THE DARK LIGHT

Ah, supreme good! You dwell in the dark light so that for great brightness we cannot see your powerful splendour.

San Juan de la Cruz

Coplas del alma que pena por ver a Dios

Vivo sin vivir en mí,
Y de tal manera espero,
Que muero porque no muero.

En mí yo no vivo ya,
Y sin Dios vivir no puedo;
Pues sin él y sin mí quedo,
Este vivir ¿qué será?
Mil muertes se me hará,
Pues mi misma vida espero,
Muriendo porque no muero.

Esta vida que yo vivo
Es privación de vivir;
Y así, es contino morir
Hasta que viva contigo.
Oye, mi Dios, lo que digo,
Que esta vida no la quiero;
Que muero porque no muero.

Estando absente de ti,
¿Qué vida puedo tener,
Sino muerte padescer,
La mayor que nunca vi?
Lástima tengo de mí,
Pues de suerte persevero,
Que muero porque no muero.

Coplas of the soul which pines to see God

I live without living in myself, and my hope is such that I am dying because I do not die.

I do not live in myself now; and I cannot live without God; and since I am deprived of Him and me, this life, what is it? It will become for me a thousand deaths, since I am hoping for my own true life, dying because I do not die.

This life I live is a deprivation of living; and thus it is a continual death until I live with You. Hear me, my God, hear what I say, for I do not want this life; I am dying because I do not die.

Being absent from You, what Life can I have without suffering the greatest death I ever saw? I pity myself, because I persevere in such a way that I die because I do not die.

El pez que del agua sale,
Aun de alivio no caresce,
Que en la muerte que padesce,
Al fin la muerte le vale.
¿Qué muerte habrá que se iguale
A mi vivir lastimero,
Pues si más vivo más muero?

Cuando me pienso aliviar
De verte en el Sacramento,
Háceme más sentimiento
El no te poder gozar;
Todo es para más penar,
Por no verte como quiero,
Y muero porque no muero.

Y si me gozo, Señor,
Con esperanza de verte,
En ver que puedo perderte
Se me dobla mi dolor:
Viviendo en tanto pavor,
Y esperando como espero,
Muérome porque no muero.

Sácame de aquesta muerte,
Mi Dios, y dame la vida;
No me tengas impedida
En este lazo tan fuerte;
Mira que peno por verte,
Y mi mal es tan entero,
Que muero porque no muero.

The fish that comes out of water does not lack some sort of relief, for the death which he suffers in the end avails him. What death can there be to equal my pitiful life, since the longer I live the more I die?

When I think I will alleviate my pain through seeing You in the Sacrament, not being able to enjoy You makes more suffering for me; since I do not see You as I want to, everything is more anguish to me, and I am dying because I do not die.

And if I rejoice, Lord, in the hope of seeing You, seeing that I can lose You doubles my grief; living in so much fear, and hoping with such great hope, I am dying because I do not die.

Rescue me from this death, my God, and give me life; do not keep me in such a powerful bond; see how I pine to see You, and how my pain is so total that I am dying because I do not die.

The Love of God

Lloraré mi muerte ya,
Y lamentaré mi vida
En tanto que detenida
Por mis pecados está.
¡Oh mi Dios! ¿cuándo será?
Cuando yo diga de vero:
Vivo ya porque no muero.

Kuhlmann

UNIO MYSTICA (62. Kuhlpsalm, II)
[Kühlpsalm is a pun on the author's name]

Recht dunkelt mich das Dunkel,
Weil Wesenheit so heimlichst anbeginnt!
O seltner Glückskarfunkel!
Es strömt, was äusserlich verrinnt,
Und wird ein Meer, was kaum ein Bächlein gründt.

Je dunkler, je mehr lichter:
Je schwärzer A.L.L.S., je weisser weisst sein Sam.
Ein himmlisch Aug ist Richter:
Kein Irdscher lebt, der was vernahm;
Es glänzt je mehr, je finster' es ankam.

Ach Nacht! Und Nacht, die taget!
O Tag, der Nacht vernünftiger Vernunft!
Ach Licht, das Kaine plaget
Und helle strahlt der Abelzunft!
Ich freue mich ob deiner finstern Kunft.

I shall mourn my death now, and I shall lament my life while it is prolonged because of my sins. O my God, when will it be, when will I truly say: 'I live because I am not dying'?

Darkness darkens me rightly, because thus essence begins most secretly! O rare carbuncle of fortune! What trickles away outwardly, now streams, and what hardly makes up a brook becomes an ocean.
   The darker the lighter: the blacker A.L.L., the whiter whitens its seed. A heavenly eye is judge: no mortal lives who perceived anything of it; it shines the more, the darker it approached.
   Ah night! And night that becomes day! O day, of night the reasonable reason! Ah light that torments Cain and shines brightly on the Abelclan! I rejoice at your dark coming.

O längst erwart'tes Wunder,
Das durch den Kern des ganzen Baums auswächst!
Du fängst neu Edens Zunder,
Ei, Lieber, sieh, mein Herze lechzt!
Es ist genug! Hör wie es innig ächzt!

O unaussprechlichst Blauen!
O lichtste Röt! O übergelbes Weiss!
Es bringt, was ewigst, schauen,
Beerdt die Erd als Paradeis;
Entflucht den Fluch, durchsegnet jeden Reis.

O Erdvier! Welches Strahlen!
Der Finsterst ist als vor die lichtste Sonn.
Kristallisiertes Prahlen!
Die Welt bewonnt die Himmelswonn:
Sie quillt zurück, als wäre sie der Bronn.

Welch wesentliches Bildnis?
Erscheinst du so, geheimste Kraftfigur?
Wie richtigst, was doch Wildnis?
O was vor Zahl? Ach welche Spur?
Du bists, nicht ich! Dein ist Natur und Kur!

Die Kron ist ausgefüllet,
Die Tausend sind auch ueberall ersetzt:
Geschehen, was umhüllet;
Sehr hoher Röt, höchst ausgeätzt,
Dass alle Kunst an ihr sich ausgewetzt.

O long expected miracle which grows through the core of the entire tree. You capture anew Eden's tinder. Ah, dear love, see how my heart languishes! It is enough! Listen, how it sighs within me!

O most ineffable blue-becoming! O brightest redness! O more than yellow white! It brings to beholding what is most eternal, earthing the earth as paradise, uncursing the curse, through blessing every twig.

O square of earth! What radiance! the darkest is as was the brightest sun. Crystal brilliance! Heavenly bliss blesses and fills the world with joy: it wells back as if it were the source.

What essential image? Do you manifest yourself thus, most mysterious figure of strength? How do you right what is a wilderness? O what number? Ah, which trace? It is you, not I. Yours is nature as well as choice!

The crown is complete, the thousand are replaced everywhere; what [was] concealed, has happened; intensest red, so sublimely etched that all art is blunted beside it.

The Love of God

Die Lilien und Rosen
Sind durch sechs Tag gebrochen spat und früh:
Sie kränzen mit Liebkosen
Nun dich und mich aus deiner Müh.
Dein Will ist mein, mein Will ist dein, vollzieh.

Im jesuelschen Schimmer
Pfeiln wir zugleich zur jesuelschen Kron:
Der Stolz ist durch dich nimmer!
Er liegt zu Fuss im höchsten Hohn.
Ein ander ist mit dir der Erb und Sohn.

VERZUECKUNG

Hosanntriumph! Werd ich im Geist verzückt!
Halleluja! Ist Christi Reich geschmückt?
Auf, Heilgen, auf, zum Moses, Lammes Lied!
Auf, Patriarchen, auf! Auf Zwölfapostelstühle!
Auf, auf! Auf, harft in allgemeinem Fried!
Der grosse Welttag ist nun in der Abendkühle.
Auf, allgemeines Bruderheer!
Auf, harft mit mir am gläsern Meer!
Auf, lobet und preiset und danket dem Herrn,
Im Himmel, auf Erden, von nahe und fern!

The lilies and roses have been picked from morning till night for six days; caressingly they now crown you and me out of your pain. Your will is mine, my will is yours: accomplish [it].

In Jesuelic radiance we arrow together towards the Jesuelic crown: through you pride is no more! It lies on the ground—covered with deepest shame. Another is heir and son with you.

ECSTASY

Hosannatriumph! Ecstasy fills my spirit! Halleluia! Is Christ's realm adorned? Arise, saints, arise, on towards Moses, song of the lamb! Arise, you patriarchs, arise! Arise twelvapostlechairs! Arise, arise! Arise, and harp in universal peace! The great world day is now in the cool of the evening. Arise, universal army of brothers! Arise, harp with me by the glassy shores! Arise, praise and glorify and thank the Lord, in heaven, on earth, from near and far!

230

Crashaw

THE FLAMING HEART
UPON THE BOOK AND PICTURE OF THE SERAPHICALL SAINT TERESA

Well meaning readers! you that come as freinds
And catch the pretious name this peice pretends;
Make not too much hast to' admire
That fair-cheek't fallacy of fire.
That is a SERAPHIM, they say
And this the great TERESIA.
Readers, be rul'd by me; & make
Here a well-plac't & wise mistake
You must transpose the picture quite,
And spell it wrong to read it right;
Read HIM for her, & her for him;
And call the SAINT the SERAPHIM.
    Painter, what didst thou understand
To put her dart into his hand!
See, euen the yeares & size of him
Showes this the mother SERAPHIM.
This is the mistresse flame; & duteous he
Her happy fire-works, here, comes down to see.
O most poor-spirited of men!
Had thy cold Pencil kist her PEN
Thou couldst not so unkindly err
To show us This faint shade for HER.
Why man, this speakes pure mortall frame;
And mockes with female FROST love's manly flame.
One would suspect thou meant'st to paint
Some weak, inferiour, woman saint.
But had thy pale-fac't purple took
Fire from the burning cheeks of that bright Booke
Thou wouldst on her have heap't up all
That could be found SERAPHICALL;
What e're this youth of fire weares fair,
Rosy fingers, radiant hair,
Glowing cheek, & glistering wings,
All those fair & flagrant things,
But before all, that fiery DART
Had fill'd the Hand of this great HEART.
    Doe then as equall right requires,
Since HIS the blushes be, & her's the fires,
Resume & rectify thy rude design;
Undresse thy Seraphim into MINE.

Redeem this injury of thy art;
Give HIM the vail, give her the dart.
　Give Him the vail; that he may cover
The Red cheeks of a rivall'd lover.
Asham'd that our world, now, can show
Nests of new Seraphims here below.
　Give her the DART for it is she
(Fair youth) shootes both thy shaft & THEE
Say, all ye wise & well-peirc't hearts
That live & dy amidst her darts,
What is't your tastfull spirits doe prove
In that rare life of Her, and love?
Say & bear wittnes. Sends she not
A SERAPHIM at every shott?
What magazines of immortall ARMES there shine!
Heavn's great artillery in each love-spun line.
Give then the dart to her who gives the flame;
Give him the veil, who kindly takes the shame.
　But if it be the frequent fate
Of worst faults to be fortunate;
If all's præscription; & proud wrong
Hearkens not to an humble song;
For all the gallantry of him,
Give me the suffring SERAPHIM.
His be the bravery of all those Bright things,
The glowing cheekes, the glistering wings;
The Rosy hand, the radiant DART;
Leave HER alone THE FLAMING HEART.
　Leave her that; & thou shalt leave her
Not one loose shaft but love's whole quiver.
For in love's feild was never found
A nobler weapon then a WOUND.
Love's passives are his activ'st part.
The wounded is the wounding heart.
O HEART! the æquall poise of love's both parts
Bigge alike with wounds & darts.
Live in these conquering leaves; live all the same;
And walk through all tongues one triumphant FLAME
Live here, great HEART; & love and dy & kill;
And bleed & wound; and yeild & conquer still.
Let this immortall life wherere it comes
Walk in a crowd of loves & MARTYRDOMES.
Let mystick DEATHS wait on't; & wise soules be
The love-slain wittnesses of this life of thee.
O sweet incendiary! shew here thy art,
Upon this carcasse of a hard, cold, hart,

Let all thy scatter'd shafts of light, that play
Among the leaves of thy larg Books of day,
Combin'd àgainst this BREST at once break in
And take away from me my self & sin.
This gratious Robbery shall thy bounty be;
And my best fortunes such fair spoiles of me.
O thou undanted daughter of desires!
By all thy dowr of LIGHTS & FIRES;
By all the eagle in thee, all the dove;
By all thy lives & deaths of love;
By thy larg draughts of intellectuall day,
And by thy thirsts of love more large then they;
By all thy brim-fill'd Bowles of feirce desire
By thy last Morning's draught of liquid fire;
By the full kingdome of that finall kisse
That seiz'd thy parting Soul, & seal'd thee his;
By all the heav'ns thou hast in him
(Fair sister of the SERAPHIM)
By all of HIM we have in THEE;
Leave nothing of my SELF in me.
Let me so read thy life, that I
Unto all life of mine may dy.

Sor Juana

En que expresa los efectos del Amor Divino, y propone morir amante, a pesar de todo riesgo

Traigo conmigo un cuidado,
y tan esquivo, que creo
que, aunque sé sentirlo tanto,
aun yo misma no lo siento.

  Es amor; pero es amor
que, faltándole lo ciego,
los ojos que tiene, son
para darle más tormento.

In which she expresses the effects of divine love, and despite all risks proposes to die a lover

I carry with me a care, and such an elusive care that I believe, although I know so well how to feel it, I myself do not feel it.

  It is love but it is love which lacking blindness has eyes only to give it more torment.

233

The Love of God

El término no es *a quo*,
que causa el pesar que veo:
que siendo el término el Bien,
todo el dolor es el medio.

Si es lícito, y aun debido
este cariño que tengo,
¿por qué me han de dar castigo
porque pago lo que debo?

¡Oh cuánta fineza, oh cuántos
cariños he visto tiernos!
Que amor que se tiene en Dios,
es calidad sin opuestos.

De lo lícito ni puede
hacer contrarios conceptos,
con que es amor que al olvido
no puede vivir expuesto.

Yo me acuerdo, ¡oh nunca fuera!,
que he querido en otro tiempo
lo que pasó de locura
y lo que excedió de extremo;

mas como era amor bastardo,
y de contrarios compuesto,
fué fácil desvanecerse
de achaque de su sér mesmo.

Mas ahora, ¡ay de mí!, está
tan en su natural centro,
que la virtud y razón
son quien aviva su incendio.

The terminus which causes the sorrow I see is not *a quo*; for since good is its end all grief is the means.

If this tenderness I feel is lawful, and even obligatory, why should I be punished for paying what I owe?

O how much delicacy, how many tendernesses have I seen! For the love which we feel for God is a quality which has no opposites.

From the lawful one cannot deduce contradictory concepts and so it follows that this is a love which cannot live subject to forgetfulness.

I remember, alas, that some time ago I sought [a love] which out-ran madness and exceeded the extremes;

but since it was a bastard love composed of contraries it was easy for it to vanish away from the very suffering of being itself.

But now, alas, it is so clearly fixed in its natural centre that both virtue and reason themselves fan its flames.

Quien tal oyere, dirá
que, si es así, ¿por qué peno?
Mas mi corazón ansioso
dirá que por eso mesmo.

¡Oh humana flaqueza nuestra,
adonde el más puro afecto
aun no sabe desnudarse
del natural sentimiento!

Tan precisa es la apetencia
que a ser amados tenemos,
que, aun sabiendo que no sirve,
nunca dejarla sabemos.

Que corresponda a mi amor,
nada añade; mas no puedo,
por más que lo solicito,
dejar yo de apetecerlo.

Si es delito, ya lo digo;
si es culpa, ya la confieso;
mas no puedo arrepentirme,
por más que hacerlo pretendo.

Bien ha visto, quien penetra
lo interior de mis secretos,
que yo misma estoy formando
los dolores que padezco.

Bien sabe que soy yo misma
verdugo de mis deseos,
pues muertos entre mis ansias,
tienen sepulcro en mi pecho.

Whoever hears this will say, if it is so, why do I suffer? But my anxious heart will say, for that very reason.

O our human frailty! Whence comes it that the purest emotion still does not know how to rid itself of natural sentiment?

The desire which we have to be loved is so demanding that even though we know it won't work we never know how to leave it.

That my love is requited in no way helps; for however much I struggle I cannot stop myself from desiring it.

If it is a crime, I admit it; if a sin I confess it; but I cannot repent even when I try to do so.

He who has penetrated the interior of my secrets can well see that I myself am creating the griefs I suffer from.

He well understands that I myself am the executioner of my desires for, when they are dead at the hands of my despairs, they are sepulchred in my bosom.

The Love of God

Muero, ¿quién lo creerá?, a manos
de la cosa que más quiero,
y el motivo de matarme
es el amor que le tengo.
    Así alimentando, triste,
la vida con el veneno,
la misma muerte que vivo,
es la vida con que muero.
    Pero valor, corazón:
porque en tan dulce tormento,
en medio de cualquier suerte
no dejar de amar protesto.

Gryphius

AN GOTT DEN HEILIGEN GEIST

O Feuer wahrer Lieb! O Brunn der guten Gaben!
O Meister aller Kunst! O höchste Heiligkeit!
O dreimal grosser Gott! O Lust, die alles Leid
Vertreibt! O keusche Taub! O Furcht der Höllenraben!

Die, eh das wüste Meer mit Bergen rings umgraben,
Ehr Luft und Erden ward, eh das gestirnte Kleid
Dem Himmel angelegt, vor Anbeginn der Zeit,
Die zwei, die ganz dir gleich, von sich gelassen haben!

I die, who will believe it, at the hands of the very thing I most desire and the motive for killing me is my own love.

So, sadly, feeding my life with poison, the same death I live is the life I die.

But courage, heart; I swear not to give up loving since I am in such a sweet torment, in the midst of whatever fortune does to me.

TO GOD THE HOLY GHOST

O fire of true love, O well of wholesome gifts! O master of all art! O supreme holiness! O thrice great God! O pleasure which drives away all suffering! O chaste dove! O terror of hell's ravens!

Those who, before the wild ocean was surrounded by mountains, before there were air and earth, before heaven had been dressed in its star-studded robe, before the beginning of time, those two, totally like you, who parted from each other!

O Weisheit ohne Mass! O reiner Seelen Gast!
O teure Gnadenquell! O Trost in herber Last!
O Regen, der in Angst mit Segen uns befeuchtet!

Ach lass ein Tröpflein nur von deinem Lebenstau
Erfrischen meinen Geist! Hilf, dass ich doch nur schau
Ein Fünklein deiner Glut! So bin ich ganz erleuchtet.

George Herbert

THE PEARL

I know the wayes of Learning; both the head
And pipes that feed the presse, and make it runne;
What reason hath from nature borrowed,
Or of it self, like a good huswife, spunne
In laws and policie; what the starres conspire,
What willing nature speaks, what forc'd by fire;
Both th' old discoveries, and the new-found seas,
The stock and surplus, cause and historie:
　　　　　　　　　　Yet I love thee.

I know the wayes of Honour, what maintains
The quick returns of courtesie and wit:
In vies of favours whether partie gains,
When glorie swells the heart, and moldeth it
To all expressions both of hand and eye,
Which on the world a true-love-knot may tie,
And bear the bundle, wheresoe're it goes:
How many drammes of spirit there must be
To sell my life unto my friends or foes:
　　　　　　　　　　Yet I love thee.

I know the wayes of Pleasure, the sweet strains,
The lullings and the relishes of it;
The propositions of hot bloud and brains;
What mirth and musick mean; what love and wit
Have done these twentie hundred yeares, and more:
I know the projects of unbridled store:

O wisdom without bounds! O guest of pure souls! O precious well of grace!
O solace of heavy burden! O rain which moistens us with blessing when we are
anguished!

Ah, let a small drop of your vital dew refresh my spirit! Help me so that I may
glimpse but a spark of your fire! Then I shall be wholly illumined.

The Love of God

My stuffe is flesh, not brasse; my senses live
And grumble oft, that they have more in me
Then he that curbs them, being but one to five:
                Yet I love thee.

I know all these, and have them in my hand:
Therefore not sealed, but with open eyes
I flie to thee, and fully understand
Both the main sale, and the commodities;
And at what rate and price I have thy love;
With all the circumstances that may move:
Yet through these labyrinths, not my groveling wit,
But thy silk twist let down from heav'n to me,
Did both conduct and teach me, how by it
                To climbe to thee.

DENIALL

When my devotions could not pierce
            Thy silent eares;
Then was my heart broken, as was my verse:
   My breast was full of fears
            And disorder:

My bent thoughts, like a brittle bow,
            Did flie asunder:
Each took his way; some would to pleasures go,
   Some to the warres and thunder
            Of alarms.

As good go any where, they say,
            As to benumme
Both knees and heart, in crying night and day,
   Come, come, my God, O come,
            But no hearing.

O that thou shouldst give dust a tongue
            To crie to thee
And then not heare it crying! all day long
   My heart was in my knee,
            But no hearing.

Therefore my soul lay out of sight,
                    Untun'd, unstrung:
My feeble spirit, unable to look right,
          Like a nipt blossome, hung
                    Discontented.

O cheer and tune my heartlesse breast,
                    Deferre no time;
That so thy favours granting my request,
          They and my minde may chime,
                    And mend my ryme.

THE COLLAR

I struck the board, and cry'd, No more.
                    I will abroad.
What? Shall I ever sigh and pine?
My lines and life are free; free as the rode,
     Loose as the winde, as large as store.
               Shall I be still in suit?
Have I no harvest but a thorn
To let me bloud, and not restore
What I have lost with cordiall fruit?
               Sure there was wine
Before my sighs did drie it: there was corn
               Before my tears did drown it.
     Is the yeare onely lost to me?
               Have I no bayes to crown it?
No flowers, no garlands gay? all blasted?
               All wasted?
Not so, my heart: but there is fruit,
               And thou hast hands.
Recover all thy sigh-blown age
On double pleasures: leave thy cold dispute
Of what is fit, and not. Forsake thy cage,
               Thy rope of sands,
Which pettie thoughts have made, and made to thee
     Good cable, to enforce and draw,
               And be thy law
While thou didst wink and wouldst not see.
               Away; take heed:
               I will abroad.
Call in thy deaths head there: tie up thy fears.
               He that forbears
               To suit and serve his need,
                    Deserves his load.

The Love of God

But as I rav'd and grew more fierce and wilde
                    At every word,
Me thoughts I heard one calling, *Child !*
                    And I reply'd, *My Lord.*

Gaudiosi

DE LE GRANDEZZE DI DIO

Ignoto Dio ch'in ogni parte splendi,
che senza loco in ogni loco stai,
tu che, non mosso, il movimento dai,
che compreso non sei, tutto comprendi;
    tu che 'n ciel regni e negli abissi stendi
l'essenza tua non circoscritta mai;
unica luce in triplicati rai,
che non sei foco e l'universo accendi;
    fosti sempre e sarai; ma propriamente
l'infinito esser tuo non fu, né fia:
sempre, astratto dai secoli, presente.
    Se tenta il volo inaccessibil via,
tu le forze avvalora, e si sostente
su lo spirito tuo la penna mia.

CRISTO SPIRANTE

Sotto l'incarco de gli strazi ed onte,
stanca cedea l'umanità smarrita;
quando, chinata il Redentor la fronte,
sovra l'arbor vital lasciò la vita.

ON THE GRANDEUR OF GOD

Unknown God, who shinest on everything, who art without place in every place, thou who motionless givest movement, thou who comprehending all art not comprehended (thyself);
    thou who reignest in Heaven and extendest thy never circumscribed essence to the abyss; unique light and a triple ray, who art not fire yet settest burning the universe;
    who wast for ever and wilt be; but properly thy infinite essence neither was nor will be; for ever present, yet absent from the centuries.
    If the wing attempts the inaccesible road, thou givest it its strength, and my wing sustains itself upon thy spirit.

ON THE DYING CHRIST

Lost weary humanity gave in under the burden of torments and shames when our Redeemer with bent head gave up his life upon the tree of life.

240

Ed ecco al suo spirar si scote il monte,
s'oscura il cielo, e da la terra uscita
schiera d'alme prigioni in Flegetonte
del morto Dio l'onnipotenza addita.
  Fu chi giurò per l'increato Sole
ch'al forte punto, al portentoso instante,
cader dovea questa superba mole.
  Gloria del nostro Dio che, se spirante
fa meraviglie inusitate e sole,
che farà glorïoso e trionfante?

Crashaw

ADORO TE

With all the powres my poor Heart hath
Of humble love & loyall Faith,
Thus lowe (my hidden life!) I bow to thee
Whom too much love hath bow'd more low for me.
Down down, proud sense! Discourses dy.
Keep close, my soul's inquiring ey!
Nor touch nor tast must look for more
But each sitt still in his own Dore.

Your ports are all superfluous here,
Save That which lets in faith, the eare.
Faith is my skill. Faith can beleive
As fast as love new lawes can give.
Faith is my force. Faith strength affords
To keep pace with those powrfull words.
And words more sure, more sweet, then they
Love could not think, truth could not say.

And see the mountain shakes at his last breath, the sky darkens and from the earth comes a company of souls imprisoned in Phlegethon, given strength by the omnipotence of the dead God.

It was he who swore by the uncreated sun that at that precise moment, at that portentous instant, this proud mass of earth had to fall.

Glory to our God who, if even when dying can work rare and unique miracles, what will He be able to do in glory and triumph?

The Love of God

O let thy wretch find that releife
Thou didst afford the faithfull theife.
Plead for me, love! Alleage & show
That faith has farther, here, to goe
And lesse to lean on. Because than
Though hidd as GOD, wounds writt thee man,
Thomas might touch; None but might see
At least the suffring side of thee;
And that too was thy self which thee did cover,
But here ev'n That's hid too which hides the other.

Sweet, consider then, that I
Though allow'd nor hand nor eye
To reach at thy lov'd Face; nor can
Tast thee GOD, or touch thee MAN
Both yet beleive; and wittnesse thee
My LORD too & my GOD, as lowd as He.

Help lord, my Faith, my Hope increase;
And fill my portion in thy peace.
Give love for life; nor let my dayes
Grow, but in new powres to thy name & praise.

O dear memoriall of that Death
Which lives still, & allowes us breath!
Rich, Royall food! Bountyfull BREAD!
Whose use denyes us to the dead;
Whose vitall gust alone can give
The same leave both to eat & live;
Live ever Bread of loves, & be
My life, my soul, my surer selfe to mee.

O soft self-wounding Pelican!
Whose brest weepes Balm for wounded man.
Ah this way bend thy benign floud
To'a bleeding Heart that gaspes for blood.
That blood, whose least drops soveraign be
To wash my worlds of sins from me.
Come love! Come LORD! & that long day
For which I languish, come away.
When this dry soul those eyes shall see,
And drink the unseal'd sourse of thee.
When Glory's sun faith's shades shall chase,
And for thy veil give me thy FACE.

AMEN

Gryphius

UEBER DIE GEBURT JESU

Nacht, mehr denn lichte Nacht! Nacht, lichter als der Tag!
Nacht, heller als die Sonn! in der das Licht geboren,
Das Gott, der Licht in Licht wohnhaftig, ihm erkoren!
O Nacht, die alle Nächt und Tage trotzen mag!

O freundenreiche Nacht, in welcher Ach und Klag
Und Finsternis und was sich auf die Welt verschworen
Und Furcht und Höllenangst und Schrecken war verloren!
Der Himmel bricht; doch fällt nunmehr kein Donnerschlag.

Der Zeit und Nächte schuf, ist diese Nacht ankommen
Und hat das Recht der Zeit und Fleisch an sich genommen
Und unser Fleisch und Zeit der Ewigkeit vermacht.

Die jammertrübe Nacht, die schwarze Nacht der Sünden,
Des Grabes Dunkelheit muss durch die Nacht verschwinden.
Nacht, lichter als der Tag! Nacht, mehr denn lichte Nacht!

Fletcher

From CHRISTS VICTORIE ON EARTH

. . . .

Upon a grassie hillock he was laid,
With woodie primroses befreckeled,
Over his head the wanton shadowes plaid
Of a wilde olive, that her bowgh's so spread,
As with her leav's she seem'd to crowne his head,
   And her greene armes [t'] embrace the Prince of peace,
   The Sunne so neere, needs must the winter cease,
The Sunne so neere, another Spring seem'd to increase.

ON THE BIRTH OF JESUS

Night, more than light night! Night, lighter than day! Night, brighter than the sun! in which the light was born which God, himself light dwelling in light, has chosen. O night which may defy all nights and days!

O joyful night in which [cries of] alas! and woe!, and darkness, and everything that has conspired against the world, and fear and dread of hell and terror vanished! The heavens burst asunder; yet no thunderclap is heard.

He who created time and nights, has come this night and taken upon himself the law of time and of the flesh, and has transferred our flesh and our time to eternity.

That miserably dismal night, that black night of sins, that darkness of the grave, must vanish through this night. Night, lighter than day! Night, more than light night!

The Love of God

His haire was blacke, and in small curls did twine,
As though it wear the shadowe of some light,
And underneath his face, as day, did shine,
But sure the day shined not halfe so bright,
Nor the Sunnes shadowe made so darke a night.
   Under his lovely locks, her head to shroude,
   Did make Humilitie her selfe growe proude,
Hither, to light their lamps, did all the Graces croude.

One of ten thousand soules I am, and more,
That of his eyes, and their sweete wounds complaine,
Sweete are the wounds of love, never so sore,
Ah might he often slaie mee so againe.
He never lives, that thus is never slaine.
   What boots it watch? those eyes, for all my art,
   Mine owne eyes looking on, have stole my heart,
In them Love bends his bowe, and dips his burning dart.

As when the Sunne, caught in an adverse clowde,
Flies crosse the world, and thear a new begets,
The watry picture of his beautie proude,
Throwes all abroad his sparkling spangelets,
And the whole world in dire amazement sets,
   To see two dayes abroad at once, and all
   Doubt whither nowe he rise, or nowe will fall:
So flam'd the Godly flesh, proude of his heav'nly thrall.

His cheekes as snowie apples, sop't in wine,
Had their red roses quencht with lillies white,
And like to garden strawberries did shine,
Wash't in a bowle of milke, or rose-buds bright
Unbosoming their brests against the light:
   Here love-sicke soules did eat, thear dranke, and made
   Sweete-smelling posies, that could never fade,
But worldly eyes him thought more like some living shade.

For laughter never look't upon his browe,
Though in his face all smiling joyes did bide,
No silken banners did about him flowe,
Fooles make their fetters ensignes of their pride:
He was best cloath'd when naked was his side,
   A Lambe he was, and wollen fleece he bore,
   Wove with one thread, his feete lowe sandalls wore,
But bared were his legges, so went the times of yore.

244

As two white marble pillars that uphold
Gods holy place whear he in glorie sets,
And rise with goodly grace and courage bold,
To beare his Temple on their ample jetts,
Vein'd every whear with azure rivulets,
  Whom all the people on some holy morne,
  With boughs and flowrie garlands doe adorne,
Of such, though fairer farre, this Temple was upborne.

Not lovely Ida might with this compare,
Though many streames his banks besilvered,
Though Xanthus with his golden sands he bare,
Nor Hibla, though his thyme depastured,
As fast againe with honie blossomed.
  Ne Rhodope, ne Tempes flowrie playne,
  Adonis garden was to this but vayne,
Though Plato on his beds a flood of praise did rayne.

For in all these, some one thing most did grow,
But in this one, grew all things els beside,
For sweet varietie herselfe did throw
To every banke, here all the ground she dide
In lillie white, there pinks eblazed wide;
  And damask't all the earth, and here shee shed
  Blew violets, and there came roses red,
And every sight the yeelding sense, as captive led.

The garden like a Ladie faire was cut,
That lay as if shee slumber'd in delight,
And to the open skies her eyes did shut;
The azure fields of heav'n wear sembled right
In a large round, set with the flo[w'r]s of light,
  The flo[w'r]s-de-luce, and the round sparks of deaw,
  That hung upon their azure leaves, did shew
Like twinkling starrs, that sparkle in th[e] eav'ning blew.

Upon a hillie banke her head shee cast,
On which the bowre of Vaine-Delight was built,
White, and red roses for her face wear plac't,
And for her tresses Marigolds wear spilt:
Them broadly she displaid, like flaming guilt,
  Till in the ocean the glad day wear drown'd,
  Then up againe her yellow locks she wound,
And with greene fillets in their prettie calls them bound.

The Love of God

What should I here depeint her lillie hand,
Her veines of violets, her ermine brest,
Which thear in orient colours living stand,
Or how her gowne with silken leaves is drest;
Or how her watchmen, arm'd with boughie crest,
   A wall of prim hid in his bushes bears,
    Shaking at every winde their leavie spears,
While she supinely sleeps, ne to be waked fears?

Over the hedge depends the graping Elme,
Whose greener head, empurpuled in wine,
Seemed to wonder at his bloodie helme,
And halfe suspect the bunches of the vine,
Least they, perhaps, his wit should undermine.
   For well he knewe such fruit he never bore:
    But her weake armes embraced him the more,
And with her ruby grapes laught at her paramour.

Under the shadowe of these drunken elmes
A Fountaine rose, where Pangloretta uses,
(When her some flood of fancie overwhelms,
And one of all her favourites she chuses)
To bath herselfe, whom she in lust abuses,
   And from his wanton body sucks his soule,
    Which drown'd in pleasure, in that shaly bowle,
And swimming in delight, both am[o]rously rowle.

The font of silver was, and so his showrs
In silver fell, onely the guilded bowles
(Like to a fornace, that the min'rall powres)
Seem'd to have moul't it in their shining holes:
And on the water, like to burning coles,
   On liquid silver, leaves of roses lay:
    But when PANGLORIE here did list to play,
Rose water then it ranne, and milke it rain'd they say.

The roofe thicke cloudes did paint, from which three boyes
Three gaping mermaides with their eawrs did feede,
Whose brests let fall the streame, with sleepie noise,
To Lions mouths, from whence it leapt with speede,
And in the rosie laver seem'd to bleed.
   The naked boyes unto the waters fall,
    Their stonie nightingales had taught to call,
When Zephyr breath'd into their watry interall.

And all about, embayed in soft sleepe,
A heard of charmed beasts aground wear spread,
Which the faire Witch in goulden chaines did keepe,
And them in willing bondage fettered,
Once men they liv'd, but now the men were dead,
    And turn'd to beasts, so fabled Homer old,
    That Circe, with her potion, charm'd in gold,
Us'd manly soules in beastly bodies to immould.

Through this false Eden, to his Lemans bowre,
(Whome thousand soules devoutly idolize)
Our first destroyer led our Saviour.
Thear in the lower roome, in solemne wise,
They daunc't a round, and powr'd their sacrifice
    To plumpe Lyæus, and among the rest,
    The jolly Priest, in yvie garlands drest,
Chaunted wild Orgialls, in honour of the feast.

. . . .

Milton

AT A SOLEMN MUSIC

Blest pair of *Sirens*, pledges of Heav'ns joy,
Sphear-born harmonious Sisters, Voice, and Verse,
Wed your divine sounds, and mixt power employ
Dead things with inbreath'd sense able to pierce,
And to our high-rais'd phantasie present
That undisturbed Song of pure concent,
Ay sung before the saphire-colourd throne
To him that sits thereon
With Saintly shout, and solemn Jubily,
Where the bright Seraphim in burning row
Their loud up-lifted Angel trumpets blow,
And the Cherubic host in thousand quires
Touch their immortal Harps of golden wires,
With those just Spirits that wear victorious Palms,
Hymns devout and holy Psalms
Singing everlastingly;
That we on Earth with undiscording voice
May rightly answer that melodious noise;
As once we did, till disproportiond sin
Jarrd against natures chime, and with harsh din
Broke the fair music that all creatures made
To their great Lord, whose love their motion swayd

247

In perfet Diapason, whilst they stood
In first obedience, and their state of good.
O may we soon again renew that Song,
And keep in tune with Heav'n, till God ere long
To his celestial consort us unite,
To live with him, and sing in endless morn of light.

Crashaw

A HYMN TO THE NAME AND HONOUR OF THE ADMIRABLE SAINTE TERESA

Love, thou art Absolute sole lord
Of LIFE & DEATH. To prove the word,
Wee'l now appeal to none of all
Those thy old Souldiers, Great & tall,
Ripe Men of Martyrdom, that could reach down
With strong armes, their triumphant crown;
Such as could with lusty breath
Speak lowd into the face of death
The Great LORD's glorious name, to none
Of those whose spatious Bosomes spread a throne
For LOVE at larg to fill: spare blood & sweat;
And see him take a private seat,
Making his mansion in the mild
And milky soul of a soft child.
    Scarse has she learn't to lisp the name
Of Martyr; yet she thinks it shame
Life should so long play with that breath
Which spent can buy so brave a death.
She never undertook to know
What death with love should have to doe;
Nor has she e're yet understood
Why to show love, she should shed blood
Yet though she cannot tell you why,
She can LOVE, & she can DY.
    Scarse has she Blood enough to make
A guilty sword blush for her sake;
Yet has she'a HEART dares hope to prove
How much lesse strong is DEATH then LOVE.
    Be love but there; let poor six yeares
Be pos'd with the maturest Feares
Man trembles at, you straight shall find
LOVE knowes no nonage, nor the MIND.
'Tis LOVE, not YEARES or LIMBS that can
Make the Martyr, or the man.

LOVE touch't her HEART, & lo it beates
High, & burnes with such brave heates;
Such thirsts to dy, as dares drink up,
A thousand cold deaths in one cup.
Good reason. For she breathes All fire.
Her weake brest heaves with strong desire
Of what she may with fruitles wishes
Seek for amongst her MOTHER's kisses.
　Since 'tis not to be had at home
She'l travail to a Martyrdom.
No home for hers confesses she
But where she may a Martyr be.
　Sh'el to the Moores; And trade with them,
For this unvalued Diadem.
She'l offer them her dearest Breath,
With CHRIST's Name in't, in change for death.
Sh'el bargain with them; & will give
Them GOD; teach them how to live
In him: or, if they this deny,
For him she'l teach them how to DY.
So shall she leave amongst them sown
Her LORD's Blood; or at lest her own.
　FAREWEL then, all the world! Adieu.
TERESA is no more for you.
Farewell, all pleasures, sports, & joyes,
(Never till now esteemed toyes)
Farewell what ever deare may bee,
MOTHER's armes or FATHER's knee
Farewell house, & farewell home!
SHE's for the Moores, & MARTYRDOM.
　SWEET, not so fast! lo thy fair Spouse
Whom thou seekst with so swift vowes,
Calls thee back, & bidds thee come
T'embrace a milder MARTYRDOM.
　Blest powres forbid, Thy tender life
Should bleed upon a barbarous knife;
Or some base hand have power to race
Thy Brest's chast cabinet, & uncase
A soul kept there so sweet, ô no;
Wise heavn will never have it so
THOU art love's victime; & must dy
A death more mysticall & high.
Into love's armes thou shalt let fall
A still-surviving funerall.
His is the DART must make the DEATH
Whose stroke shall tast thy hallow'd breath;

The Love of God

A Dart thrice dip't in that rich flame
Which writes thy spouse's radiant Name
Upon the roof of Heav'n; where ay
It shines, & with a soveraign ray
Beates bright upon the burning faces
Of soules which in that name's sweet graces
Find everlasting smiles. So rare,
So spirituall, pure, & fair
Must be th'immortall instrument
Upon whose choice point shall be sent
A life so lov'd; And that there be
Fitt executioners for Thee,
The fair'st & first-born sons of fire
Blest SERAPHIM, shall leave their quire
And turn love's souldiers, upon THEE
To exercise their archerie.

   O how oft shalt thou complain
Of a sweet & subtle PAIN.
Of intolerable JOYES;
Of a DEATH, in which who dyes
Loves his death, and dyes again.
And would for ever so be slain.
And lives, & dyes; and knowes not why
To live, But that he thus may never leave to DY.

   How kindly will thy gentle HEART
Kisse the sweetly-killing DART!
And close in his embraces keep
Those delicious Wounds, that weep
Balsom to heal themselves with. Thus
When These thy DEATHS, so numerous,
Shall all at last dy into one,
And melt thy Soul's sweet mansion;
Like a soft lump of incense, hasted
By too hott a fire, & wasted
Into perfuming clouds, so fast
Shalt thou exhale to Heavn at last
In a resolving SIGH, and then
O what? Ask not the Tongues of men.
Angells cannot tell, suffice,
Thy selfe shall feel thine own full joyes
And hold them fast for ever. There
So soon as thou shalt first appear,
The MOON of maiden starrs, thy white
MISTRESSE, attended by such bright
Soules as thy shining self, shall come
And in her first rankes make thee room;

250

Where 'mongst her snowy family
Immortall wellcomes wait for thee.
  O what delight, when reveal'd LIFE shall stand
And teach thy lipps heav'n with his hand;
On which thou now maist to thy wishes
Heap up thy consecrated kisses.
What joyes shall seize thy soul, when she
Bending her blessed eyes on thee
(Those second Smiles of Heav'n) shall dart
Her mild rayes through thy melting heart!
  Angels, thy old freinds, there shall greet thee
Glad at their own home now to meet thee.
  All thy good WORKES which went before
And waited for thee, at the door,
Shall own thee there; and all in one
Weave a constellation
Of CROWNS, with which the KING thy spouse
Shall build up thy triumphant browes.
  All thy old woes shall now smile on thee
And thy paines sitt bright upon thee
All thy sorrows here shall shine,
All thy SUFFRINGS be divine.
TEARES shall take comfort, & turn gemms
And WRONGS repent to Diademms.
Ev'n thy DEATHS shall live; & new
Dresse the soul that erst they slew.
Thy wounds shall blush to such bright scarres
As keep account of the LAMB's warres.
  Those rare WORKES where thou shalt leave writt,
Love's noble history, with witt
Taught thee by none but him, while here
They feed our soules, shall cloth THINE there.
Each heavnly word by whose hid flame
Our hard Hearts shall strike fire, the same
Shall flourish on thy browes. & be
Both fire to us & flame to thee;
Whose light shall live bright in thy FACE
By glory, in our hearts by grace.
  Thou shalt look round about, & see
Thousands of crown'd Soules throng to be
Themselves thy crown. Sons of thy vowes
The virgin-births with which thy soveraign spouse
Made fruitfull thy fair soul, goe now
And with them all about thee bow
To Him, put on (hee'l say) put on
(My rosy love) That thy rich zone

The Love of God

Sparkling with the sacred flames
Of thousand soules, whose happy names
Heav'n keeps upon thy score. (Thy bright
Life brought them first to kisse the light
That kindled them to starrs.) and so
Thou with the LAMB, thy lord, shalt goe;
And whereso'ere he setts his white
Stepps, walk with HIM those wayes of light
Which who in death would live to see,
Must learn in life to dy like thee.

Le Moyne

L'AMOUR DIVIN *from* HYMNE PREMIER

Les merveilles de l'amour divin en Dieu, en la Nature, et dans les Amours inferieurs

Feu sans matiere et sans fumée;
Sainte flamme des saints amans;
Source des doux embrasements,
Dont la Nature est allumée;
Vive ardeur d'un double flambeau;
Entre-deux du bon et du beau;
Beau souffle de deux belles bouches,
Nœud du Pere et du Fils, Esprit, inspire moy!
Mon cœur obscur et froid attend que tu le touches,
Et que pour te louër, tu l'emplisses de toy.

Esprit saint, jette sur ma teste
Un rayon de ces sacrez feu,
Qu'autrefois les peuples hebreux
Virent au front de leur prophete.

The marvels of divine love in God, Nature, and inferior Loves

Fire without material, and without smoke; holy flame of holy lovers, source of the sweet blazes with which Nature is lit; living ardour from a double torch; space between the good and the beautiful, lovely breath from two lovely mouths, knot of the Father and Son, Spirit inspire me! My dark cold heart waits for you to touch it, and so as to praise you, waits for you to fill it with yourself.

Holy Spirit, cast upon my head a beam of those sacred fires which once the Hebrew peoples saw on the brow of their prophet. Away with those deceitful

252

Loin de moy ces trompeurs flambeaux,
Qui sont allumez dans les eaux,
Qu'épand le fabuleux Parnasse,
Loin de moy les lauriers de ce prophane mont:
Ardent buisson d'Oreb, mettez-vous en leur place,
Et venez aujourd'huy me couronner le front.

Puis-je comprendre tes merveilles,
Beau Principe des beaux amours,
Ardeur moyenne entre deux jours,
Eclair de deux flammes pareilles?
Feu qui n'es jamais consumé,
Cœur de l'Amant et de l'Aimé,
Baiser du Fils, baiser du Pere;
Beau terme où se conclud leur commerce divin;
Et qui procedes d'eux, par un divin mystere,
Comme un angle infini de deux lignes sans fin.

Loin du soleil et de la lune,
Au dessus des plus hauts esprits,
Les feux du Pere et ceux du Fils
Te sont une source commune.
Là tes éclairs se font des leurs;
Tes flammes sont de leurs chaleurs
L'expression continuelle;
De tous les deux en toy le regard est complet;
Et tu fais au milieu la rencontre eternelle
D'un modelle fecond, et d'un fecond portrait.

torches lit in the waters rising from fabled Parnassus, away with the laurels of
that profane mountain: burning bush of Horeb, put yourself in their place, and
today come to crown my brow.

Can I comprehend your marvels, beautiful Principal of beautiful loves,
central ardour between two days, the light of two similar flames? O, Fire which
is never consumed, heart of the Lover and the Beloved, kiss of the Son, kiss of
the Father; beautiful term where their divine commerce concludes, and you who
proceed from them, by a divine mystery, like an infinite angle between two
endless lines.

Far from the sun and the moon, above the highest spirits, the fires of the
Father and those of the Son are your common source. There your lights are
made from theirs: your flames are the continual expression of their heats: the
vision of both of them reaches completion in you: and between them you make
the eternal meeting of a fertile model and a fertile painting.

253

The Love of God

Ainsi le feu dans un nuage,
Se prend aux rayons du soleil
Lors que pour se faire un pareil
Luy-mesme il y peint son image;
Le portrait à peine est formé,
Qu'il en est l'amant et l'aimé,
Comme l'ouvrier et le modelle;
D'une part et de l'autre, un mesme jour reluit;
Et l'ardeur d'entredeux est l'amour mutuelle
Du soleil produisant, et du soleil produit.

Dans le Bien premier est ta source;
Tu t'épans sur les seconds biens;
Et par là mesme tu reviens
Au point où commence ta course.
Tu roules eternellement,
Et formes par ton mouvement
Un cercle de flames fecondes;
Par amour tu descends, tu montes par amour;
Et tes effusions sublimes et profondes,
Ont en toy le principe et la fin de leur tour.

Ainsi la chaleur descenduë
De l'astre qui fait les saisons
Monte avec les exhalaisons,
Sur qui le jour l'a répanduë.
La feconde Mere des mers
S'écoule ainsi dans l'univers
Par cent secretes ouvertures;
Et sans vuider ses humides tresors,
Elle rentre chez soy par autant d'embouchures,
Qu'elle fait de ruisseaux pour s'épandre au dehors.

Thus the fire in a cloud is kindled by the rays of the sun when, to make for himself an equal, he paints his own image there; the portrait is hardly finished when he is both the lover of it, and its beloved, like the craftsman and his model; the same day shines from both parts; and the ardour between them is the mutual love of the sun which produces, and the sun which is produced.

Your source is in the primary Good; you spread over the secondary goods; and through them you return to the point where your journey begins. You roll eternally, and form by your movement a circle of fertile flames: by love you descend; by love you ascend, and your sublime and profound effusions have the beginning and end of their circuit in you.

So does the heat, descended from the star which makes the seasons ascend with the exhalations which the day has poured out. The fertile Mother of the seas spreads through the universe by a hundred secret openings: and without emptying her humid treasures, she returns to herself by as many openings as she makes into streams to flood into the outer world.

Dans ces longs et vastes espaces,
Qui par ton cours sont limitez,
Tu fais toy mesme les bontez
Des natures sur qui tu passes;
Leur estre se forme sous toy;
Ta plenitude y met de quoy
Remplir leur vuide et leur matiere;
Tu coules sur l'esprit, tu coules sur le corps;
Et tes écoulemens sont comme une riviere,
Qui dore son gravier, et qui pare ses bords.

Ta chaleur active et feconde,
Dans le sein d'une vaste nuit,
Ouvrit la source et le conduit,
D'où sortit le globe du monde.
Les corps par elle, et les esprits
Receurent leur ordre et leur prix,
Leur figure et leur consistence;
Et selon que sur eux s'étendit sa vertu,
L'esprit fut élevé dans la circonférence,
Et le corps demeura dans le centre abatu.

Avant qu'elle fût épanchée,
Tous les astres estoient encor
Comme une obscure graine d'or,
Que la miniere tient cachée;
Elle en fit des corps glorieux;
De feconds et mobiles yeux;
Et des ames universelles;
Et si-tost qu'à leur masse un beau feu se fut pris,
Une cendre en tomba, qui fit par étincelles
Le jour du diamant, et l'éclat du rubis.

. . . .

In these long and vast spaces, which are limited by your path, you yourself make the bounties of natures over which you pass: their being is formed under you: your fullness puts there that which fills their void and their matter; you flow over the spirit, you flow over the body, and your flowings are like a river which gilds its bed and adorns its banks.

Your active fertile heat, in the heart of a vast night opened the source and the channel from which the globe of the world emerged. Through it bodies and souls received their orders, and their value, their shape and consistency; and according to how its virtue extended upon them, the spirit was elevated to the circumference, and the body remained sunk in the centre.

Before it [the heat of the Holy Spirit] was disseminated, all the stars were still like a dark speck of gold that the mine conceals; it made of it glorious bodies, fertile moving eyes; and universal souls; and as soon as a great fire was lit in their mass, a cinder fell from it, which made, in its sparks, the day of the diamond, the glorious light of the ruby.

Crashaw

THE WEEPER

I

Hail, sister springs!
Parents of sylver-footed rills!
    Ever bubling things!
    Thawing crystall! snowy hills,
Still spending, never spent! I mean
Thy fair eyes, sweet MAGDALENE!

II

    Heavens thy fair eyes be;
    Heavens of ever-falling starres.
    'Tis seed-time still with thee
    And starres thou sow'st, whose harvest dares
Promise the earth to counter shine
Whatever makes heavn's forhead fine.

III

    But we'are deceived all.
    Starres indeed they are too true;
    For they but seem to fall,
    As Heavn's other spangles doe.
It is not for our earth & us
To shine in Things so pretious.

IV

    Upwards thou dost weep.
    Heavn's bosome drinks the gentle stream.
    Where th'milky rivers creep,
    Thine floates above; & is the cream.
Waters above th' Heavns, what they be
We' are taught best by thy TEARES & thee.

V

    Every morn from hence
    A brisk Cherub somthing sippes
    Whose sacred influence
    Addes sweetnes to his sweetest Lippes.
Then to his musick. And his song
Tasts of this Breakfast all day long.

VI

 Not in the evening's eyes
 When they Red with weeping are
 For the Sun that dyes,
 Sitts sorrow with a face so fair,
No where but here did ever meet
Sweetnesse so sad, sadnesse so sweet.

VII

 When sorrow would be seen
 In her brightest majesty
 (For she is a Queen)
 Then is she drest by none but thee.
Then, & only then, she weares
Her proudest pearles; I mean, thy TEARES.

VIII

 The deaw no more will weep
 The primrose's pale cheek to deck,
 The deaw no more will sleep
 Nuzzel'd in the lilly's neck;
Much reather would it be thy TEAR,
And leave them Both to tremble here.

IX

 There's no need at all
 That the balsom-sweating bough
 So coyly should let fall
 His med'cinable teares; for now
Nature hath learn't to'extract a deaw
More soveraign & sweet from you.

X

 Yet let the poore drops weep
 (Weeping is the ease of woe)
 Softly let them creep,
 Sad that they are vanquish't so.
They, though to others no releife,
Balsom maybe, for their own greife.

XI

 Such the maiden gemme
 By the purpling vine put on,
 Peeps from her parent stemme
 And blushes at the bridegroome sun.
This watry Blossom of thy eyn,
Ripe, will make the richer wine.

XII

When some new bright Guest
Takes up among the starres a room,
And Heavn will make a feast,
Angels with crystall violls come
And draw from these full eyes of thine
Their master's Water: their own Wine.

XIII

Golden though he be,
Golden Tagus murmures tho;
Were his way by thee,
Content & quiet he would goe.
So much more rich would he esteem
Thy sylver, then his golden stream.

XIV

Well does the May that lyes
Smiling in thy cheeks, confesse
The April in thine eyes.
Mutuall sweetnesse they expresse.
No April ere lent kinder showres,
Nor May return'd more faithfull flowres.

XV

O cheeks! Bedds of chast loves
By your own showres seasonably dash't
Eyes! nests of milky doves
In your own wells decently washt,
O wit of love! that thus could place
Fountain & Garden in one face.

XVI

O sweet Contest; of woes
With loves, of teares with smiles disputing!
O fair, & Freindly Foes,
Each other kissing & confuting!
While rain & sunshine, Cheekes & Eyes
Close in kind contrarietyes.

XVII

But can these fair Flouds be
Freinds with the bosom fires that fill thee
Can so great flames agree
Æternall Teares should thus distill thee!
O flouds, o fires! o suns o showres!
Mixt & made freinds by love's sweet powres.

XVIII

Twas his well-pointed dart
That digg'd these wells, & drest this Vine;
And taught the wounded HEART
The way into these weeping Eyn.
Vain loves avant! bold hands forbear!
The lamb hath dipp't his white foot here.

XIX

And now where're he strayes,
Among the Galilean mountaines,
Or more unwellcome wayes,
He's follow'd by two faithfull fountaines;
Two walking baths; two weeping motions;
Portable, & compendious oceans.

XX

O Thou, thy lord's fair store!
In thy so rich & rare expenses,
Even when he show'd most poor,
He might provoke the wealth of Princes.
What Prince's wanton'st pride e're could
Wash with Sylver, wipe with Gold.

XXI

Who is that King, but he
Who calls't his Crown to be call'd thine,
That thus can boast to be
Waited on by a wandring mine,
A voluntary mint, that strowes
Warm sylver showres where're he goes!

XXII

O pretious Prodigall!
Fair spend-thrift of thy self! thy measure
(Mercilesse love!) is all.
Even to the last Pearle in thy treasure.
All places, Times & objects be
Thy teare's sweet opportunity.

XXIII

Does the day-starre rise?
Still thy starres doe fall & fall
Does day close his eyes?
Still the FOUNTAIN weeps for all.
Let night or day doe what they will,
Thou hast thy task; thou weepest still.

XXIV

Does thy song lull the air?
Thy falling teares keep faith full time.
Does thy sweet-breath'd praire
Up in clouds of incense climb?
Still at each sigh, that is, each stop,
A bead, that is, A Tear, does drop.

XXV

At these thy weeping gates,
(Watching their watry motion)
Each winged moment waits,
Takes his Tear, & gets him gone.
By thine Ey's tinct enobled thus
Time layes him up; he's pretious.

XXVI

Not, so long she lived,
Shall thy tomb report of thee;
But, so long she greived,
Thus must we date thy memory.
Others by moments, months, & yeares
Measure their ages; thou, by Teares.

XXVII

So doe perfumes expire.
So sigh tormented sweets, opprest
With proud unpittying fire.
Such Teares the suffring Rose that's vext
With ungentle flames does shed,
Sweating in a too warm bed.

XXVIII

Say, ye bright brothers,
The fugitive sons of those fair Eyes
Your fruitfull mothers!
What makes you here? what hopes can tice
You to be born? what cause can borrow
You from Those nests of noble sorrow?

XXIX

Whither away so fast?
For sure the sordid earth
Your Sweetnes cannot tast
Nor does the dust deserve your birth.
Sweet, whither hast you then? o say
Why you trip so fast away?

XXX

We goe not to seek,
  The darlings of Auroras bed,
  The rose's modest Cheek
  Nor the violet's humble head.
Though the Feild's eyes too WEEPERS be
Because they want such TEARES as we.

XXXI

Much lesse mean we to trace
  The Fortune of inferior gemmes,
  Preferr'd to some proud face
  Or pertch't upon fear'd Diadems.
Crown'd Heads are toyes. We goe to meet
A worthy object, our lord's FEET.

Southwell

MARIE MAGDALENS COMPLAINT AT CHRISTS DEATH

Sith my life from life is parted:
  Death come take thy portion.
Who survives, when life is murdred,
  Lives by meere extortion.
All that live, and not in God:
Couch their life in deaths abod.

Seely starres must needes leave shining,
  When the sunne is shaddowed.
Borrowed streames refraine their running,
  When head springs are hindered.
One that lives by others breath,
Dieth also by his death.

O true life, sith thou hast left me,
  Mortall life is tedious.
Death it is to live without thee,
  Death, of all most odious.
Turne againe or take me to thee,
Let me die or live thou in mee.

Where the truth once was, and is not,
  Shaddowes are but vanitie:
Shewing want, that helpe they cannot:
  Signes, not salves of miserie.
Paynted meate no hunger feedes,
Dying life each death exceedes.

261

With my love, my life was nestled
  In the sonne of happinesse:
From my love, my life is wrested
  To a world of heavinesse.
O, let love my life remove,
Sith I live not where I love.

O my soule, what did unloose thee
  From thy sweete captivitie?
God, not I, did still possesse thee:
  His, not mine, thy libertie.
O, too happie thrall thou wart,
When thy prison, was his hart.

Spitefull speare, that breakst this prison,
  Seate of all felicitie,
Working thus, with double treason,
  Loves and lifes deliverie:
Though my life thou drav'st away,
Maugre thee my love shall stay.

Crashaw

UPON THE BLEEDING CRUCIFIX—A Song

I
Jesu, no more! It is full tide.
From thy head & from thy feet,
From thy hands & from thy side
All the purple Rivers meet.

II
What need thy fair head bear a part
In showres, as if thine eyes had none?
What need They help to drown thy heart,
That strives in torrents of it's own?

III
Thy restlesse feet now cannot goe
For us & our eternall good,
As they were ever wont. What though?
They swimme. Alas, in their own floud.

IV

Thy hands to give, thou canst not lift;
Yet will thy hand still giving be.
It gives but ô, it self's the gift.
It gives though bound; though bound 'tis free.

V

But ô thy side, thy deep-digg'd side!
That hath a double Nilus going.
Nor ever was the pharian tide
Half so fruitfull, half so flowing.

VI

No hair so small, but payes his river
To this red sea of thy blood
Their little channells can deliver
Somthing to the Generall floud.

VII

But while I speak, whither are run
All the rivers nam'd before?
I counted wrong. There is but one;
But ô that one is one all ore.

VIII

Rain-swoln rivers may rise proud,
Bent all to drown & overflow.
But when indeed all's overflow'd
They themselves are drowned too.

IX

This thy blood's deluge, a dire chance
Dear LORD to thee, to us is found
A deluge of Deliverance;
A deluge least we should be drown'd.

N'ere wast thou in a sense so sadly true,
The WELL of living WATERS, Lord, till now.

The Love of God

Southwell

CHRISTS BLOODY SWEAT

Fat soile, full spring, sweete olive, grape of blisse,
That yeelds, that streams, that pours, that dost distil,
Untild, undrawne, unstampt, untouch't of presse,
Deare fruit, cleare brookes, faire oile, sweete wine at will:
Thus Christ unforct prevents in shedding blood
The whips, the thornes, the nailes, the speare, and roode.

He Pelicans, he Phenix fate doth prove,
Whom flames consume, whom streames enforce to die,
How burneth bloud, how bleedeth burning love?
Can one in flame and streame both bathe and frie?
How could he joine a Phenix fiery paines
In fainting Pelicans still bleeding vaines?

Elias once to prove gods soveraigne powre
By praire procur'd a fier of wondrous force
That blood and wood and water did devoure,
Yea stones and dust, beyonde all natures course:
Such fire is love that fedd with gory bloode
Doth burne no lesse then in the dryest woode.

O sacred Fire come shewe thy force on me
That sacrifice to Christe I maye retorne,
If withered wood for fuell fittest bee,
If stones and dust, if fleshe and blood will burne,
I withered am and stonye to all good,
A sacke of dust, a masse of fleshe and bloode.

Donne

SONNET

At the round earths imagin'd corners, blow
Your trumpets, Angells, and arise, arise
From death, you numberlesse infinities
Of soules, and to your scattred bodies goe,
All whom the flood did, and fire shall o'erthrow,
All whom warre, dearth, age, agues, tyrannies,
Despaire, law, chance, hath slaine, and you whose eyes,
Shall behold God, and never tast deaths woe.

264

But let them sleepe, Lord, and mee mourne a space,
For, if above all these, my sinnes abound,
'Tis late to aske abundance of thy grace,
When wee are there; here on this lowly ground,
Teach mee how to repent; for that's as good
As if thou'hadst seal'd my pardon, with thy blood.

SONNET

Batter my heart, three person'd God; for, you
As yet but knocke, breathe, shine, and seeke to mend;
That I may rise, and stand, o'erthrow mee,'and bend
Your force, to breake, blowe, burn and make me new.
I, like an usurpt towne, to'another due,
Labour to'admit you, but Oh, to no end,
Reason your viceroy in mee, mee should defend,
But is captiv'd, and proves weake or untrue.
Yet dearely'I love you, and would be lov'd faine,
But am betroth'd unto your enemie:
Divorce mee,'untie, or breake that knot againe,
Take mee to you, imprison mee, for I
Except you'enthrall mee, never shall be free,
Nor ever chast, except you ravish mee.

Von Grimmelshausen

NACHTLIED DES EINSIEDLERS from *Simplicius Simplicissimus*

Komm Trost der Nacht, o Nachtigall,
Lass deine Stimm mit Freudenschall
Aufs lieblichste erklingen;
Komm, komm, und lob den Schöpfer dein,
Weil andre Vöglein schlafen sein
Und nicht mehr mögen singen!
Lass dein Stimmlein
Laut erschallen, dann vor allen
Kannst du loben
Gott im Himmel hoch dort oben.

THE HERMIT'S NIGHT SONG

Come, comforter in the night, O nightingale, let your voice ring out most pleasingly with joyous sound; come, come, and praise your creator, because all other birds are asleep and do not want to sing any more! Let your small voice ring out loud, for you above all others can praise God in heaven on high.

The Love of God

Obschon ist hin der Sonnenschein
Und wir im Finstern müssen sein,
So können wir doch singen;
Von Gottes Güt und seiner Macht,
Weil uns kann hindern keine Nacht,
Sein Lob zu vollenbringen.
Drum dein Stimmlein
Lass erschallen, dann vor allen
Kannst du loben
Gott im Himmel hoch dort oben.

Echo, der wilde Widerhall,
Will sein bei diesem Freudenschall
Und lässet sich auch hören.
Verweist uns alle Müdigkeit,
Der wir ergeben allezeit,
Lehrt uns den Schlaf betören.
Drum dein Stimmlein
Lass erschallen, dann vor allen
Kannst du loben
Gott im Himmel hoch dort oben.

Die Sterne, so am Himmel stehn,
Lassen sich zum Lob Gottes sehn,
Und tun ihm Ehr beweisen;
Auch die Eul, die nicht singen kann,
Zeigt doch mit ihrem Heulen an,
Dass sie Gott auch tu preisen.
Drum dein Stimmlein
Lass erschallen, dann vor allen
Kannst du loben
Gott im Himmel hoch dort oben.

Although the sun had gone, and we must be in darkness, we can still sing of God's goodness and of His power, for no night can prevent us from performing His praise. Therefore let your small voice ring out loud, for you above all others can praise God in heaven on high.

Echo, that boisterous mimic, wants to take part in this joyous sound and lets her voice be heard too. She rebukes us for the tiredness to which we are given at all times, and teaches us to delude sleep. Therefore let your small voice ring out loud, for you above all others can praise God in heaven on high.

The stars in the sky display themselves for the glory of God and do homage to Him; even the owl which cannot sing demonstrates its [desire to] praise God by its screeching. Therefore let your small voice ring out loud, for you above all others can praise God in heaven on high.

Nur her mein liebstes Vögelein,
Wir wollen nicht die fäulste sein
Und schlafend liegen bleiben,
Sondern bis dass die Morgenröt
Erfreuet diese Wälder öd,
Im Lob Gottes vertreiben.
Lass dein Stimmlein
Laut erschallen, dann vor allen
Kannst du loben
Gott im Himmel hoch dort oben.

Sor Juana

De la más fragrante Rosa
nació la Abeja más bella,
a quien el limpio rocío
dió purísima materia.

Nace, pues, y apenas nace,
cuando en la misma moneda,
lo que en perlas recibió,
empieza a pagar en perlas.

Que llore el Alba, no es mucho,
que es costumbre en su belleza;
mas ¿quién hay que no se admire
de que el Sol lágrimas vierta?

Si es por fecundar la Rosa,
es ociosa diligencia,
pues no es menester rocío
después de nacer la Abeja;

Come along, dearest little bird, we have no wish to be the laziest, to lie asleep in bed, but pass the time in praise of God until dawn gladdens these desolate woods. Let your small voice ring out loud, for you above all others can praise God in heaven on high.

From the most fragrant rose was born the loveliest bee, to whom the limpid dew gave the purest material.

He is born then and no sooner is he born than in the same currency he begins to pay in pearls what in pearls he received.

Let dawn weep, it matters not, for that is a habit of her beauty. But who is there who does not marvel that the sun sheds tears?

If it is to fertilize the rose it is a useless labour, for after the birth of the bee dew is not necessary;

267

y más, cuando en la clausura
de su virginal pureza,
ni antecedente haber pudo
ni puede haber quien suceda.

¿Pues a qué fin es el llanto
que dulcemente le riega?
Quien no puede dar más Fruto,
¿qué importa que estéril sea?

Mas ¡ay!, que la Abeja tiene
tan íntima dependencia
siempre con la Rosa, que
depende su vida de ella;

pues dándole el néctar puro
que sus fragancias engendran,
no sólo antes la concibe,
pero después la alimenta.

Hijo y Madre, en tan divinas
peregrinas competencias,
ninguno queda deudor
y ambos obligados quedan.

La Abeja paga el rocío
de que la Rosa la engendra,
y ella vuelve a retornarle
con lo mismo que [la alienta].

Ayudando el uno al otro
con mutua correspondencia,
la Abeja a la Flor fecunda,
y ella a la Abeja sustenta,

Pues si por eso es el llanto,
llore Jesús, norabuena,
que lo que expende en rocío
cobrará después en néctar.

and furthermore, when he was in the cloister of her virginal purity he could
have neither predecessor nor successor.

But to what purpose is that weeping that sweetly waters her? Why should
sterility matter to her who can bear no more fruit?

But ah! the bee always lives in such intimate dependence upon the rose, for he
depends for his life upon her.

For in giving him the pure nectar which her fragrances engender not only does
she first conceive him but afterwards she feeds him.

Son and mother in such strange divine competition that none remains the
debtor and both remain in debt.

The bee pays for the dew from which the rose engendered him and she repays
him with what she feeds him with.

The one helps the other in mutual inter-dependence; the bee fertilizes the
flower and the flower feeds the bee.

Therefore if the weeping is for this, let Jesus cry, bless Him, for what he
spends in dew he will be paid for later in nectar.

Silesius

EPIGRAMS from *The Cherubinic Traveller*

Gott ergreift man nicht

Gott ist ein lauter Nichts, ihn rührt kein Nun noch Hier:
Je mehr du nach ihm greifst, je mehr entwird er dir.

Das Bildnis Gottes

Ich trage Gottes Bild: wenn er sich will besehn,
So kann es nur in mir, und wer mir gleicht, geschehn.

Gott ist mein Punkt und Kreis

Gott ist mein Mittelpunkt, wenn ich ihn in mich schliesse:
Mein Umkreis dann, wenn ich aus Lieb in ihn zerfliesse.

Ich bin wie Gott und Gott wie ich

Ich bin so gross als Gott, er ist als ich so klein:
er kann nicht über mich, ich unter ihm nicht sein.

Du musst zum Kinde werden

Mensch, wirst du nicht ein Kind, so gehst du nimmer ein,
Wo Gottes Kinder sind: die Tür ist gar zu klein.

Du musst, was Gott ist, sein

Soll ich mein letztes End und ersten Anfang finden,
So muss ich mich in Gott und Gott in mir ergründen.

God cannot be grasped
God is a very nothing, not moved by the here and now: the more you reach out
for Him, the more he recedes from you.

God's image
I bear God's image: if he wants to look at Himself, this can take place only in
me and in those who are like me.

God is my point and circle
God is my centre point when I enclose Him in myself: my circle when I dissolve
into Him with love.

I am like God and God is like me
I am as great as God, he is as small as I: he cannot be above me, I cannot be
below him.

You must become a child
Man, unless you become a child, you will never enter where God's children are:
the door is far too low.

You must be what God is
If I am to find my ultimate end and my first beginning, I must fathom myself in
God and God in me.

The Love of God

Vaughan

THE MORNING-WATCH

O Joyes! Infinite sweetnes! with what flowres,
And shoots of glory, my soul breakes, and buds!
     All the long houres
     Of night, and Rest
     Through the still shrouds
     Of sleep, and Clouds,
   This Dew fell on my Breast;
     O how it *Blouds*,
And *Spirits* all my Earth! heark! In what Rings,
And *Hymning Circulations* the quick world
     Awakes, and sings;
     The rising winds,
     And falling springs,
     Birds, beasts, all things
    Adore him in their kinds.
     Thus all is hurl'd
In sacred *Hymnes*, and *Order*, The great *Chime*
And *Symphony* of nature. Prayer is
     The world in tune,
     A spirit-voyce,
     And vocall joyes
   Whose *Eccho is* heav'ns blisse.
     O let me climbe
When I lye down! The Pious soul by night
Is like a clouded starre, whose beames though said
     To shed their light
     Under some Cloud
     Yet are above,
     And shine, and move
    Beyond that mistie shrowd.
    So in my Bed
That Curtain'd grave, though sleep, like ashes, hide
My lamp, and like, both shall in thee abide.

Taylor

MEDITATION EIGHT

I kenning through astronomy divine
    The world's bright battlement, wherein I spy
A golden path my pencil cannot line
    From that bright throne unto my threshold lie.
      And while my puzzled thoughts about it pore,
      I find the bread of life in't at my door.

When that this bird of paradise put in
    This wicker cage (my corps) to tweedle praise
Had pecked the fruit forbid: and so did fling
    Away its food, and lost its golden days,
      It fell into celestial famine sore,
      And never could attain a morsel more.

Alas! alas! poor bird, what wilt thou do?
    This creature's field no food for souls e'er gave:
And if thou knock at angels' doors, they show
    An empty barrel: they no soul bread have.
      Alas! poor bird, the world's white loaf is done,
      And cannot yield thee here the smallest crumb.

In this sad state, God's tender bowels run
    Out streams of grace: and he to end all strife,
The purest wheat in heaven, his dear-dear Son
    Grinds, and kneads up into this bread of life:
      Which bread of life from heaven down came and stands
      Dished in thy table up by angels' hands.

Did God mould up this bread in heaven, and bake,
    Which from his table came, and to thine goeth?
Doth he bespeak thee thus: this soul bread take;
    Come, eat thy fill of this, thy God's white loaf?
      It's food too fine for angels; yet come, take
      And eat thy fill! it's heaven's sugar cake.

What grace is this knead in this loaf? This thing
    Souls are but petty things it to admire.
Ye angels, help; this fill would to the brim
    Heav'ns whelm'd-down crystal meal bowl, yea and higher.
      This bread of life dropped in thy mouth doth cry:
      Eat, eat me, soul, and thou shalt never die.

The Love of God

HOUSEWIFERY

MAKE me, O Lord, thy spinning wheel complete;
    Thy holy word my distaff make for me.
Make mine affections thy swift flyers neat,
    And make my soul thy holy spool to be.
    My conversation make to be thy reel,
    And reel the yarn thereon spun of thy wheel.

Make me thy loom then, knit therein this twine:
    And make thy holy spirit, Lord, wind quills:
Then weave the web thyself. The yarn is fine.
    Thine ordinances make my fulling mills.
    Then dye the same in heavenly colors choice,
    All pinked with varnished flowers of paradise.

Then clothe therewith mine understanding, will,
    Affections, judgment, conscience, memory;
My words and actions, that their shine may fill
    My ways with glory and thee glorify.
    Then mine apparel shall display before ye
    That I am clothed in holy robes for glory.

Greville

CHORUS QUINTUS TARTARORUM

From *Mustapha*

Vain superstition! Glorious style of weakness!
Sprung from the deep disquiet of man's passion,
To desolation, and despair of Nature:
Thy texts bring princes' titles into question:
Thy prophets set on work the sword of tyrants:
They manacle sweet truth with their distinctions:
Let virtue blood: teach cruelty for God's sake;
Fashioning one God; yet him of many fashions,
Like many-headed error, in their passions.
    Mankind! Trust not these superstitious dreams,
Fear's idols, pleasure's relics, sorrow's pleasures.
They make the wilful hearts their holy temples:
The rebels unto government their martyrs,
    No: thou child of false miracles begotten!
False miracles, which are but ignorance of cause,
Lift up the hopes of thy abjected prophets:
Courage, and worth abjure thy painted heavens.

Sickness, thy blessings are; misery, thy trial;
Nothing, thy way unto eternal being;
Death, to salvation; and the grave to Heaven.
So blest be they, so angel'd, so eterniz'd
That tie their senses to thy senseless glories,
And die, to cloy the after-age with stories.
   Man should make much of life, as Nature's table,
Wherein she writes the cypher of her glory.
Forsake not Nature, nor misunderstand her:
Her mysteries are read without faith's eyesight:
She speaketh in our flesh; and from our senses,
Delivers down her wisdoms to our reason.
If any man would break her laws to kill,
Nature doth, for defence, allow offences.
She neither taught the father to destroy:
Nor promis'd any man, by dying, joy.

Index of Authors